Concepts of Leisure

Concepts
of Leisure
Philosophical
Implications

JAMES F. MURPHY

San Jose State University

PRENTICE-HALL, INC.

Englewood Cliffs, New Jersey

Library of Congress Cataloging in Publication Data

MURPHY, JAMES FREDRICK,   comp.
    Concepts of leisure: philosophical implications.

    Bibliography: p.
    1. Leisure. I. Title.
BJ1498.M87   790'.0135   73-12713
ISBN   0-13-166439-5

© 1974 by **Prentice-Hall, Inc.,** Englewood Cliffs, N.J.

Printed in the United States of America

10   9   8   7   6   5   4   3

Prentice-Hall International, Inc., *London*
Prentice-Hall of Australia, Pty. Ltd., *Sydney*
Prentice-Hall of Canada, Ltd., *Toronto*
Prentice-Hall of India Private Limited, *New Delhi*
Prentice-Hall of Japan, Inc., *Tokyo*

To Mary S. Wiley and Ardith B. Frost,
pioneers and spiritual leaders of recreation education

Contents

Preface

Profound sociotechnological changes have radically altered the American society of the last quarter of the twentieth century. Perhaps the most significant change has been the increasing shift in emphasis from work to nonwork concerns. We are in transition from an industrial to a technological or postindustrial society, from a rural to an urban society, and from a work-oriented society to one in which leisure and its associated institutions, values, and behavior are becoming the essentials that determine other factors.

In this text I have attempted to represent the varied dimensions of leisure through a discussion of primary views and interpretations. Each concept or dimension of leisure is complemented by selected readings designed to elaborate that particular view of leisure. This is an introductory text, oriented primarily toward undergraduate students majoring in recreation and leisure studies. Students of sociology and related social science and humanities disciplines as well may find the volume of value. It is not an exhaustive discussion of all possible leisure perspectives. Instead, its intent is to introduce various interpretations of leisure so that the student can make independent judgments of their value.

The field of recreation and leisure service encompasses many singular, often distorted, interpretations of the leisure behavior and life styles of various groups of people. Increasingly, however, we are witnessing a wide divergence of leisure expression. If Alvin Toffler, Marshall McLuhan, Margaret Mead, and other futurists are correct, we may expect increasing individual deviation during leisure, in sharp contrast to the common view of leisure as unobligated, socially purposeful, discretionary time.

The first chapter of this book provides an overview of six philosophical interpretations of leisure, notions of time and the changes in our society that have resulted in erosion of the Protestant work ethic and movement toward a leisure ethic. It stresses that developing a philosophy of leisure is essential so that the individual has a meaningful pattern of living. Chapters 2 through 6 discuss five of the philosophical approaches or concepts of leisure and provide reading selections giving additional insights, controversies, and added references for clarification. Each view of leisure is explored more fully in an attempt to develop a basic interpretation and understanding. Chapter 7 discusses work and leisure and their relationship, the framework for speculating about the future orientation of a postindustrial society. Chapter 8 reviews sociohistorical developments which have eradicated "economic" man and led to *Homo americansis,* a high-consumption, materialistic man typical of an affluent, post-scarce economy. Chapter 8 also presents the sixth concept of leisure, the holistic approach, as the central (although not necessary) focus of leisure in a postindustrial society.

As American society places less and less emphasis on the work rhythm of life, it assumes more of the characteristic features of a post-work (or at least post-scarce) economy with an abundance of manufactured and mass-produced goods. However, society and the recreation and leisure service field are ill-equipped to understand the consequences of some of the sweeping sociotechnological changes which have occurred, given the emphasis on the discretionary-time perspective of leisure. An orientation primarily toward work concerns, such as the values, time orientation, and hierarchical technocratic and bureaucratic organization of industrialism, seems inappropriate in a technological, postindustrial society. The need for decentralized, spontaneous, instant feedback and for community-oriented services is blurring and replacing previous distinctions recognized between line and staff, planner and recipient, and work "time" and leisure "time." In an industrializing nation the material object was unique and man was expendable. As we move into a postindustrial society, the material object has become expendable and automation has returned value to man.

I hope that this book will help the reader understand the dimensions of leisure so that he may develop a sound leisure philosophy. In our rapidly changing society, students, practitioners, and educators must continually reassess the values which guide the delivery of leisure opportunities, thus moving the field of recreation and leisure service to a higher plateau of understanding and commitment.

Acknowledgments

I am extremely grateful to Walter Welch, Assistant Vice-President, Prentice-Hall, who has continually demonstrated confidence both in my ability to communicate ideas and in the potential of this book. I also appreciate the help of Joseph J. Bannon, Head, Department of Recreation and Park Administration, University of Illinois, and Robert Hanson, Professor, Department of Recreation, San Diego State University, who reviewed the text proposal and expressed their support for the book during its preparation.

I am grateful to the authors and publishers who permitted me to use their material to supplement and enrich the book. Without their assistance I would have been unable to present the concepts of leisure so completely and authoritatively. I also extend sincere appreciation to Carolyn Davidson, who magnificently edited the copy and improved the quality of the manuscript.

I extend special gratitude to S. Raquel Roe, graduate student in the Department of Recreation and Leisure Studies, San Jose State University, who helped immensely by diagramming the interrelationships of the concepts of time and leisure. Her assistance was important to the conceptual presentation of the book.

Thanks also to Dr. Paul D. Brown, Chairman, Department of Recreation, San Jose State University, who has always allowed me to pursue areas of "creative" endeavor. His support and friendship are sincerely appreciated.

Finally, but with no less appreciation, I thank my wife Betty and my daughter Erin for their love and moral support during the course of the project and their willingness to allow me to forge ahead in the study of leisure. I hope that my quest may help to conceptualize leisure and thereby discover its many dimensions and implications for a postindustrial society.

Concepts of Leisure

chapter one

Philosophical Dimensions of Leisure

The relationships among our major social institutions, including work, religion, the family, education, and leisure, have changed considerably during the past seventy years. At the turn of the twentieth century leisure was not recognized as a separate, distinguishable institution in American society. The family assumed the major responsibility for giving children and members of the extended family their basic play orientation, equipment, and environment. While the family remains the center of the child's play experience, the broader society has assumed more responsibility for allocating facilities, equipment, and instruction and for enhancing leisure opportunities for community members.

The recreation and leisure service field has been guided largely by principles and practices propagated and administered during the formative years of the American recreation movement. Our sociopolitical environment has changed significantly since that time, particularly with the advent of television, Telstar, and computers. The rapidity of sociotechnological change has left many Americans numb. Guidelines which provided understanding and direction have become obsolete in the "electric age."

1

BUILDING A PHILOSOPHY OF LEISURE

The leisure service practitioner, recreation educator, student, and ordinary lay citizen *must* have meaningful guidelines to direct their lives and the lives of others. These guidelines must be founded on a sound philosophical premise. Earle F. Zeigler notes that the philosopher attempts to appraise existing knowledge, beliefs, and human relations. "Subsequently he evolves a systematic and coherent plan that may give the ordinary person an understanding of life. It may help to give him a focus so that he can determine that which is important and significant. Thus it can help him decide what he should do in the years ahead."[1]

The recreation and leisure service field, an integral part of the human service profession, has largely failed to provide the prospective educator and practitioner the opportunity to develop a meaningful, comprehensive interpretation of leisure, because of the lack of significant guidelines and a rather narrow conceptualization of leisure. The knowledge, values, and beliefs which guided the recreation movement in the United States in 1900 were characteristic of a still largely agricultural, segregated, rural, blue-collar nation operating on a scarce economy and oriented toward work. The rewards of industrial technology for the masses would not be realized for several decades. Our highly affluent society has an imperative need for recreation and leisure service personnel to reassess the values which guide the field. In an economy of plenty, the segment of time which is becoming the central life interest for a growing number of people is leisure—not work.

Fundamental questions about our perceptions of the world, human relations, free will, good and evil, and so on must be answered within a philosophical framework to lend meaning to our existence. Meaningful leisure opportunities become operable when people comprehend the value of exercising self-expression and satisfying individually determined needs within a given milieu. It is important that we answer questions related to leisure and that we examine our philosophical positions on education, technology, the economy, political structure, religion, the family, and so on. "What we decide as professionals, and what laymen will accept, will exert considerable influence on the place of . . . recreation in our educational systems [and other institutions as well] and, subsequentially, in our communities at large for our mature citizens."[2]

---

[1]Earle F. Zeigler, *Philosophical Foundations for Physical, Health, and Recreation Education* (Englewood Cliffs, N.J.: Prentice-Hall, Inc., 1964), p. 11.

[2]Ibid., p. 11.

CONCEPTUALIZING LEISURE

Leisure evolved in ancient Greece with the "cultivation of self" interpretation developed by Aristotle. This *traditional* or *classical view* of leisure emphasizes contemplation, enjoyment of self in search of knowledge, debate, politics, and cultural enlightenment. In this sense, leisure is seen as *qual.* freedom from the necessity of being occupied. Sebastian de Grazia[3] and Josef Pieper[4] advocate this qualitative concept, which identifies leisure as a *condition or state of being, a condition of the soul, which is divorced from time.* David E. Gray states that the classical concept of leisure "is an act of aesthetic, psychological, religious and philosophical contemplation."[5]

The dominant concept of leisure, the *discretionary time view* or quantita- *quant.* tive perspective, holds that leisure is the portion of time which remains when work and the basic requirements for existence have been satisfied. Don Fabun[6] suggests that at present we have only one view of how time should be spent, as emulated by the industrial worker: hours to be gotten through in order to receive sustenance. We have constructed a society in which participation in work has almost become the goal of life. According to Fabun, the challenge of our economic system is to recognize and then implement the consequences of the changed energy flow of production, to find new ways of looking at work and leisure and the role of each in society.

The concept of leisure as related to social class structure is largely the result of the writing of Thorstein Veblen,[7] an American sociologist. Veblen showed how ruling classes, during particular eras, became identifiable mostly through their possession of leisure. Additional research has attempted to classify and conceptualize leisure according to social class, race, and occupational determinants. Reuel White,[8] Alfred Clarke,[9] Joel Gerstl,[10] and others have explored the influence of leisure behavior on

[3]Sebastian de Grazia, *Of Time, Work and Leisure* (Garden City, N.Y.: Doubleday & Company, Inc., 1964).

[4]Josef Pieper, *Leisure: The Basis of Culture* (New York: Pantheon Books, Inc., 1952).

[5]David E. Gray, "This Alien Thing Called Leisure" (paper presented at Oregon State University, Corvallis, Oregon, 8 July 1971).

[6]Don Fabun, *The Dynamics of Change* (Englewood Cliffs, N.J.: Prentice-Hall, Inc., 1967).

[7]Thorstein Veblen, *The Theory of the Leisure Class* (New York: The New American Library, 1953).

[8]Reuel White, "Social Class Difference in the Uses of Leisure," *American Journal of Sociology,* 61 (September 1955), 145–50.

[9]Alfred Clarke, "The Use of Leisure and Its Relation to Levels of Occupational Prestige," *American Sociological Review,* 21 (June 1956), 301–7.

[10]Joel Gerstl, "Leisure, Taste, and Occupational Milieu," *Social Problems,* 9 (Summer 1961), 56–58.

different occupations and of social status on leisure behavior. A number of leisure activities are very closely related to social class level, particularly those in which participation requires a certain level of education. The kind of work one engages in also constitutes a significant variable in leisure expression. The diffusion of culture, the spreading influence of mass media, and growing affluence have brought diverse forms of leisure within the reach of the masses, diminishing the socioeconomic dimension of leisure; however, the notion of *life style* (material and nonmaterial attributes of one's cultural orientation) has emerged as an important factor in determining leisure interests.[11]

Another concept of leisure, the *anti-utilitarian view*, is articulated by Walter Kerr in *The Decline of Pleasure.* Kerr suggests that leisure is a state of mind that is a worthy end in itself. As noted by Gray, this concept rejects "the position that every investment of human energy must produce a useful result. It rejects the work ethic as the only source of value and permits the investment of self in pursuits that promise no more than the expression of self."[12] "Doing your own thing" has merit according to this view of leisure, which sees the industrial and technological revolutions as antagonistic influences.

Leisure is also viewed as a form of nonwork *activity* in which people engage during their free time—apart from the obligations of work, family, and society. According to Joffre Dumazedier,[13] leisure in this sense serves three essential functions: relaxation, entertainment, and personal development. Bennett Berger[14] views leisure chiefly as a form of behavior; he stresses that it is voluntary activity carried on in free time, in sharp contrast with work, which is required, utilitarian, and rewarded in economic terms.

Finally, a sixth view of leisure, the *holistic* perspective, sees leisure as a construct, "with such elements as an antithesis to the work of the participant, a perception of the activity as voluntary or free, a pleasant expectation or recollection, a full range of possibilities from withdrawal in sleep or drink to highly creative tasks."[15] According to the holistic view, elements of leisure are to be found in work, family, education, religion, and so on. Conversely, elements from those constructs are often to be found

[11]Richard Kraus, *Recreation and Leisure in Modern Society* (New York: Appleton-Century-Crofts, 1971), p. 295.

[12]Gray, "This Alien Thing Called Leisure."

[13]Joffre Dumazedier, *Toward a Society of Leisure* (New York: The Free Press, 1967), pp. 16–17.

[14]Bennett Berger, "The Sociology of Leisure: Some Suggestions," *Industrial Relations,* 1 (February 1962), 31–45.

[15]Max Kaplan, "Aging and Leisure" (paper presented at the American Psychological Association, Washington, D.C., 4 September 1971).

in leisure. This view of leisure incorporates all possible interpretations of leisure into one definition.

The holistic view of leisure changes the whole perspective of organized recreation and leisure service, eliminating the dichotomy between work and leisure which has been a formidable barrier to many people's enjoyment of leisure opportunities. According to the holistic concept of leisure, the meanings of work and leisure are inextricably related. Conceivably we can no longer view leisure as solely discretionary time and work as action.[16] Leisure must be viewed as action, too. This view suggests a need for a *value reorientation,* to confer honor on leisure as honor was conferred on work during the nineteenth century.

It is difficult to classify leisure according to any one of the foregoing concepts or dimensions. Kraus states:

> A more realistic approach [in classifying leisure] would be to suggest that leisure represents all free time and that it provides the potential for freedom of choice. Within leisure one may engage in a wide range of activities—including those which are negative, passive, and destructive or those which are positive, active, self-enhancing, and constructive for the community as a whole.[17]

Our social system has created longer adolescence, more years of retirement, and monotonous assembly-line jobs—but our value system has not conferred honor on increased leisure.[18] "Leisure service managers will have the dubious task of making interpretations about people's non-work behavior with emphasis upon the facilitation of opportunities for recreation that cover the full range of commitment and intensity."[19]

NOTIONS OF TIME

In assessing the various conceptions of leisure it is important to understand notions of time. There are essentially three kinds of time: *cyclical* or *natural* time, *mechanical* or *clock* time, and *personal* or *psychological* time. Each of these time perspectives conditions the individual to behave in a certain way and affects his understanding of others' movement in space.

Cyclical time. The nomadic hunting life was conditioned largely by the

---

[16]James F. Murphy, "Dimensions of Leisure" (paper presented at the National Congress for Recreation and Parks, Anaheim, California, 4 October 1972).

[17]Kraus, *Recreation and Leisure in Modern Society,* p. 259.

[18]Berger, "The Sociology of Leisure," 31–45.

[19]James F. Murphy, John G. Williams, E. William Niepoth, and Paul D. Brown, *Leisure Service Delivery System: A Modern Perspective* (Philadelphia: Lea and Febiger, 1973).

rising and setting of the sun. There were no clocks to divide the day into hours, minutes, and seconds. Tribal life was oriented around daily, monthly, and seasonal rhythms of the natural universe. Nomads understood the summer solstice and the vernal equinox, the spring, summer, fall, and winter seasons to be circular conceptions of time which were *constant* and *recurring*. Thomas F. Green states:

> According to this image, time is measured in relation to the constant and recurring passage of the sun, the fluctuations of the tides, the stages of the moon, or even the cycles of the seasons.[20]

Time was never lost or wasted; according to this conception of time the periods of the day were not seen as linear, sequential divisions. The image of time was based on the repetition of activities, both social and natural.

> In this case, time repeats itself, so that one cannot speak of "wasting" time. The time that has passed is never really lost; it will come again. . . . Time is not cumulative—that is, the idea that one might now undertake something that will reach its completion at some time in the distant future is not dominant.[21]

Circular, eternally returning time gives man a strong sense of belief and commitment to the natural world. Ecologically, man understood his relationship to the physical world and was better able to live harmoniously in his natural surroundings. De Grazia notes that the ancient Greeks delightedly accepted the eternal harmonious order that could be discovered through contemplation.[22]

Mechanical time. Hunting, food gathering, play, and rest occupied the daily lives of nomads and preindustrial people in a total life rhythm. The governance of cyclical, natural time was inherently *leisurely*. The mechanization of time occurred when nomads and food-gatherers with specific work tasks needed to meet other men and engage in barter and trade of goods and wares. This required a more finite division of time between sunrise and noon, noon and sunset. The death of cyclical time and the notion of recurrence vanished with the triumph of Christianity.

Mechanical clocks are known to have existed in the thirteenth century, but the earliest survivors belong to the fourteenth century.[23] The week

---

[20]Thomas F. Green, *Work, Leisure, and the American Schools* (New York: Random House, Inc., 1968), p. 49.

[21]Ibid., p. 49.

[22]De Grazia, *Of Time, Work and Leisure*, p. 26.

[23]J. B. Priestley, *Man and Time* (New York: Dell Publishing Co., Inc., 1968), p. 27.

is an arbitrary time division, simply a convenient time period between the day and the month. The Greeks divided the month into three ten-day periods and the Romans had an eight-day week between market days.

In the industrial world time is generally viewed as *linear,* without beginning or end, never pausing or veering off course. Nels Anderson states, "The time by which most of us regulate our lives is called *mechanical* because it reflects the interdependence of man and the rhythm of his machines."[24] According to this image of time, regulated by the clock, it becomes possible to speak of "wasting" time, letting time "escape," and "putting in" time.

> In this conception, time is linear rather than circular; every moment of time is new, and therefore also contains the possibility of something new. A time can pass, and when it passes it cannot be recovered. One can therefore plan to achieve something in the future that is indeed genuinely new. . . . One *must* plan for the future, for the span of a lifetime is brief enough, and what shape it will take is not given, but can be contrived. There is some urgency that it be shaped well.[25]

The acceptance of artificial time-keeping devices diluted man's inner biological rhythm of movement through space and oriented it to the mechanical beat of the clock. By varying the years, months, and days it seemed possible to arrange for more optimum work and play schedules.

Would the industrial worker be happier, after a long and more rewarding period of working at his job, to have an ampler weekend in which to enjoy leisure at his own pace? Is it possible for the contemporary industrial worker to decide for himself when he wants to work or play, and in fact ignore the official week?[26]

According to de Grazia, technology is no friend of leisure.

> The machine, the hero of a dream, the bestower of free time to men, brings a neutralized idea of time that makes it seem free, and then chains it to another machine, the clock. . . . Clock time cannot be free. . . . Clocked time requires activities and decisions that must always be referred back to and synchronized with the machine and its ramifications in an industrial culture.[27]

[24]Nels Anderson, *Dimensions of Work* (New York: David McKay Co., Inc., 1964), p. 106.

[25]Green, *Work, Leisure, and the American Schools,* p. 52.

[26]See Phillip Bosserman, "Implications for Youth," in *Technology, Human Values and Leisure,* ed. Max Kaplan and Phillip Bosserman (Nashville: Abingdon Press, 1971), pp. 162–63, for examples of alternative work schedules.

[27]De Grazia, *Of Time, Work and Leisure,* p. 310.

The man-made environment of mechanical clock time reinforces the artificial rhythms of the industrial work day, communications networks, transportation systems, and scheduled routines of schools, churches, offices, and recreation facilities. Without the clock, free time as we know it in industrial society would not have emerged. Work and leisure, fused in preindustrial society, have become *opposing* conceptions in our highly industrialized culture. The contemporary arrangement of time has become rigorously circumscribed by industrial work time. Because work time needs to be filled with productive occupation, leisure time is seen largely as empty time, not innately meaningful.

Psychological time. A third concept is psychological or inner time. The inner sense of space and movement which dictates our behavior and receptiveness to events, independent of natural time, the clocks, and the calendars, is the time we really live with. Clock time artificially schedules our days, but psychological time lets us commit ourselves intensely, joyously, harmoniously to life. Although clock time may bring us more success and importance, few of us feel that it necessarily enriches experience.

Many people feel contained by the one-way temporal process epitomized by industrial time clocks. They yearn to escape the artificial entanglements of work time and to explore more fully the natural world unbound by stoplights, the six o'clock news, school buzzers, alarm clocks, sirens, and factory time clocks. Psychological time is concerned not with the specificity of quantitative time, but rather with quality.

> No matter how the empirical self adopts itself to the concept of passing time, a one-way horizontal track, the essential self (which expects something different and better) tries to escape from the contradictions, the ruthless opposites, and knows nothing but a sense of frustration, a profound dissatisfaction.[28]

Mechanical, chronological time conveys the idea that in time there can be no sense of completeness, no enduring satisfactions. Everything in mechanical time, no matter what its scale, is here today and gone tomorrow. The passing and continuous passage of time includes only fragments of ourselves. This one-way track of passing time fosters a curious apathy, boredom, a lack of zest, a flavorless sense of living. Unfortunately, the passing time is all we have. The individual must learn to perceive time and space as an opportunity to add experience and knowledge, through a broadening and deepening consciousness.

Attempting to escape time's limitations, frustrations, and contradictions, Western man devours everything around him. The Eastern philoso-

[28]Priestley, *Man and Time*, p. 173.

phy of time and the universe refuses to be devoured by events and time. Eastern cultures believe in a self that does not waste away, a detachment that allows them to "behave as if they believed, paradoxically, that in this world everything is important and nothing is important."[29]   Although psychological time is little help to the scientist or computer analyst surrounded by clocks, calendars, and precise instruments, the outer or mechanical time measured by those instruments is essentially unreal; reality can be found only in our inner sense of duration or psychological time.[30] *The basis of leisure in postindustrial society clearly gains significance when its meaning is attached to the industrial rhythm of life, but its attributes and character emerge only when interpreted by the individual who makes of it what is pertinent and valuable to his personal life regimen.*

SOCIETAL VALUE SYSTEMS

The Industrial Revolution, sanctified by the Protestant Ethic, introduced economic, cultural, political, and value changes in America, including machines, new sources of power, and a factory system of production and free time.[31]

We are presently experiencing a crisis in values with respect to work, leisure, and community life. Berger refers to this as "the problem of leisure." A large number of people still feel a Puritan sense of guilt in relation to leisure, although the masses have been able to realize a fairly stable standard of living. They want to be useful and productive members of the community, and traditionally this has meant that they were employed. The technological transition of American society from a predominantly agricultural society (late phase of the feudal era) to a postindustrial society has been readily accepted by most people, but most members of society have been unprepared for the cultural changes which have affected our ways of behaving, values, and interpersonal relationships and have literally destroyed the social foundations.[32]

Berger provides particular insight; he states that "the problems of leisure and of alienation of work . . . are problems created by the inconsistencies between normative and social systems."[33] The problem is exacerbated

---

[29]Ibid., p. 176.

[30]Ibid., p. 45.

[31]John Bowditch and Clement Ramsland, eds., *Voices of the Industrial Revolution* (Ann Arbor: University of Michigan Press, 1961).

[32]Jack D. Douglas, ed., *The Technological Threat* (Englewood Cliffs, N.J.: Prentice-Hall, Inc., 1971), p. 4.

[33]Bennett Berger, "The Sociology of Leisure: Some Suggestions," in *Work and Leisure*, ed. Erwin O. Smigel (New Haven: College and University Press, 1963), p. 32.

when a value system is rendered incapable of conferring honor on the typical social situations that confront people. When inconsistencies exist between what the social system requires (earlier retirement, assembly-line jobs, longer adolescence, and so on) and what the value system prescribes (need for the individual to be productive, occupationally oriented, and so on), social problems emerge. "Though the Protestant Ethic is by no means in its grave, there is growing consensus that the major moral satisfactions in life are to be sought through leisure, not work. Or, . . . leisure is to be sought through activities unconnected with leisure."[34]

The social structure of the industrial society, governed by an economic principle of rationality, clashes with the emerging values of the culture, an anti-utilitarian, hedonistic, pleasure-seeking rationale based on openness, choice, flexibility, change, and spontaneity. This inconsistency has resulted in the development of a host of subcultures and subcommunity deviations which view life primarily from the perspective of free time.

In *The Greening of America,* Charles Reich portrayed a new character type, Consciousness III, which represents the anti-utilitarian philosophy, believing in doing what one wants to do rather than responding passively to outside pressures, and which provides an arena for fellowship, spontaneity, authenticity, and creativity.[35] Reich's conception of contemporary man is essentially oriented around a *leisure society* founded on free time, a diversity of life styles, and growth and self-fulfillment. Human fulfillment is the conscious goal of a postindustrial society founded on free time; in contrast, industrial society emphasizes conformity, standardization, and routinization. The postindustrial leisure-based society is the result of a synthesis of preindustrial social aspects, including community interaction, psychological security, ritualized aspects of culture, tolerance, freedom, and social fluidity. Figure 1 portrays the concepts of leisure, work, and time and their dynamic interrelationships.

David Riesman notes, "In preindustrial cultures leisure is scarcely a 'problem' because it is built into the ritual and ground plan of life for which people are conditioned in childhood. Often they possess a relatively timeless attitude toward events."[36] The nature of work is a condition of life in survivalist societies; therefore it is not viewed particularly as labor. In industrial, post-scarce societies work has *intrinsic* value; it is a normal outlet for man to express his energies. Play is not enough.

---

[34]Ibid., pp. 32–33.

[35]Charles Reich, *The Greening of America* (New York: Random House, Inc., 1970).

[36]David Riesman, "Leisure and Work in Postindustrial Society," *The Technological Threat,* ed. Jack D. Douglas (Englewood Cliffs, N.J.: Prentice-Hall, Inc., 1971), p. 77.

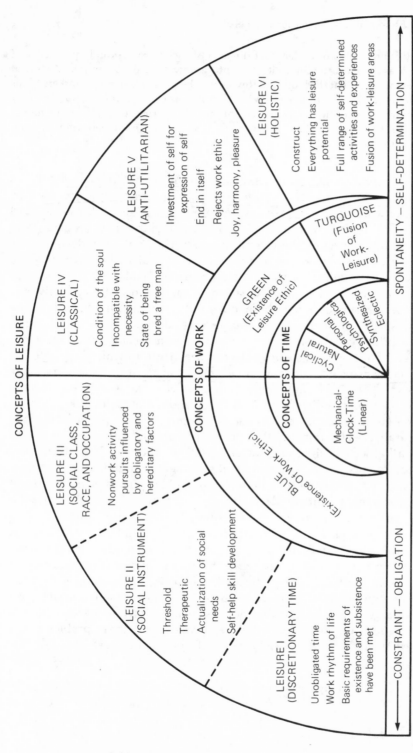

Figure 1. Toward a dynamic conceptualization of leisure.

It is probably no accident that the idea of social progress and the sanctity of work as a means to achieve it grew into a now virtually unexamined ethic at the same time that the Industrial Revolution began to need more 'workers.' This kind of work was not like the work that had gone on before; it was specially oriented in space (in the factory or foundry) and structured in time (the necessity for the worker to be in a certain place, at certain times, performing certain prescribed activities).[37]

In industrial society, leisure is separate from the rest of man's life. It has become not a part of life, but a means to life—a thing of *extrinsic* value, useful only because it relaxes and restores the individual for work. Karl Mannheim suggests that the masses "want to feel that they are useful and important members of the community, with a right to understand the meaning of their work and of the society in which they live."[38] The essence of the method of translation which will make the value system functional once more lies in the creation and acceptance of specifically new values which would support, humanize, and spiritualize unobligatory time —time spent outside the workshop, factory, or office.

The primary antagonism among values is associated with the work process: "The real struggle lies between the attitudes which are rooted in good craftsmanship and values which emanate from machine-made goods."[39] The shift from primary groups to secondary group contacts, the transition from handicrafts to large-scale industrial techniques, and the segmentation of leisure as a separate, distinguishable part of life have necessitated readjustment of the social structure and value system to embrace *all* aspects of life as having *self-fulfilling* potential. The rejection by numbers of people of the antiquated work ethic, founded in the scarce economy of an industrializing nation in the middle and late 1800s, has not proven as free, enriching, and satisfying as promised, and is not purposeful to the goals and aspirations of a postindustrial society.

The present quality of life (perpetuated by a highly objective, rational work ethic), as it is reflected in a ravaged environment, polluted cities and waterways, decaying slums, and unstable race relations, reveals a need for a change in the behavior which has brought us to the brink of disaster. These conditions confronting our emerging leisure-centered society, requiring urgent reorientation and development of a whole new set of attitudes, skills, and behavior which will ameliorate these problems and constructively support a society primarily evolved around *nonwork* concerns.

[37]Fabun, "The Theory of the Leisure Masses," in *The Dynamics of Change;* pp. 13–14.
[38]Karl Mannheim, "The Crisis in Valuation," in *The Technological Threat,* ed. Douglas, p. 57.
[39]Ibid., p. 62.

VALUE CONFLICT—LEISURE SOCIETY VALUE SYSTEMS

H. Douglas Sessoms notes two main interpretations of the conceptualization of leisure.[40] The first holds leisure to be free time. This view embraces the discretionary time, social class race, and occupation, and activity dimensions of leisure. The second views leisure as a state of being, incorporated into the classical and anti-utilitarian views of leisure. The holistic concept of leisure embraces both schools of thought. The former concept views leisure as based on the existence of an already accepted time notion—time free from subsistence obligations and existence requirements. The latter perspective deals with attitudes toward existence, not with behavior or the period in which an experience occurs. It is a conditional state of mind that has nothing to do with mechanical time.

Sessoms states that our present value system is based on the mechanical time approach; leisure behavior is recognized as occurring in a set time period, although some people, notably hippies and other "outsiders," ignore this time framework and view life as existence in which leisure may occur whenever they feel it exists.

The specific challenge to the recreation and leisure service field and society in general is that if the leisure orientation of the postindustrial society is based on an extension of the time-orientation value system, the transition from our present work structure will be relatively easy. However, if the leisure-oriented society of the future requires the creation of new values and behavior patterns, the adjustment will be more difficult for people, organizations, and institutions.

Values are patterns of behavior and beliefs we hold important to our way of life. Leisure behavior is a part of our value structure; leisure activities we choose result from that value structure. Traditionally, psychic fulfillment has been derived from accomplishments at work. Now, however, work is becoming less important and people are turning increasingly to other forms of expression for achievement, mastery, self-worth, and pleasure. The challenge to postindustrial society seems to be to *provide moral reinforcement for people to express and act out leisure attitudes and behavior whenever they desire, during free time or at work, and the opportunity to be identified by their leisure life styles and cultural tastes rather than by their occupations.*

[40]H. Douglas Sessoms, "Leisure Society Value Systems: The Effects of a Leisure-Oriented Society Upon Individuals—The Role of Parks and Recreation" (paper presented at the National Congress for Recreation and Parks, Chicago, Illinois, September 1969).

leisure society
value systems

H. DOUGLAS SESSOMS

BACKGROUND INFORMATION

Implied in the topic of the effects of a leisure-oriented society upon individuals and the role of the park and recreation profession in such a situation is the existence of a leisure-oriented society. The writings of industrial sociologists and economists such as Robert Dubin, Stephen Miller and Robert Theobald suggest that we are moving in this direction. In fact, one of our own, Charles K. Brightbill, in his last work, dealt with educating for a leisure-centered society. Also, implied in the topic is that in a leisure-oriented society a different value system will be at work than that which we now have, and that the roles of parks and recreation will be affected through the dynamics of that new value system. The validity of these implications has not been established.

In order to get at the issue and to evaluate the possible reality of a "leisure-oriented society," we must define our terms, especially the notion of leisure. Scores of writers have attempted this yet no universally accepted definition of leisure currently exists. At best, two schools of thought seem to exist. The first holds leisure to be free time. It is an operational concept, based upon the existence of an already accepted time notion. It is generally referred to in relationship to work and subsistence obligations. It is that time one has after he had done those things he must do. The second school of thought holds leisure to be a state of being. It is a philosophical notion and has nothing to do with time. It is difficult to operationalize for research purposes as it deals with attitudes toward existence, not behavior nor the period in which an experience takes place. It is a state of being free from obligations but free only in the sense of one's perception of what he must

H. Douglas Sessoms, "Leisure Society Value Systems: The Effects of a Leisure-Oriented Society upon Individuals—The Role of Parks and Recreation." Paper read at the National Congress for Recreation and Parks, September 1969, Chicago, Illinois.

14

or ought to do. The two concepts are related inasmuch as they both deal with the notion of freedom but are quite different in the way they function. For one, leisure behavior occurs in a set time period; the other has leisure being whenever one feels it exists.

Our present value system is based upon the time approach. As a people, we hold dear those structures which are measurable and subject to organizational change; we are not aesthetically oriented. Pragmatism is our philosophy; technology is our language. We consume the day, dividing it into hours, and label our experiences according to when they occur. There are family obligations, work obligations, subsistence obligations, recreation, church work, *ad infinitum.* We program our lives according to the time blocks available: the work week, vacation time, retirement.

Many of these time blocks—retirement, vacation periods, and after work—are often referred to as periods of leisure, yet they may have little to do with a feeling of being. They are time periods resulting from our having done other activities; they have been perceived to be occasions for recreation or some other self-directed activity.

There is a group, however, which tends to ignore this time framework and views life as existence; their whole behavior is recreationally oriented. At least, we perceive it to be a life of freedom, the state of being which the philosophers refer to as leisure. Of course, I'm speaking of the Hippies and our inherent dislike for what they represent. We consider them irresponsible, ignoring the basic values of organization and interdependency. We say if all were to enjoy the life of the Hippie, then who will tend the shop, uphold the structures of society? The potentials of a leisure-oriented society trouble us for the freedom we hold to be the essence of the recreational experience can only exist when someone else or some thing is allowing us to act independently of necessity.

Our present and past efforts to understand leisure have been based upon a time-oriented value system. If our leisure-oriented society is to be an extension of that value system, then our fears should be dispelled for we are dealing with the same basic value system we've dealt with from the time of the industrial revolution. Few major changes in values will occur. We will not drastically alter the organizational structures which result from and support that value system. We will simply create new patterns or ways to exhibit them. In other words, the protestant ethic, the values of our work-oriented society, will remain. Both work and leisure behavior will stem from the dominant beliefs about life and the way it is to be lived.

If by a leisure-oriented society we are referring to the creation of a new value system, one based upon the philosophical notion of leisure, then we do have a lot of change in store. To achieve it will require the creation of a totally different life-style, one which is incompatible with out present western civilization concept of order and organization. Remember, organization is a time-oriented value, and its components of interdependency and deferred gain are foreign to those who live for the moment. Our concept of civilization is based upon the notion of obligation and interdependence. Life is structured, broken into time periods in which specific sets of activities—work, play, family—are pursued. It does not allow for personal freedom in the sense of the Hippie nor the pre-industrial society man.

Frankly, I do not see us moving toward this value system although some romantics would have us believe it is the ideal one. In it, the concepts of work and leisure are non-existent, for all of life is the struggle to survive and all experiences an extension of that struggle. Immediate gratification is inherent in that system but the "now" generation, which some may see as a forerunner of a non–time-oriented society, exists only because the rest of us work and make their "freedom" possible. Man has always tolerated its leisured class. The issue then seems to be can we create in our time-oriented society opportunities for the enjoyment of some of the sensory feelings accompanying the free state of leisure while not destroying the organizations which allow for extended periods of non-work? That course of action implies a value judgment, but what are values?

When the sociologist refers to values, he's referring to those patterns of behavior and belief which man holds to be important to his welfare. They are his concepts of desired experiences and are manifested in his expressed preferences. They give direction for choosing alternative courses of behavior and are used as a means for evaluating the relative importance of man's experiences.

Values are conceptions of the desirable and are subject to various interpretations. Each of us has different perceptions of what is important, what life ought to be, and these perceptions are the product of our experiences and our social-economic-ethnic group background. In a society as heterogeneous as ours, a multitude of value structures exist, yet all of them are somewhat similar as all reflect the dominant value structure of urban America.

From its beginning the park and recreation movement has held that recreation and play experiences were of value. Our early pioneers wrote that recreation should be provided for it built character, added to the good life, instilled feelings of democracy, self-reliance, and the like. In fact, organized recreation programs were created to provide opportunities for the learning of these values and to negate such unacceptable behavior as delinquency and poor sportsmanship. Of course, each generation of park and recreation professionals has created programs reflecting the value structures of its generation. Consequently, program modifications have occurred but these modifications have been minimal when compared to the beliefs we have held since our professional birth. For example, we believe that organized recreation programs are basically for those with free time, i.e., children and the aged; that recreation is activity, primarily sports activities; that art is cultural and should be provided by some other institution. At least our program behavior suggests this and the public seems to agree with this perception and expects us to behave accordingly.

There are many value conflicts within our society and consequently, within our profession. We are a reflection of the larger system and share the same concerns and hopes as does the rest of society. What is the role of the recreation and park professional? Should he encourage and support the life-style and value-orientation of the "now" generation and provide rock festivals and pathways for motorized vehicles? Or should he discourage the young from admiring and emulating the behavior of priests and priestesses of these activities by denying these opportunities? What does he offer as alternative models and avenues of expression? Can we as recreators do anything to negate the Easy Rider lifestyle and its value orientation or is this a concern for parks and recreation?

CLARIFICATION OF THE ISSUES

Another way of facing the issue is to ask to what extent do Americans value recreation behavior? Is it important enough to accommodate a non–work-centered society or is it important only as long as there is work to give one status? It is my contention that Americans do not value leisure (free time) for its own sake, that is as time for self-fulfillment, discovery, and personal freedom. It is valued as time for the expression of achievement, for the accomplishments of work for both work and leisure are simple time occasions in which we express and act out our basic values. If the work time opportunities diminish so that we are no longer able to gain the necessary rewards in that environment, we will then use the free time environment for those purposes. We believe a man's worth is demonstrated in what he does and traditionally that has been his work. If, as a result of his technology, he no longer needs to spend as many hours on the job, then he will value his recreation behavior for the same reasons he values work—it affords him the occasion to display his worth.

Remember, values are patterns of behavior and belief we hold to be important to our way of life. Leisure behavior is a part of that value structure; the activities we choose for our leisure result from that value structure. There is no independent leisure value system. The dominant value system ranks for us the activities we may pursue in our leisure, and please note I am using leisure as synonymous with free time. Of course, our leisure priorities and behavior are modified by individual and class value orientations.

What we have in leisure are more opportunities to express the existing values. Quickly, let me mention and discuss some of those values. First of all we value action, goal-oriented action. We are a nation of workers and believe time is of value only when something is accomplished. In the past we considered production a desirable goal. More recently we have shifted from action in the sense of production to action in the sense of consumption. We now are a nation of consumers and this shift has implications for recreation, but remember both patterns stem from our belief that action counts.

We value vitality. Those who are most vital are most active; they can produce more or, in a sense, consume more. The young have been proclaimed as those most vital and therefore those to be most imitated and praised. They are glorified for they are the biggest consumers and the group to whom the message is beamed.

We also value individualism. We have long considered the frontier style of life as the American ideal and because we do not want to inhibit individual behavior, we have shifted from an individualism based upon self-reliance to one of permissiveness, based upon affluence and the goals of social welfarism. We tend to confuse the concepts of freedom and license and experience much ambivalence when enforcing the norms of behavior which seemingly inhibit self-expression. We want people to conform but at the same time express their individuality. When you combine this desire with our ability to consume and the immaturity of the model we most glorify, you can understand some of the frustrations of the older generation when they perceive a new value system to be in operation. Actually, the system is not new. We are still adhering to the same values but are developing new ways to express them. Motion is motion whether it be the Model T of the '20s or the dune buggies of the '70s.

Another set of values which we hold dear are those related to civil rights. We believe individuals have the right for equal opportunity but in trying to provide for this, we sometimes equate equality of possession with equal opportunities for expression. Consequently, we want to provide all with the same experience and fail to take into consideration the many individual differences which do exist. Mass programming and mediocrity result from these efforts.

Materialism is another one of our basic beliefs. Because of it, it is not surprising that we are more willing to put investments in facilities and organizational structures than we are in services. We tend to judge individual worth in terms of material possessions, those goods which can be consumed. The value of materialism is supported by the desire for immediate gratification. When we were less affluent, we sought to acquire material possessions but disciplined ourselves to wait until we were able to pay cash for them before we purchased them. With our improved manufacturing and marketing procedures, coupled with a decline in the virtue of thrift, a prerequisite behavior for the former state, we shifted orientations. Immediate pleasure and deferred payment became legitimate. A boom in recreation equipment and apparel resulted with the accompanying demand for occasions for their use.

Finally, as a dominant value we are students of organization. We believe material goods, civil rights, individual freedom, etc. are best achieved when we organize our time for their acquisition. Therefore we create delivery systems to make available the opportunities to re-enforce the validity of these values. Organized recreation is one such system.

True, there have been shifts in the American value system. Some of the values which were formerly held to be important now seem less critical. They are being replaced by other patterns and beliefs, yet the greatest shifts have been not in the values themselves but in the way the values are expressed. Some might say that these shifts constitute a new value system or that they may alter the existing dynamics to the point that a new system will develop. I agree this is possible but at present, the same forces appear to be at work. The new patterns seem to be an extension of those developed in the past.

Some of the shifts which do appear to have change consequences do concern me and have implications for our role in the future. The shift from production to consumption was accompanied by decline in the concepts of thrift. Pollution is a natural by-product of the consumptive society for consumption can exist only when there is high production and few rewards for thrift. The emphasis on youth as the epitome of vitality encourages egocentric and immediate gratification behavior but when you are in a consumption-oriented society, immediate gratification is a desirable goal. The problems arise when the want and search of pleasure leaves in its wake the residue of experience: pollution, the decline of quality, the loss of order, the tinkling of brass and the clash of cymbals. The values of civil rights, when interpreted as equality of possession or "doing your own thing" without responsibility and obligation, raise some interesting questions. Do we make available opportunities to smoke marijuana because the prohibiting of it infringes upon the right of the individual? Do we provide each neighborhood with the same program regardless of its wants to assure all we are treating each equally? To deny is to put our judgment above those we serve unless we value their judgment more than we value our own. Values are learned and once accepted become the molders of behavior. Who is to lead? Who is to follow in this domain?

When groups and individuals rebel against the value system, they often demonstrate their rebellion by choosing patterns directly opposite, the negative image, to the value they say they wish to destroy, thereby re-enforcing their belief in that value. For example, the kids who rebel against the establishment create highly complex political and social organizations to perpetuate their rebellion. Those who have observed the student protests are amazed by the ability of the young to organize for disorganization. They learned the lessons of their fathers well.

When we ask the question of recreation's role in a leisure-oriented society, we're really asking which system or subsystem is to be supported and furthered. There are so many subsystems in operation and so many ways of demonstrating our values we are to encourage. The choice of an alternative itself is based upon a value system. Are we to be universal in our approach or do we support a pattern of particularism?

Before getting to the alternatives there are a couple of summarizing comments I wish to make. Discovered and colonized during the beginning years of the industrial revolution, the growth of America has paralleled the growth of western technology. Work has been and still is a basic force. Success is equated with what one has as a result of what one does. With much of man's labor now being performed by machines, more free time is available for man to demonstrate his possessions. For quite some time individual productivity provided psychic fulfillment but due to advances in technology, these opportunities are less available; consequently, other forms of behavior are being sought to provide this gratification. Recreation is one potential medium with leisure time being the period in which those expressions are made. It is impossible for recreation to assume the same virtues as work unless there are monetary rewards associated with it. However, recreation activities do provide opportunities for self-expression, and inasmuch as free time is a period in which consumptive behavior may be observed by others, its potential value increases. Although recreation is a means of expressing the values associated with work, productivity and consumption, it is not an independent value system. The only means for creating a new value system based upon leisure as a state of being is when labor no longer has monetary value and personal freedoms abound.

The concept of freedom is an interesting one, for in a group situation, freedom exists only as long as the behavior of one individual does not infringe upon the freedom of another. In order to assure rights or freedoms, groups enact laws and create structures to regulate the behavior of their members. In a societal situation, freedom is always prescriptive and our concepts of what is permitted vary from time to time. The concept of leisure as a state of being is incompatible with a society based upon interdependent relationships. When one performs specialized activity which benefits the group, the group depends upon that person to provide those services. The individual providing the services can no longer be free, nor can any of the other members of the group be free since they, too, must provide for all. When we say one has a right to recreate that implies the responsibility of the group to make available opportunities for recreation. Inasmuch as recreation is viewed as an activity on a time continuum, occurring during leisure, free time must be made available for those pursuits, but who is to provide freedom from work?

Finally, I believe play to be one of the driving forces of life, one which results in the adult activities we label as work and recreation. Children learn and are socialized through play. Their play behavior reflects the values of the culture and re-enforces those values. It is a form of social control; in fact, we allow children to play only those games and activities which are sanctioned by the value system to which we subscribe. I believe recreators should always look at play in terms of their value framework, that is if we really program activities to result in certain payoffs such as creative expression, individualism and character development. Socialization occurs whether we plan for it or not. The question is do we want to play a role in the shaping of behavior, and if so, what behavior do we wish to develop and re-enforce?

ALTERNATIVES—THE ROLE OF PARKS AND RECREATION

What should be recreation's stand regarding values, particularly those related to leisure behavior? Several possible courses of action are available. First, we might accept that parks and recreation has no role to play, that the shifts in lifestyle occur because of the larger dynamics at work. We may hold that as a service profession we should provide those experiences which the public seeks and do this in the most efficient manner possible. We should let the value system be shaped by the builders of images, the producers of the products for consumption. Our role then would be to provide the occasions and environment—the mini-bike trails, the camp sites, the recreation complexes—for the consumption of those goods. Values would be the domain of educational, religious, governmental and business institutions, not of the park and recreation profession. Although we should be sensitive to the shifts of lifestyle and accommodate those modifications, this alternative would have us assume the role of the purist and not become involved in the decision making process.

The second alternative is to have the National Recreation and Park Association assume the role of spokesman for the park and recreation movement. The Association would develop statements about values and recreation's contribution to the dominant lifestyle of our people. Priorities would be set by the profession's representative; we would speak our piece through it and take stands on such issues as the desirability of motorized vehicles, the design of playground equipment and children's toys, and the development of the intercoastal water areas. These stands should be specific and should be viewed as the voice of the profession. What do we say about the values associated with the motor bike, the Barbie-type dolls, the design of private camp sites? Do we want to set the profession between the manufacturers of equipment and their users? These stands would suggest political action and would be offered as recommended positions. Each recreation professional or agency could adhere to the position taken by the profession or could disregard or modify it depending upon local needs and value interpretations. In a sense, I am suggesting that National Recreation and Park Association should become a recreation advocate, the Ralph Nader of recreation behavior. It is not a new role for the Association but this suggested action does imply a greater commitment to the issues of values, to their study, and to the conflicts which will result from taking a public, professional stand.

A third possible role we may take is similar to the one just mentioned as it includes that position but goes one step further. It gives the NRPA the power and authority to speak to the profession as well as on its behalf. Such a role would have all professionals adhere to the position taken by our national organization and suggests the development and enforcement of a code of behavior for park and recreation professionals. Implied in that code of behavior would be the role the park and recreation professionals would assume. Such a course of action would require the development of position statements, thoroughly discussed within the profession, and a strict adherence to the position taken by the national organization once it has spoken. This alternative suggests: (1) a universal rather than a particular approach to the problem of values; (2) our role in a society with more free time; and (3) the opportunities and experiences the recreation and park profession are expected to provide.

The final alternative would be to have the profession, with the National Recreation and Park Association as its spokesman, assume the advocate role and call for a White House Conference on Leisure where the goals and objectives for living in a free-time–oriented society could be established. Sister organizations, such as the National Education Association, the American Association of Landscape Architects, the National Wildlife Federations, would be asked to join with the NRPA in asking for the Conference. By assuming this role, the profession would be acting as the initiator of concerns rather than the reactor to crises and the positions taken by other interests. It would have the profession recognizing both the breadth of values that relate to leisure behavior and the genuine concerns other institutions have regarding that behavior. What is the role of the school in educating for a leisure-centered society? What are the responsibilities of business and industry in providing the tools and supplies for leisure living? What is the role of religious organizations in legitimizing the values of free-time expression? What should be expected from governmental agencies in developing opportunities for leisure activities? The assumption of this leadership role and the convening of a White House Conference on Leisure should produce the platform upon which the profession could move to assure the quality of living we believe to be in the best interest of all our citizens.

RECOMMENDED COURSE OF ACTION

Of the four possible courses of action identified the last appears to be the most feasible. As stated throughout this presentation, leisure behavior is only one form of human behavior and is conditioned by the same forces which govern our non-leisure actions. No one institution or agency has claim over the individual when he practices his recreation and society has not given the recreation and park profession the authority to speak for it on these matters. The assumption of this authority might result in approval but there is little evidence to support this view. Consequently, I feel the National Recreation and Park Association should not act alone in defining the role of parks and recreation in a leisure-oriented society. Any concerned action which may result from the efforts of NRPA will succeed only when other institutions are involved in the study of lifestyles and the programs to be created to affect the quality of living we desire. Ours is the role of the advocate, the initiator, the leader, and we are the ones uniquely qualified by commitment and training to assume the task.

Each of the alternatives I posed is based upon a value orientation. The first, to do nothing and allow others to shape the destiny of American behavior, to sit back and accept the role of a purist, is permissible in our society but one to which I would prefer not to subscribe. The second and third alternatives suggest a legislative and somewhat autocratic approach which I find desirable but unfeasible at this time. For these alternatives to be successful, the profession must develop a greater degree of unity and identity than it now possesses. Also, the political power of parks and recreation professionals would have to be strengthened considerably. Public recognition of our field as the legitimate providers and authorities of recreation, and the professionals' acceptance of the NRPA as the voice of the profession, are prerequisites. I hope it will not be too long before these alternatives are real possibilities. The fourth proposal is consistent with both our status and value systems. It is predicated upon our ability to organize and involve others and may lead to the realization of positions two and three.

Some might argue that to involve others in determining the role of recreation in a leisure-oriented society is to sell our profession short. They may hold this alternative to be a non-professional one for aren't recreators and park professionals in the best position to suggest the values we are to support in a leisure society? I say not and hope I have developed a rationale for my decision. Recreation is not a right for which government has the responsibility to provide all opportunities. It is one form of free-time behavior and organized recreation has been charged to provide only a segment of the experiences which one defines as recreation. Then, too, the political realities are such that it would be folly to think the park and recreation movement alone could establish the basic value system for a world in which free-time activities will increasingly play a more important role. We must work with others in defining the style of life which we will support and which we will provide the opportunities to shape.

Values are a national concern. By calling for a White House Conference on Leisure, we may create the climate for a critical analysis of the realities of the American dream. The issues of values have too far-ranging conse-quences to be thought of as the responsibility of any one group. Yet these issues must be faced. What we offer in the form of recreation experiences will result from the dominant values of our society and shape the future behavior of generations. People have played and will continue to play and will learn from the kinds of play they are afforded. As Pieper wrote, leisure is the basis of culture. I believe the future belongs to those who are willing to accept the challenge and I know of no group I would rather see take the leadership in the study of leisure behavior, its use and potential, than the recreation and park profession.

some implications
of time

NELS ANDERSON

Never has man had such a relationship to time. On the one hand, some new perspectives of time give new meanings to work, while on the other hand, new ways of work give new meanings to time in a chicken-egg interdependence. Also leisure, as we have recognized, has come on the scene, affecting our relationships to both work and time. All of this is recent and still very much in process.

Moreover, the implications of time may be seen in our ways of community living, in the changing role of distance in our daily rounds, and in the nature of our person-to-person contacts. Also changing is man's relationship to his total measure of time and to the different cycles in his life: family cycle, work cycle, and the span of his years. Perhaps time acquires no new values for modern man, but those values impress themselves differently on his consciousness.

FROM NATURAL TO MECHANICAL TIME

Huxley wrote, "The time of which we have knowledge is artificial, machine-made time. Of natural, cosmic time, as it is measured out by sun and moon, we are for the most part almost wholly unconscious. Pre-industrial people know time in its daily, monthly and seasonal rhythms. They are aware of sunrise, noon and sunset; of the full moon and the new; of equinox and solstice; of spring and summer, autumn and winter."[1] Time

Copyright © 1964 by David McKay Company, Inc. From the book *Dimensions of Work* by Nels Anderson. Reprinted by the permission of the publisher, David McKay Company, Inc.

[1]Aldous Huxley, "Time and the Machine," *The Olive Tree and Other Essays* (London, Chatto, 1947), pp. 122–24. He adds this about the urbanite: "He is the inhabitant of an artificial universe that is, to a great extent, walled off from the world of nature. Outside the walls time is cosmic and moves with the motion of sun and stars. Within, it is an affair of revolving wheels and is measured in seconds and minutes."

to modern man is largely a matter of clock and calendar and only secondarily a matter of the criteria mentioned by Huxley.

Most philosophers of earlier times, so De Grazia observes, had a *circular* conception of time: the spring returns every fourth season, bringing all plant life back to vigor again; each species renews itself in the birth of its young; even history is seen as repeating itself. Time in the industrial world is generally seen as *linear,* going on without beginning or end, never backtracking, and never veering from course.[2] Understandably the first conception, often called *natural* time, was an unconscious adaptation to the rhythms of the natural universe. The time by which most of us regulate our lives is called *mechanical* because it reflects the interdependence of man and the rhythms of his machines.

Mechanical time is not dissociated from nature but, as noted by Toynbee, it links itself with nature in a more cosmic way.[3] Time and nature are converted into abstractions. Time for the farmer involves a more elemental relationship between him and the forces called natural, and his notions about such time are mixed into various folk beliefs; he may plant his crops or breed his animals according to the right phase of the moon. There are right times as well as right ways of performing each type of work. He, like the fisherman or hunter, has his body of knowledge (in which fact and fancy are agreeably intermingled) for starting, doing, or stopping work. In what may be called the time pattern of his work all sorts of nonwork and leisure interests are to be found. The seasons determine when to work, when to pray, and when to dance, and there is room in his thinking for weather lore. None of this has place in the rational uses of mechanical time. It is also called *pure* time because for practical purposes it must be reduced to an abstraction.

Mechanical time came into use because, among other reasons, the industrial civilization demands more precision, promptness, and regularity than natural time can provide. Sombart mentions the urgency of deliveries rightly timed as well as money values of time in commercial transactions. One loses if another comes late, or both lose.[4] It is mechanical time the engineer must use in planning or directing a project, and the same time must be used by the mechanic to measure the speed or output of a machine or the co-ordination of machines in a series. When the scientist would

[2]Sebastian de Grazia, *Of Time, Work and Leisure* (New York, Twentieth Century Fund, 1962), p. 319. Circular time is also identified as biological and as such is self-regulating.

[3]Arnold J. Toynbee, *A Study of History* (London, Oxford, 1955), Vol. 7, p. 294. In finding ways to measure time precisely, man is doing no more nor less than was necessary in his measurement of space, volume, and weight.

[4]Werner Sombart, *Der Bourgeois* (München und Leipzig, Duncker & Humblot, 1913), p. 421. A summary of the evolution of the clock is given, with observations about its importance for commerce and science.

measure relationships between durations and other abstractions (space, distance, momentum, volume) he must use mechanical time.

The approximate timing in the sphere of nature is not sufficient where interdependence exists in work activity and where goings, comings, and meetings in time and space must be precise. Except for mechanical time, the industrial urban civilization could hardly function. Indeed, degrees of difference between countries with respect to development can be told in terms of their respective commitment to a rational use of mechanical time. This Presthus found in his study of a public authority for industrial work in Turkey.[5]

We associate mechanical time with a special kind of environment, natural time with another, and each has its own kind of tempo. The environment of mechanical time is largely man-made: buildings, paved streets, water systems, sewage systems, lighting and communications networks, even the parks, are man-made. In this environment the rhythms of natural time in many respects may be and usually are disregarded. A plant or office may work "around the clock," messages go and come at any hour, and transportation is continuous. Daytime is preferred for most activities, but many are performed in the night (cleaning, moving things) so that daytime work can move with the minimum of interruption.

[5]Robert V. Presthus, "Weberian versus Welfare Bureaucracy in Traditional Society," *Administrative Science Quarterly,* Vol. 6, No. 1, June 1961, pp. 14–15, adds this regarding different assumptions and valuations of time: "Whereas Western man is *personally* concerned with time, by which he measures out his life in hours, days and years, man in underdeveloped society feels little or no personal affinity with time, over which he seems to have so little influence. This conception of time is bound up with fatalism, with an often well-documented conclusion that man has little control over his personal destiny. Thus the Western belief that man can shape his future by the application of logic, rationality and time is often out of context."

a society of leisure

KENNETH ROBERTS

LEISURE IN A COMPARATIVE PERSPECTIVE

In many fields of social research one finds that, when the results of investigations into different aspects of a problem are all drawn together, the effect is to produce a confused mass of detail rather than a precisely delineated model of the contours of the problem. Attempting simply to add together the results of different empirical studies is rarely a satisfactory way of obtaining general conclusions about a topic, and this is certainly the case with the research that has been conducted in the field of leisure. Collecting together the available information upon what people do during their free time, the relationship of leisure to work and family roles, and the way in which leisure organizations work, does not produce any obvious conclusions about the role that leisure plays in contemporary society. In itself the available research material does not enable us to draw general conclusions about the place of leisure in contemporary social life, partly because there remain many aspects of leisure which research has yet hardly touched upon; but when the findings of studies of leisure in contemporary society are set against our knowledge of the role that leisure has played within other cultures, certain distinctive characteristics of leisure in modern society instantly become apparent.

All known human societies have possessed activities enabling people to find enjoyment, amusement, self-fulfilment, and self-enrichment. The experiences that modern man gains from his leisure are cultural universals, but the ways in which these experiences have been obtained have varied immensely.[1] The distinctive feature of leisure in modern industrial society is the extent to which it has become a differentiated institution. This point

From Kenneth Roberts, *Leisure,* by permission of Humanities Press, Inc., New York, and Longman Group Limited.

[1]For evidence that the experiences which we describe as leisure are cultural universals see N. P. Miller and D. M. Robinson, *The Leisure Age: Its Challenge to Recreation* (Belmont, Calif.: Wadsworth, 1963).

was touched upon in the last chapter when the development of an industry specifically geared to catering for the public's leisure needs was noted, but the extent to which leisure has become a differentiated institution goes far beyond the fact that such an industry exists. There are particular periods during the day, the week, and the year, which people define as leisure time. Leisure is differentiated not only in terms of there being organizations specifically designed to cater for it, but also in terms of its possessing a definite place in the rhythm of life. In addition to this, leisure is now recognized as a distinct cultural entity. People are aware that certain experiences are leisure experiences—for instance, seeking amusement and recreation are recognized as leisure activities—and enjoying one's leisure is valued for its own sake. In terms of the values through which people view life, in terms of the way in which time is distributed, and in terms of the social structure, leisure is a clearly differentiated institution.

In pre-industrial societies the experiences that modern man derives from his leisure were normally provided in alternative ways. In the civilization of ancient Greece the dominant cultural ideal urged the citizens to cultivate a balanced way of life. In fact the concept of leisure to the ancient Greeks referred to a balanced way of life which included enjoyment and self-fulfilment but also encompassed work, political activity and religious observance. The idea of valuing activities in themselves simply because they produced amusement would have been foreign to the Greeks' basic approach to life. Such experiences were valued, for enjoyment and amusement were certainly not frowned upon, but they were valued only in so far as they contributed to the total way of life that was the cultural ideal. The point is that in Greek civilization the citizens had no concept of leisure such as the one that we are familiar with today. People did not recognize the enjoyment of free time as being a desirable activity in its own right; enjoyable experiences were intertwined with their culture's prescribed total style of life, and there were no organizations or institutions whose specific job was to provide recreation and entertainment. Activities such as the theatre and athletics had a religious and political significance in addition to the recreational significance that they possess in our own civilization.

The civilization of Greece was not unusual in not differentiating leisure from other areas of life, for until the twentieth century the notion of valuing leisure for its own sake was virtually unknown.[2] Medieval pursuits such as jousting and archery, as has already been mentioned, were forms of military training in addition to being enjoyable pastimes. In these

---

[2]For information about leisure in non-industrial societies see I. Craven, "Leisure," *Encyclopaedia of the Social Sciences*, Vol. V (New York: The Macmillan Company, 1933), p. 402; and P. C. McIntosh, *Sport in Society*, Watts, 1963.

sports rules were adopted to avert injury and to increase the enjoyment derived from the activities, but they were not a form of pure leisure such as is experienced in contemporary society. In urban areas in medieval times certain recreational pursuits were instituted by the citizens purely for their own amusement, and similar institutions were also found in Ancient Rome, but before the modern industrial era it was very unusual to find leisure existing as a culturally and structurally distinct part of society.

Even in nineteenth-century Britain leisure was not valued as a part of life and a type of activity that was desirable for its own sake. The sports that were incorporated into public school life during the nineteenth century were promoted not because the schools were concerned that their pupils should enjoy themselves, but because it was believed that team games could exercise a wider beneficial moral and social influence. Encouraging children to do things purely for their own amusement would not have been considered to be a sound educational practice. Many of the sports that achieved widespread popularity towards the end of the nineteenth century were initially sponsored by organizations that had a faith in the desirable moral effects of physical recreation. Some of the football clubs currently competing in the Football League were initially founded by religious organizations in the belief that this type of sporting activity could be an effective means of providing moral discipline and training for its working-class participants.

When municipal authorities became involved in the provision of parks and open spaces upon which games could be played, the spending of public money on such facilities was justified in terms of the contribution to the physical health of the population that it would make, and a healthy population, it was argued, was desirable for both economic and military reasons. Spending public money simply in order that people could enjoy themselves would not have been considered justified.

The youth clubs that various voluntary associations began to found during the nineteenth century were not instituted with the idea of simply facilitating the recreation and amusement of juveniles. The aim of the founders of the youth movement was to help to make young people into useful adult members of society and to steer them clear of immoral and anti-social influences. The para-military organization of many of the early youth clubs betrays the fact that their concern was more with the training of the young for a disciplined adulthood than with merely providing opportunities for recreation.[3] It is really only since the Second World War that the idea of providing youth clubs to which young people can go simply to relax and to enjoy themselves has received any significant support.

[3]W. M. Evans, *Young People in Society*, Blackwell, 1965.

These attitudes towards sport and recreation that were found in nine-teenth-century Britain cannot be explained purely in terms of the influence of puritanism and the protestant ethic upon British culture. The explanation is that the existence of leisure as a separate part of people's lives, catered for by its own social institutions, was virtually unknown before the twentieth century. Leisure as it is experienced today is really a product of industrial society. It is not just that the productive power of industrialism has given to the population time and money to cultivate leisure interests on an unprecedented scale, but that it has also created a new cultural awareness of leisure that was previously impossible. Industrialization has created not only the spare-time and surplus income that is available for discretionary spending: it has also instituted a rhythm of life in which set hours are devoted to work, after which man's time is free. Social obligations, centered upon an individual's occupation, are compressed in terms of time, and people are left with a part of their lives to use purely in accordance with their own inclinations and interests. As a consequence of this, institutions have developed to cater for people's leisure needs, and leisure thereby has become a differentiated element within the structure of society. But apart from this structural separation of leisure the population has been made aware that certain activities are leisure activities and that certain occasions are leisure time. The population has been made consciously aware of leisure as a distinct element in its rhythm of life, and particular pursuits can now be valued purely for their worth as leisure activities. Leisure values, in this way, are incorporated into society's culture, and people are able to think about and experience leisure in a way that was formerly impossible.

Nowadays sports and games are valued for the satisfaction and enjoyment that they yield as leisure activities. The fact that since the war the former Central Council of Physical Training has been renamed the Central Council of Physical Recreation symbolizes the way in which social attitudes towards sports and games have changed. Anyone can legitimately participate in sports provided that they derive pleasure from the experience, even if they are physically disabled and cannot hope to achieve a normal standard of competence. Being a professional entertainer no longer has a disreputable stigma attached to it, as was once the case. Youth clubs and all other types of leisure activities are judged in terms of the pleasure and enjoyment they yield. People no longer have to seek an ulterior motive in order to justify having fun. The new emerging cultural attitudes towards leisure were given intellectual justification by Huizinga, who argued in his book, *Homo Ludens*,[4] that play was a type of activity that met basic human needs and was therefore an indispensable element in all human civiliza-

[4] J. Huizinga, *Homo Ludens: A Study of the Play Element in Culture*, Routledge, 1950.

tions. Today such cultural attitudes towards play and leisure have been firmly institutionalized. Indeed, Margaret Mead[5] has argued that to have fun and to enjoy oneself have now become mandatory social obligations, and that work is now regarded by many people as a place where they can relax and escape from the pressure of the new social values which demand that the individual derives the maximum possible enjoyment from his free time.

The existence of leisure as a distinct part of the structure of contemporary society is one of the distinguishing features of the role that leisure plays in the life of modern man. It is a distinguishing and basic feature whose significance can be seen only when the facts that have been collected about the rhythm of life and leisure, and about the importance of organizations catering for the public's leisure needs in contemporary society, are contrasted with the different patterns of life that have been normal in pre-industrial civilizations. Traditional attitudes towards self-indulgence and recreation still persist to some extent within the culture of British society. But the extent to which leisure has established for itself a distinctly recognized and valued place in contemporary life is not difficult to appreciate when the contrast is made with the values and structures of earlier societies.

As leisure has gradually established a definite place in people's lives its autonomy from the influence of other institutions has correspondingly increased. The extent to which the activities people elect to devote their leisure to are independent from the other social roles that they play has been commented upon throughout the earlier chapters; but in societies in which the experiences and activities that people would nowadays describe as leisure were interwoven with the roles that they played in institutions performing additional social functions, styles of recreation had to be closely related to the other positions that people occupied within society. In medieval Britain different forms of recreation were associated with particular social classes. Hunting and jousting were upper-class activities, the lower orders of society being excluded not only by economic factors but also by the law, since to participate in the pursuits of the upper classes would have indicated that an individual of lower status was attempting to step outside the role in society to which he had been allocated and adopt a style of life that was the prerogative of the higher social strata. The styles of life associated with different positions in society all contained their own patterns of recreational experience. Even in the nineteenth century styles of recreation were closely linked to social status. A person's class position was central to the entire pattern of his life, and most of the new sports that

[5]M. Mead, "The Pattern of Leisure in Contemporary American Culture," *Annals of the American Academy of Political and Social Science,* Vol. 313, p. 11.

were later popularized during the second half of the nineteenth century were initially devised by and for a particular status group. The class origins of some of our modern popular sports are indicated in their rules. The rule relating to gentlemanly conduct in association football indicates that initially this was a sport devised for the recreation of the gentlemanly strata of society.

Today, forms of recreation that were initially associated with particular classes are more likely to draw followers from all sections of society. People from all classes and of all ages are able to select from a range of possible leisure activities which are open to all members of society. Relationships between occupational and family roles and leisure do exist, but the relationships between them are mostly weak and there is no longer a stringent social expectation that people will use their free time in ways appropriate to their stations in society. Leisure activities are valued for their own sake and people adopt particular activities purely for the pleasure derived from them. Whether a particular form of recreation is considered appropriate for a person of a particular class, sex or age still has some influence, but it is becoming increasingly weak. The differentiation of leisure within society in terms of culture and structure, and the autonomy of leisure from the influence of other social institutions, are distinctive features of modern society.

LEISURE AS THE BASIS OF CONTEMPORARY LIFE

The fact that leisure now occupies an autonomous place in the life of contemporary man justifies treating it as a subject which deserves the attention of sociologists. There are some sociologists, however, who consider that the sociological significance of leisure goes far beyond its mere existence as a distinct aspect of life in contemporary society. It has been argued that leisure occupies such a central place in the life of contemporary man that its analysis is a pre-condition for the development of any sociology that seeks to understand the structure and functioning of modern society. It has been argued that advanced industrial societies are becoming societies of leisure, in which leisure and its associated institutions and values are becoming the key elements around which the remainder of the social system evolves. Whilst all those sociologists who have examined the problem agree that the development of industrialism has given leisure a distinct place in the lives of the members of modern society, the idea that leisure is a factor of key importance in determining the shape of the entire social structure of contemporary society is decidedly contentious, and conflicting views have been expressed as to just how influential leisure is.

Those sociologists who claim that society is becoming leisure-based do so not on the grounds that the quantity of the leisure that people are able to enjoy is increasing at such a rate that it is becoming the dominant element in their lives; nor do they claim that the ways in which people spend their leisure are completely uninfluenced by the other roles that they play within society. The claim that societies of leisure are in the process of becoming established is based upon the view that the self-consciousness of modern man is based mainly upon the interests and activities which he pursues during his leisure, and that therefore the values and attitudes which are associated with leisure will exercise a generalized influence throughout all spheres of people's lives. In modern societies people play numerous specific roles. In playing some roles individuals merely conform outwardly with the demands that are made upon them, whilst in other roles they feel that they are really a part of what they are doing; they identify with their roles and consider the values and attitudes associated with them to be their own. In playing some roles people act the required part without any sense of personal commitment, whilst when playing other roles they consider that the parts they are acting enable them to display qualities with which they are willing to identify their real selves. Those who argue that society is becoming leisure-centred do so on the grounds that it is in their leisure lives that individuals feel that they are expressing their real personalities. The individual's self-concept is based upon, and reinforced by, the activities he undertakes during his leisure. In other spheres of life, for example when the individual is at work, he feels relatively detached from the role that he is playing and does not identify his own personality with the qualities which his job demands that he displays. The argument that society is becoming leisure-based goes on to assert that, since individuals internalize the qualities and values associated with their leisure lives, they will attempt to play all the other roles that they enter, in so far as they are allowed sufficient latitude, in accordance with their leisure-centred self-concepts. Attitudes and values generated during leisure are therefore carried by individuals into other social situations, and in this way are able to exercise a generalized influence upon patterns of social life. In order to function effectively other social institutions have to accommodate their own values and structures to the leisure-based orientations of the public. Thus leisure, as the source of man's sense of self-identity, becomes the basis of all social life.

Support for this view of the importance of leisure in contemporary society is to be found in the writings of a considerable number of sociologists who base their conclusions upon evidence collected in several different modern industrial societies. Upon the basis of evidence collected in European societies Dumazedier[6] has argued strongly that it is his leisure

[6]J. Dumazedier, *Towards a Society of Leisure* (New York: The Macmillan Company, 1967).

that is the major determinant of man's self-consciousness, and that the style of life the individual develops during his leisure forms the basis for the adoption of values and attitudes that affect his behaviour in all other spheres of life. Anderson,[7] also drawing extensively upon research conducted in Europe, argues that it is now leisure that gives the members of contemporary society a meaning in life. From being an unplanned and initially unwelcome product of industrialism, leisure has emerged to play a central role in modern society. Other aspects of life, such as work, have become relatively meaningless and people structure their lives around their leisure interests and needs.

Similar arguments have been offered by American sociologists such as David Riesman and the co-authors of *The Lonely Crowd.*[8] For the 'other-directed' man, the product of mature industrial society, leisure and consumption are held to occupy the central place in his style of life. In his subsequent writings, Riesman[9] has argued that the values embodied in other American institutions will have to be modified to accommodate these new orientations of contemporary man if they are to continue to function effectively. In the sphere of education, for instance, Riesman argues that the schools will have to concern themselves increasingly with preparing the young for their future leisure lives, rather than for occupational roles, if education is to continue to be a meaningful experience. Lowenthal's[10] analysis of the subjects of biographies in American popular magazines showed that during the twentieth century the interest of biographers, and presumably the members of the public who read popular magazines, had switched away from the businessman and towards entertainers and popular artists. These are American society's new cultural heroes, demonstrating that it is leisure and those personalities who cater for it that now capture the attention and interest of the public. Leisure has become the part of life to which people attach the greatest interest and importance.

Writing about British society Burns[11] has drawn almost identical conclusions to these. He has argued that leisure is ceasing to be overshadowed by work and is becoming the element that gives the individual a meaning in everyday life. One of the themes of Zweig's study of *The Worker in an Affluent Society*[12] was that relationships formed at work with both col-

[7]N. Anderson, *Work and Leisure* (Routledge, 1967).

[8]D. Riesman, et al., *The Lonely Crowd: A Study of the Changing American Character* (New Haven, Conn.: Yale University Press, 1967).

[9]D. Riesman, "Leisure and Work in Post-industrial Society," in E. Larrabee and R. Meyersohn, eds., *Mass Leisure,* Glencoe Free Press, 1958.

[10]L. Lowenthal, "Biographies in Popular Magazines: From Production Leaders to Consumption Idols," in A. and E. Etzioni, eds., *Social Change: Sources, Patterns, and Consequences,* Basic Books, 1964.

[11]T. Burns, "A Meaning in Everyday Life," *New Society,* 25 May 1967.

[12]F. Zweig, *The Worker in an Affluent Society: Family Life and Industry,* Heinemann, 1961.

leagues and supervisors were becoming irrelevant to the worker's own conception of his place in society. The workers that Zweig interviewed felt that the nature of their jobs gave no indication of the type of people that they really were. It was the interests that they cultivated and the styles of life that they adopted during their leisure upon which the workers based their sense of self-identity. The nature of their consumption patterns, rather than the characteristics of their jobs, was what the workers felt to be the most important indicator of their position in society. As a result, Zweig argued, traditional class divisions and lines of conflict were being blurred and a new system of stratification based upon styles of life developed outside the workplace was emerging. Status groups, rather than socio-economic classes, to use Max Weber's terminology, were becoming the basis of the individual's consciousness and sense of prestige. Many studies of young people and their attitudes have emphasized the leisure-centredness of their lives.[13] It is leisure that offers the most satisfying, and to young people the most important, experiences of their lives, and the young person tends to judge other spheres of activity in terms of the significance that they possess for the style of leisure he wishes to develop.

There are sociologists who strenuously dispute the view that life in contemporary society is becoming leisure-centred. Whilst admitting that leisure has come to occupy a distinct place in the structure of modern society and in the lives of its members, they dispute that it is leisure that acts as the basis for the development of man's sense of self-identity and thereby exercises a persuasive influence upon all other areas of his life. Foremost amongst those who reject the leisure-based view of modern life are Wilensky[14] and Blumberg,[15] both of whom remain faithful to the traditional sociological view that it is their occupations which structure the styles of life and attitudes of the members of society. Wilensky argues that it is the relationships which men enter into at work and the values and attitudes that are generated within them that shape their style of life. The leisure activities that they prefer and are capable of participating in are determined by the nature of their jobs. Wilensky used this approach to argue that the nature of work in contemporary industry is so stultifying for many employees that it effectively prevents them from developing satisfying forms of recreation. The evidence upon which Wilensky's claims are based, however, is rather thin, and much of the data that he has collected does not appear to support his main arguments. Blumberg maintains that work occupies such a large proportion of man's time that it must

---

[13]For evidence of young people's indifference about work and education in contrast to the importance they attach to their free time see M. P. Carter, *Home, School and Work*, Pergamon, 1962.

[14]H. L. Wilensky, "Work as a Social Problem," in H. S. Becker, ed., *Social Problems: A Modern Approach* (New York: John Wiley, 1969).

[15]P. Blumberg, *Industrial Democracy: The Sociology of Participation*, Constable, 1968.

have a pervasive effect upon the entire pattern of his life. It is for this reason that Blumberg considers that making work more satisfying is the main task facing contemporary civilization, and he rejects the view that work need no longer be treated as a social problem on account of the greater importance that people attach to their leisure. Blumberg's faith in the paramount importance of work is, however, based more upon persuasive argument than empirical evidence.

On such a broad issue as whether or not leisure is acting as the basis of man's self-consciousness, and whether or not it is thereby influencing other areas of social life it would be wrong to expect a definitive, unqualified answer. The extent to which people do identify with the qualities demanded by the leisure roles that they play, and the extent to which other aspects of their lives are consequently influenced, will be matters of degree, and the extent to which leisure acts as the basis of people's lives can be expected to vary between different sections of society. It has been demonstrated that other roles that people play, at work and in the family for example, do exert some influence upon the use to which leisure is put, and although this influence is often of a marginal nature it is clear that leisure is not a totally autonomous sphere of life. Even though some investigators found evidence pointing to the conclusion that leisure does influence people's conduct in other areas of social life, the extent of this influence exercised by leisure has never been systematically measured in any empirical investigation. Under these circumstances it would be foolish either to embrace or reject in an unqualified manner the view that life in contemporary society is becoming leisure-based. The fact that the research necessary to establish the extent to which leisure does influence the structure of other institutions has not yet been conducted indicates the extent to which this area of study has been neglected. The potential importance of leisure in society has been overlooked and remains unassessed, but, despite the absence of really conclusive evidence, my own view is that the information which is available suggests that there is a substantial amount of truth in the view that life in contemporary societies is leisure-based.

Firstly, there is the evidence presented by the sociologists referred to above on the extent to which man's self-identity is based upon his leisure activities and achievements. In addition, there is the evidence that can be drawn from studies undertaken in a variety of fields in which investigators have been obliged to use leisure-based values and attitudes in order to explain people's conduct.

Some of the evidence was quoted in the earlier chapters on the relationships between leisure and work and the family. Foote[16] and Wolfenstein[17]

---

[16]N. Foote, "Sex as Play," *Social Problems,* Vol. I, p. 159.

[17]M. Wolfenstein, "The Emergence of a Fun Morality," *Journal of Social Issues,* Vol. 7, p. 15.

have shown respectively how aspects of family life such as sexual behaviour and the rearing of children are being influenced by the leisure-based values of play and fun. In industry there are studies, such as that of Goldthorpe,[18] showing that the instrumental approach that workers adopt towards their jobs makes their occupational behaviour incomprehensible except in terms of the styles of leisure around which employees structure their careers and job attitudes.

Sociologists working in other diverse fields have also found it necessary to refer to leisure in order to explain people's behaviour in various areas of social life. Pickering,[19] for instance, has argued that the developments that have taken place in the religious behaviour of the population and the functioning of religious institutions since the nineteenth century can only be understood in terms of the extent to which life has become leisure-centred. The importance of leisure in the lives of the public, Pickering argues, has transformed religion into a leisure-time activity. With the legal obligations that formerly compelled people to attend church having been withdrawn, and with the informal social pressures that made religious observance mandatory also having weakened, attending church has become just one possible way of using free time amongst many others, and people decide whether or not to go to church in accordance with how attractive church-going appears to be compared with alternative forms of recreation. Without being aware of what was happening the churches have been forced to accommodate themselves to this new attitude towards the religious observance. Pickering notes the extent to which, since the nineteenth century, the major Christian denominations have ceased to make heavy moral demands upon their congregations, have ceased attempting to arouse respect by the use of supernatural fears and threats, and have incorporated new pleasurable elements, such as choirs and social occasions, into their range of activities. These developments that religious institutions have been obliged to accept are only explicable once the leisure-centredness of the lives of their potential congregations is acknowledged.

Criminology is another area of social research in which the central role that leisure plays in people's lives has had to be recognized, in this case in order to explain the causes of deviant behaviour. One of the most popular approaches to the explanation of criminality in recent years has been based upon the theory of anomie initially formulated by Merton,[20] who claimed that when a discrepancy exists between the goals that society

[18]J. H. Goldthorpe et al., *The Affluent Worker: Industrial Attitudes and Behavior* (Cambridge: Cambridge University Press, 1968).

[19]W. Pickering, "Religion: A Leisure Time Pursuit," in D. A. Martin, ed., *A Sociological Yearbook of Religion in Britain,* S.C.M.P., 1968.

[20]R. K. Merton, "Social Structure and Anomie," in *Social Theory and Social Structure,* Glencoe Free Press, 1957.

urges its members to aspire towards and the means that society makes available for legitimately pursuing these goals some sort of deviant behaviour is bound to result. Basing their approach upon these theoretical foundations, a number of criminologists have identified the causes of crime in the blocked educational and vocational aspirations with which many young people, especially those from disadvantaged backgrounds amongst whom recorded crime rates are known to be particularly high, are faced.[21] In Britain, however, empirical research work conducted amongst young people has found little evidence of frustration at failing to achieve desired educational and occupational goals. The vocational and educational aspirations of young people in Britain are remarkably realistic, and when disappointments are encountered young people reconcile themselves to their fortunes with little difficulty.[22] Explaining deviant behavior in terms of the inability of young people to use legitimate means to achieve the qualifications and occupations that they would ideally have liked appears to be a reasonable approach, but in Britain it is inconsistent with the facts. Downes,[23] upon the basis of his research amongst young people in London, came to the conclusion that, in so far as young people do run into difficulties in realizing their aspirations, the relevant aspirations have to do with the style of leisure that they want to adopt rather than the educational certificates and jobs that they want to achieve. With young people's lives being basically leisure-centred, it is their ambitions to indulge in particular types of recreation that will matter most, and it is frustrations in this sphere of life that will lead to the strongest reaction. If delinquency is to be explained in terms of anomie theory it is in leisure goals and the means to achieve them that the relevant discrepancy in society's value system will lie. In their free time Downes found that the young people he studied possessed an urge to experience excitement and to engage in a variety of pursuits that cost money. If money and excitement could not be obtained legitimately the young people would resort to deviant methods of obtaining those satisfactions from their leisure that they considered to be important. Like studies in many other areas of social life, this enquiry into the origins of crime was forced to take into account attitudes and values based upon leisure in order to render its subject matter comprehensible.

Leisure is an important subject for sociological study, not only because it has become an integral part of the structure of contemporary society, and

[21]For example see A. K. Cohen, *Delinquent Boys: The Culture of the Gang*, Glencoe Free Press, 1955; and R. A. Cloward and L. E. Ohlin, *Delinquency and Opportunity: A Theory of Delinquent Gangs*, Routledge, 1961.

[22]See K. Roberts, "The Entry into Employment: An Approach Towards a General Theory," *Sociological Review*, Vol. 16, p. 165.

[23]D. M. Downes, *The Delinquent Solution; A Study in Subcultural Theory*, Routledge, 1966.

because it now accounts for an expanding proportion of people's time, but also because the analysis of other institutional systems cannot proceed without taking account of the role that leisure plays in the lives of the members of society. The meagre attention that sociology has paid to the study of leisure has therefore seriously handicapped attempts to investigate and explain other aspects of life in contemporary society. As has just been indicated, a few sociologists working in varied fields have developed an appreciation of the relevance of leisure to their own subject matter, and our knowledge of topics such as delinquency and religious behaviour has been advanced by those sociologists who have realized the pervasive influence that leisure has within the structure of contemporary society. There are probably many other as yet unresolved sociological problems to which an appreciation of the importance of leisure could add some penetrating insights. In industrial sociology for instance, many investigations have noted the failure of schemes instituted with the object of increasing employee-participation in managerial decision-making to capture the interest of the workers on the shop floor. Why workers should so consistently have failed to take advantage of opportunities offered to them to play a greater part in the control of their own working lives has remained a mystery. The failure of particular schemes has been attributed to various factors: the unwillingness of managers to grant real power to the relevant works committees, mistrust of the idea of being thought of as one of management's aides on the shop floor, the failure of workers' representatives to maintain contact with the rank and file, and the worker's lack of the skills and knowledge necessary to play a really effective role in management, have all been blamed for the lack of success experienced in attempts to increase employee-participation. It could, however, be that employees remain uninvolved in such experiments because they lack interest in their working lives and are centrally concerned with their leisure, and that they prefer to involve themselves in alternative leisure activities rather than devote some additional effort to their working lives.

In studies of trade unionism a similar apathy on the part of the rank-and-file members has been noted, and various investigators have tried to discover what it is about the trade unions that prevents them capturing the active interest of the majority of their supporters. Whether it is the size of the unions that is at fault, or whether the problem is that real power in the unions is monopolized by oligarchical elites, or whether the difficulty lies in the remoteness of bargaining from the worker's own place of work, are answers to this issue that various research workers have conjured with. Again the answer might lie in the trade unionists' preference for involving themselves in more orthodox and perhaps more satisfying types of leisure activity.

In our democratic political system the failure of the public to acquire sufficient knowledge of political issues to use its power in a rational way, and the disinclination of most citizens to extend their political activities beyond voting at general elections, have been widely commented upon. It has been inferred that anti-democratic elements must still be present in our political institutions, and that some sort of political reform is necessary in order to make our society really democratic. But once again the reason why the public seeks little involvement in the political process is quite probably because people are preoccupied with their leisure. They desire no further involvement than is socially obligatory in other areas of social life, for it is their leisure from which they derive the greatest meaning and satisfaction, and if organizations such as political parties, business enterprises, trade unions, and churches wish to obtain voluntary support and commitment from the public that goes beyond the bounds of what is socially obligatory, it is necessary for these organizations to make themselves attractive as leisure activities.

It is not my intention to claim that leisure is the one factor that determines the shape of people's lives and the structure of society. Other roles that individual's play do influence their self-consciousness, and leisure itself is affected by other elements in the social system. The evidence that does support the view that life in modern society is leisure-based is itself far from conclusive. But the information we have at our disposal does suggest that, along with other modern societies, Britain has become a society of leisure in that the activities in which people elect to participate during their free time play a significant part in the development of their sense of self-identity, and leisure thereby is accorded the power to reciprocate the influence that other institutions have upon it. Having leisure play such a role in social life is historically unusual. It is only the way in which leisure has emerged since the nineteenth century as a differentiated element in the structure of society that has made its contemporary role possible. The influence that leisure exerts upon people's lives and upon other institutions is specific to advanced industrial societies, which is why it is justifiable to call them societies of leisure. Understanding the ways in which the public uses its free time has become fundamental to understanding how other social institutions function, and sociology needs to acknowledge the importance of leisure in order to answer more general questions about the structure of contemporary society.

chapter two

Classical Dimension of Leisure

GRECO-ROMAN TRADITION

According to the classical-humanistic conceptualization, leisure "is an activity which involves pursuit of truth and self-understanding. It is an act of aesthetic, psychological, religious and philosophical contemplation."[1] This concept of leisure as the contemplative life views leisure as a life style free of work and commitments. Leisure is a *state of being,* a concept dating from the ancient *schole,* meaning leisure, implying freedom or the absence of the necessity of being occupied.

The classical interpretation of leisure was popularized by Aristotle. Aristotle believed leisure to be *essential* so that the citizens could carry on the business of government, law, debate, culture, and contemplation. Of course, slaves were required to carry on the "work" of the state. According to Richard Kraus, this "meant that leisure was given to a comparatively few patricians and made possible by the strenuous labors of many."[2] The

[1]David E. Gray, "This Alien Thing Called Leisure" (paper presented at Oregon State University, Corvallis, Oregon, 8 July 1971).

[2]Richard Kraus, *Recreation and Leisure in Modern Society* (New York: Appleton-Century-Crofts, 1971), p. 295.

42

classical view of leisure has therefore not been embraced wholeheartedly in contemporary society, since the masses now have free time (having earned it from work) for leisure pursuits. Western culture is antithetical to the classical view of leisure as intended only for the privileged elite and conditional upon the availability of slave labor.

The classical view saw leisure as the basis of culture. Sebastian de Grazia notes that the Industrial Revolution changed the concept of time, including free time, the gateway to leisure. "Time became industrialized." Large-scale industry necessitated coordinating the movement of men and materials to the regularity of machines. Leisure was seen not as a condition of life, a state of being in which a person could discover and orient himself to individual time and natural rhythms independent of any artificial or mechanical time reference. Instead, in contemporary Western society, life is oriented to the clock and time has been equated with money; like monetary rewards, time is a valuable commodity to be saved, spent, earned and counted. De Grazia states:

From the moment of our birth, everything we see and hear is touched by the clock. We learn that time is valuable, scarce. It ticks off in a straight line—runs steadily like an assembly line—is used up evenly, minute after minute, hour after hour, day after day, inexorable, impersonal, universal time. In our obsession with pacing our lives by the mechanical clock, we have all but lost the rhythmical, recurring sense of time.

The tide ebbs and flows while in infinite variation the days come and go, the moon waxes and wanes, the seasons take their turn—seed time, the harvest, the falling leaf and thawing ice, the cry of the newborn lamb. Everything in its own time lives, dies, and is born. Day after day, we bind ourselves to the clock. Machines by now have manipulated everyone into living by the dictates of the clock. An ignorant visitor from a clockless land might wonder why we reject the tyranny of men while submitting to the tyranny of time.[3]

If we are to achieve a state of leisure in the classical tradition, de Grazia suggests that we must strive to (1) rely less on commodities and purchases, (2) slow down our pace of life in more "leisurely," less hurried setting, and (3) achieve better tastes. Robert Theobald recommends that Americans begin discussing and understanding the operational requirements of our evolving postindustrial leisure-centered society. One condition essential to our understanding the consequences of a leisured society is the acceptance of diversity—"diversity in time patterns, diversity in space patterns, diver-

[3]Excerpt from the film "Of Time, Work and Leisure" (presented at the National Recreation Congress, St. Louis, Missouri, 1963).

sity in whether people wish to be involved in the technological age or prefer to live in families."[4]

In ancient Athens work was understood as the absence of leisure, rather than leisure being understood as the absence of work. "From this perspective, one works only that he may be freed from the necessity of being occupied. It would be a flagrant contradiction to this view to suggest that the problem of leisure is to find occupation for every moment."[5] In the classical sense, a leisure activity is done for its own sake and for no other purpose. But leisure, understood in this sense, involves a certain state of being, blessedness, or attitude.

The absurdity of the phrase *leisure time* is obvious; for example, one does not love one's children at a regularly appointed time and for a specific period each day. It makes little sense to speak of loving someone at a prescribed time with a prescribed feeling. Leisure, according to the Greeks, was unrelated to mechanical or clocktime (as in the Western tradition), in the same way love is unrelated to time. "Love is a condition and therefore not clockable."[6]

RELIGIOUS TRADITION—CONTEMPLATIVE LEISURE

According to Josef Pieper,[7] leisure is an attitude of mind and a condition of the soul that fosters individual capacity to perceive the reality of the world. This concept corresponds with the Greco-Roman view of leisure as the highest value of culture. According to Pieper, leisure has been and always will be the first foundation of any culture. Culture depends for its very existence on leisure, and leisure in turn is not possible unless it has a durable and consequently living link with *divine worship.*

The revitalization of leisure as an appropriate aesthetic, epistemological, and spiritual expression by various religious sects and hip young people has initiated a disciplined form of self-realization and Christian rediscovery based on community cooperation and lack of material concern. Rejuvenated interest in Eastern religious philosophy, yoga, contemplation, and communal living is a part of this spiritual movement. "The surge of interest by young people in further investigating the spiritual aspects of the uni-

[4]Robert Theobald, "Leisure—Its Meaning and Implications" (presented in panel discussion at the National Recreation Congress, St. Louis, Missouri, 1963).

[5]Thomas F. Green, *Work, Leisure, and the American Schools* (New York: Random House, Inc., 1968), p. 69.

[6]Ibid., p. 71.

[7]Josef Pieper, *Leisure: The Basis of Culture* (New York: Pantheon Books, Inc., 1952).

verse underscores the tremendous need by society for ritual and community celebration."[8]

Leisure as religion. Pieper points to attitudes such as calmness, contemplation, and wholeness as characteristic of leisure and as the soil in which freedom, education, and culture can mature. Leisure involves celebration, and celebration—something almost entirely missing from contemporary American culture—is rooted in divine worship; worship is thus regarded as the *well-spring* of leisure.

> The soul of leisure, it can be said, lies in "celebration." Celebration is the point at which the three elements of leisure come to a focus: relaxation, effortlessness, and superiority of "active leisure" to all functions.
>
> But if celebration is the core of leisure, then leisure can only be made possible and justifiable on the same basis as the celebration of a festival. That basis is divine worship.[9]

In this sense, leisure divorced from divine worship becomes idleness and laziness. The spiritual conceptualization views leisure as the foundation of life beyond the utilitarian world. Leisure, then, is an end in itself, not the means to an end. Culture thrives and is perpetuated through divine worship.

> Leisure is only possible when a man is at one with himself, when he acquiesces in his own being. Idleness and the incapacity for leisure correspond with one another. Leisure is the contrary of both.[10]

Kraus states that some people believe that leisure should extend opportunities beyond the purely utilitarian, providing opportunity for enrichment of life, for aesthetic involvement, and for personal joy, release, and reward. "All such experiences, whether they relate to the need for ritual and celebration, artistic involvement, or education, are part of the need of enriching the total quality of life."[11]

Religion and leisure provide the opportunity for man to satisfy and express his inner desires. Charles K. Brightbill feels that religion offers man an eternal chance to overcome his inner impoverishments, the occasion to develop himself using his inner resources.[12] The present widespread rebel-

[8]James F. Murphy, "A Rediscovery of the Spiritual Side of Leisure," *California Parks and Recreation,* 28 (Dec. 1972/Jan. 1973), 22.

[9]Pieper, *Leisure: The Basis of Culture,* p. 56.

[10]Ibid., p. 40.

[11]Kraus, *Recreation and Leisure in Modern Society,* p. 396.

[12]Charles K. Brightbill, "Leisure and Religion" (presented at George M. Colliver Lectures, University of the Pacific, Stockton, Calif., 29–30 November 1965).

lion, masking reality through costuming and role playing; and social protests are seemingly a manifestation of *emotionally starved* youth seeking
spiritual meaning, self-appraisal, and self-discovery. A comparison of religion and the spiritual orientation of leisure is profound: leisure may be
viewed as that part of life which comes closest to freeing man in a highly
regimented and conforming world. It enables man to pursue self-expression and enlightenment. Brightbill suggests that each individual must be
his own expert in spiritual leisure matters.

Leisure in the contemplative, spiritual sense is the central cultural focus.
It provides an inner direction, purpose, and meaning to life. Accordingly,
leisure is a receptive attitude of mind, a contemplative attitude, which
draws its vitality from serene affirmation.

> Leisure, it must be clearly understood, is a mental and spiritual attitude—it
> is not simply the result of external factors, it is not the inevitable result of spare
> time, a holiday, a weekend or a vacation. It is, in the first place, an attitude of
> mind, a condition of the soul.[13]

SUMMARY AND IMPLICATIONS

The classical conception of leisure, which draws its meaning from the
Greco-Roman and spiritual-humanistic outlooks on life, sees leisure as a
subjective feeling and condition of life. It is the state of having *cyclical-
natural* time at one's disposal. It is a free, uncalculating, qualitative, enriching state of being. The classical view of leisure connotes freedom of choice
in individual pursuits and maintenance of physical, mental, and spiritual
well-being. Its virtues lie in unfocusing and broadening one's consciousness.

The uncompelling feeling of leisure is distinguished from the necessity
of being occupied, and is incompatible with necessity, obligation, and
pressure. How man uses free time determines his leisure. Only by freeing
himself from the work routine and by eliminating boredom and its by-
product, the commodity mentality, can the individual understand what it
is to be a person of leisure, in the classical sense.

The application of the Greco-Roman interpretation of leisure to contemporary Western culture has been argued.[14] Green states:

> A social return to the conception of diurnal [cyclical, natural] time would
> make the traditional [classical] ideal of leisure viable. But such an understanding

---

[13]Pieper, *Leisure: The Basis of Culture*, p. 40.
[14]See Theobald, "Leisure—Its Meaning and Implications."

seems to me wholly unrealistic and impractical. Our society is based upon clock-time and there is every reason to suppose that a post-industrial society will not differ in that respect. . . . A people whose social existence is based upon the reality of clock-time will have enormous difficulty even conceiving of leisure in the traditional sense. To expect them to actually live it and express it in their social life seems altogether unreasonable.[15]

While most leisure theorists tend to agree with Green, it seems that educators, recreators, and social planners must discover in what ways the viable attributes of the classical interpretation of leisure can be expressed. Green suggests, "One might undertake, for instance, to meet the problem of leisure by modifying the socially expressed and psychologically held conception of time."[16] It seems apparent that a pluralistic, postindustrial society must be open to a variety of leisure dimensions to support and encourage positive free-time expressions, some independent of clock time, but all clearly recognizing a close relationship between cyclical, psychological, and clock time.

Renewal in occult, mystical, religiophilosophic belief systems reflects to a degree the loss of confidence in established symbols and cognitive models of reality, and the exhaustion of institutionalized collective symbols of identity.

To make sense of the irrational, the modes and conditions in which it occurs, as well as possible societal consequences deriving from it . . . [occult revival of today is] not [seen] as an integral component or in the formation of a new cultural matrix . . . and as a way of restructuring collective representations of social reality.[17]

Many people feel that in modern society, technology subordinates individual wishes and desires. In the classical-spiritual sense, leisure provides man the opportunity to be the sole master, designer, and interpreter of life. According to this concept of leisure, only when man effectively discards the irrelevant external societal demands of conformity, regimentation, and systematization will we be truly free and therefore open to engage wholly in leisure. Some religious sects and youth movements observe that leisure affords the individual an opportunity to "discover" himself and broaden human potential.

[15]Green, *Work, Leisure, and the American Schools*, pp. 73–74.
[16]Ibid., p. 73.
[17]Edward A. Tiryakian, "Toward the Sociology of Esoteric Culture," *American Journal of Sociology*, 78 (November 1972), 510.

the increasing scarcity of time

STAFFAN LINDER

Good-by Sir, excuse me, I haven't time.
I'll come back, I can't wait, I haven't time.
I must end this letter—I haven't time.
I'd love to help you, but I haven't time
I can't accept, having no time.
I can't think, I can't read, I'm swamped, I haven't time
I'd like to pray, but I haven't time.
                                    MICHEL QUOIST

THE PARADOXES OF AFFLUENCE

We had always expected one of the beneficent results of economic affluence to be a tranquil and harmonious manner of life, a life in Arcadia. What has happened is the exact opposite. The pace is quickening, and our lives in fact are becoming steadily more hectic. It used to be assumed that, as the general welfare increased, people would become successively less interested in further rises in income. And yet in practice a still higher economic growth rate has become the overriding goal of economic policy in the rich countries, and the goal also of our private efforts and attitudes. At the same time, much of our expenditure is no longer subject to any very careful consideration, as is clear from the successes noted by Madison Avenue. A growing proportion of the labor force is employed in the service sector, but in spite of this, our resources are in fact less well "serviced" or maintained than ever. It is becoming increasingly difficult, for instance, for elderly people to obtain the special kind of service—care and attention—that they very much need. Our so-called service economy practices in reality a throw-away system at all levels,

From Staffan Linder, *The Harried Leisure Class* (New York: Columbia University Press, 1970), pp. 1–12.

including the human level. We have long expressed hopes that the elimination of material cares would clear the way for a broad cultural advancement. In practice, not even those endowed with the necessary intellectual and emotional capacity have shown any propensity for immersing themselves in the cultivation of their minds and spirit. The tendency is rather the reverse.

These are but a few examples of the surprising phenomena occurring in the rich countries. They seem paradoxical, as they fail to fit into the picture of affluence which we have painted. The cause of these and similar modern anomalies lies in a circumstance that has been entirely ignored, namely the increasing scarcity of time. The limited availability of time and the increasing claims made on it mean that our affluence is only *partial* and not total as we seem to believe. Our affluence takes only the form of access to *goods.* The idea of "total affluence" is a logical fallacy.

TIME AS A SCARCE COMMODITY

In the natural sciences, the concept of time offers its particular mysteries. The ultimate implications of time, however, are a problem upon which we need not linger. It will be sufficient for our purposes to accept that there exists what we experience as a time dimension—a moving belt of time units which makes resources of time available to the individual as it passes. Time, unlike other economic resources, cannot be accumulated. We cannot build up a stock of time as we build up a stock of capital. As it passes, however, time puts into people's hands something that they can use. In economic terms, there exists a certain "supply of time."

But there is also a certain "demand for time." Time can be used by individuals in work, with a view to acquiring various goods. Time can also be used in consumption, i.e., the process in which goods are combined with time, in attempts to achieve the ultimate utility in the economic process —material and spiritual well-being. It is important to realize that consumption requires time just as does production. Such pleasures as a cup of coffee or a good stage play are not in fact pleasurable, unless we can devote time to enjoying them.

The scarcity of a commodity is determined by the supply in relation to the demand. Such a scarcity is normally reflected in the price. The demand for gold is high in relation to the supply, and gold, therefore, attracts a considerable price. The supply of sea water, on the other hand, is extremely great in relation to the demand, and sea water accordingly attracts no price at all. As regards the commodity in which we are interested, namely time, we have already noted that there is a certain supply and a certain demand. We can now add that the demand by individuals is usually sufficiently high in relation to the supply to make time a "scarce commodity" in the economic sense. But if time is an economic utility in short supply, then it must be subject to the economic laws that prevail in the economist's universe. It must be distributed over its different sectors of use —different activities—in accordance with the general principles of economics.

When spending money, one presumably tries to balance one's expenditures in such a way as to obtain the best possible yield. This means that one will probably refrain from spending all one's assets on a single commodity. One will instead distribute one's expenditure over a variety of different goods and services. The optimum situation will have been reached when it is impossible to increase satisfaction by reducing expenditure in one field and making a corresponding increase in another. A more technical description of this condition of equilibrium would be to say that the marginal utility of one dollar must be the same in all different sectors of expenditure.

In the same way, one tries to economize with one's time resources. They must be so distributed as to give an equal yield in all sectors of use. Otherwise, it would pay to transfer time from an activity with a low yield to one with a high yield and to continue to do this until equilibrium had been reached.

Some of my readers may object, perhaps, that this is a somewhat gross description of how people function. A moment's reflection, however, will reveal that if the reader should for this reason put down the book, such a reaction is in itself evidence that people actually try to allocate their time in order to achieve a maximum yield. Such a reader has the impression that it would be a waste of time to spend a couple of hours reading this essay and, therefore, decides to devote his time to some other, and he hopes better, pursuit.

THE INCREASING SCARCITY OF TIME

The yield on time spent working increases as the result of economic growth. Productivity per hour rises. This means that the time allocation which has represented equilibrium at our previous level of income is disrupted. The yield on time devoted to other activities must also be raised. We are aware that time in production becomes increasingly scarce with economic growth. What we will now claim in addition to this is that changes in the use of time will occur, so that the yield on time in all other activities is brought into parity with the yield on working time. In other words, economic growth entails a general increase in the scarcity of time.

The necessary increase in the yield of time in the nonwork activities can take place in many different ways. To some extent we try to achieve a change in attitudes of a kind that Walter Kerr points out in his book *The Decline of Pleasure:* "We are all of us compelled to read for profit, party for contacts, lunch for contracts, bowl for unity, drive for mileage, gamble for charity, go out for the evening for the greater glory of the municipality, and stay home for the weekend to rebuild the house."

A more basic and radical method of raising the yield on time used in consumption is to increase the amount of consumer goods to be enjoyed per time unit. Just as working time becomes more productive when combined with more capital, so consumption time can give a higher yield when combined with more consumer goods. When this happens, the proportion between consumption goods and the time for consumption changes, so that the price of such time rises to the level of the price of time in production. Admittedly, no prices are openly quoted for time in consumption, but the individual will consciously or unconsciously apply in his actions and words what we can call a "shadow price" to consumption time. This price will go up in step with the productivity of work time.

A critical reader may object that the increasing volume of consumer goods will not necessarily raise the demand for consumption time, but rather the reverse. Many consumer goods, it is claimed, save time. If a household increases its consumption by buying a washing machine, for instance, then the machine will not claim any additional time. It is true that there are many goods of this type. This must be borne in mind when deciding what to classify as "consumer goods." We normally mean all the goods bought by households. In the present study, however, we are considering a more limited category of goods. By "consumption goods," which is the term we shall be using from now on, we mean the definite end products that are combined with time in an attempt to create material or spiritual well-being. Washing machines belong to that category of goods which increases productivity in working life—in this case the work performed within households. We should not make any sharp distinction between activities within households and in production. Many of the former are by nature identical with work in production. Whether productivity rises at places of work within production proper, or in the household, it will have the same effects. The scarcity of time in working life as a whole has increased, and the yield from time in consumption must be increased to create an equilibrium between the yield on time in different sectors. This takes place by an increase in the volume of consumption goods per time unit in consumption.

As already observed, scarce commodities are distributed over different sectors of use in accordance with the principles of economics. Changes in the scarcity of different resources lead to changes in the distribution of resources. These changes, too, follow economic laws. The consequences of an increasing scarcity of time can, therefore, be studied with simple tools borrowed from the practice of economic analysis.

A BASIC PROBLEM IN SOCIAL SCIENCE

The analysis of the distribution of time, of changes in this distribution arising from economic growth, and of the implications of economic development under an increasing scarcity of time is not something of purely economic interest. It is rather a problem of more general interest, a joint problem for all the social sciences. The distribution of time and changes in this distribution are bound to affect our entire attitude to social problems, our entire philosophical outlook. An increasing scarcity of time is bound to color our basic attitude to time and pace. David M. Potter in *People of Plenty* has made the incipient superfluity of goods the starting point of speculations as to changes in the national character; the same can be done with the emerging scarcity of time.

A brief study of the literature shows that workers in the different social sciences have in fact shown some interest in the problems of time. It is equally clear, however, that no concerted attack on the problem is being made. In social anthropology, a number of attempts have been made to describe attitudes to time in different cultures. However, many standard works on the subject fail to consider attitudes to time. At all events, hardly any generalizations have been made concerning the factors which determine disparities in time attitudes among different cultures.

The sociologists, for their part, have made great efforts to perform large-scale time-budget studies. They have tried to plot how different individuals or groups divide up their time between various activities. Particularly detailed studies have been made of the use of time spent outside the place of work, time which is devoted to a variety of different activities. However, the theories formed parallel to these studies have been of an ad hoc nature. Attempts at any systematic explanation of time allocation and changes in it are lacking. Because they have ignored the importance of a time scarcity in the economic sense for the time phenomena studied, the anthropologists and sociologists have never really been able to use their own results. It is possible that an analysis of time allocation could yield a dynamic theory for use in sociological predictions. It could be a useful tool in the study of the future, a field of research which affects an increasing amount of attention.

A theory on changes in the scarcity of time could perhaps also be of use in medical research on stress. Similar openings may exist in psychology, perhaps even more in psychiatry. The present writer has found an interest in questions of the type discussed in at least one psychiatric paper. The following quotation from Professor of Psychology John Cohen speaks for itself: "The reaction of animals under conditions of temporal constraint may help to understand human disorders in the tightly time-bound cultures of our day."

It is hardly surprising that sociologists, for instance, have not come to regard the use of time as a problem of economizing with an increasingly scarce commodity. Such an approach, however, should be natural for that science which is devoted to the principles of allocating scarce resources, namely economics. Even so, a reasonable analysis of time is lacking in the economic literature. Economists typically regard consumption as an instantaneous act without temporal consequences. They regard time in working life as a scarce resource, parallel to which there exists some sort of undefined "free time." As incomes rise, one would have increasing consumption, without any consequences to the time situation of the individual, other than a reduction in work time. This would give an increasing amount of "free time." The supply would be increasing on all fronts.

By such a view, the distribution of time can never be made the subject of analysis with the tools of economic theory. It is indeed interesting to see how poorly incorporated free time is in economic theory. To give an example, one ambitious statistical study (by Gordon C. Winston) on the relationship between working time and level of income in different countries makes a distinction between the time used "either on the earning of income (work), or on a host of alternative noneconomic activities (leisure)." To speak of nonworking time as a noneconomic use of time in symptomatic. The very term free time suggests a failure to realize that consumption time is a scarce commodity.

That consumption is regarded as some sort of instantaneous act emerges most clearly from the fact that, when economists try to state the connection between the "utility" of a certain commodity and the amount of that commodity available, they never take into account the time an individual has at his disposal to consume the commodity in question. In economic theory, the pleasure an individual can be expected to derive from a couple of theatre tickets is not taken to be dependent in any way on the time he can devote to playgoing. At most, economic writers take into account the time needed for consumption by pointing out that the utility of a product depends on the length of the time period within which it is to be enjoyed. "Different levels of satisfaction are derived from consuming ten portions of ice cream within one hour and within one month." This point made by J. M. Henderson and R. E. Quandt in their textbook is, however, by no means sufficient. It is not enough to know whether portions of ice cream are to be consumed within a month or within a year. It is far more important to know how much time within a given period can be specifically devoted to enjoying the commodity whose contribution to our material well-being we are studying. If one has no time during a whole week to drink coffee, then obviously even whole sacks full of coffee will give no yield that week. Similarly, a tennis player has no use for a new racket each year, if he never has the time to play. The utility of theatre tickets cannot be established without knowing whether or not the ticket holder has time to use them. What makes the difference is not so much the period of time during which a given quantity of the commodity is available, but rather the time that is available during this period to consume the commodity in question.

Now that we have made these critical observations, we can note with satisfaction that a handful of economists has in recent years adopted a new position. Attention is beginning to be paid to the possibility that economic growth causes an increasing scarcity of time. The first, apparently, in this exclusive group was Roy Harrod, who published a short paper on this theme at the end of the fifties. However, no attention was paid to it by the profession and not even by its author either, since he has never followed up the ideas which he had presented. Harrod's thesis was that we may in time be faced with a consumption maximum, owing to an increasing scarcity of time, which is the result primarily of all the servicing and maintenance work required by consumption goods. It is Harrod's idea, puzzling at first sight, which originally triggered the thinking of the present study.

Another economist who has allowed for the fact that consumption takes time and as a result reached interesting results is Jacob Mincer. Only one economist, however, has attempted to formulate a general theory of time allocation. This is Gary Becker, whose work is presented in a paper published in 1965. The basic approach is this book and in Becker's paper are the same. Even though work on this book had reached a relatively late stage before Becker's paper became available, it has naturally been extremely valuable to be able to utilize Becker's line of thinking.

WHY THIS NEGLECT OF TIME ANALYSIS?

The absence of any theory of time allocation in the behavioral sciences must be blamed on economists who, being professionally concerned with the allocation of scarce resources, should certainly have come to regard time in this way. Instead, by ignoring the fact that consumption requires time, they have conveyed the opposite impression—that the use of time off the job is a noneconomic phenomenon and that economic growth results in a decreasing scarcity of time. How can we explain this neglect on the part of the economists? In the absence of any entirely convincing or sufficient explanation, we can only suggest various possibilities. To begin with, there could be a historical reason. When the first economists defined their sphere of interest, the scarcity of time was hardly noticeable. The overriding problem was the scarcity of goods as a result of low productivity. It was, therefore, reasonable to speak of free time in the true economic sense, i.e., time without a price. Consumption goods were lacking, and marginal time was perhaps spent in enforced passivity. Fettered by an analytic tradition, economists have failed to see time as a scarce resource, even though the situation has radically changed.

It is also possible that the actual term economic growth is misleading. When we speak of economic growth, it is easy to think of growing economic opportunities in general. We imagine total, rather than partial, affluence. Obviously, such an erroneous picture will emerge more easily if we are unaware that consumption takes time, and we stare blindly at various statistical theories reporting that we not only have more and more goods but also more and more free time. Some people may also entertain a vague idea that there has been some sort of technological advance in consumption, so that the demand for time has remained constant. But insofar as any technological advances have been made on the consumer side, they must relate to the individual's work in the household. The effects of such technological advances, however, are the same as in production proper. It is difficult to conceive of any technological advance being noted in the actual process of consumption. Productivity can be purchased only by an increase in the quantity of goods consumed per time unit, which means an increased scarcity of time.

Another possibility is that people have disregarded the claims made on consumption time because of certain basic conceptions of how our growing material affluence might be used. The optimistic view has prevailed that people would gradually be freed from toil and starvation, in order to devote themselves to cultivation of the mind and spirit in accordance with the ideals of classical antiquity. On these terms, what we now mean by consumption would take very little time. The economic target would be met as soon as we had reached a material level permitting uninterrupted philosophical exercises. Neither time nor material goods would be scarce commodities, the economic problem would vanish with the attainment of complete satisfaction in the embrace of the fine arts and beautiful thoughts. This picture has been belied by events. As economic development has continued, attractive alternative ways of using time have emerged. Mediation and speculation have been driven off the market. Whatever the cause, time has thus become de facto an increasingly scarce resource, without the economists having noticed this development.

THE SO-CALLED "LEISURE PROBLEM"

Many will surely find it peculiar that economic development should result in an increasing scarcity of time. One imagines that the situation should be the reverse. Intellectuals of the rich countries fail to analyze the increasing scarcity of time, but instead devote a great deal of attention to the so-called leisure problem.

What in fact is this much publicized but undefined leisure problem? Does it mean that people, because of the shorter working week, have got so much time on their hands that they do not know what to do with it? This would mean that time had become less and less scarce, and that there is something ludicrously amiss with the whole basic idea of this book. Instead of an increasing scarcity of time we should have a surplus.

But even if the leisure problem can not be taken to mean that people do nothing, it may nonetheless exist. However, it then consists of some people busying themselves with nothingness—a problem which is not in conflict with the argument made in this essay.

The leisure problem of the economic type, however, probably exists only in the imagination of those who are unaware that consumption takes time. If we take the position, like most economists, that consumption is instantaneous and that free time is some entirely isolated utility, then it is possible to draw peculiar conclusions. We can imagine, in this case, that we now have so much free time that we do not know what to do with it, and that certain parts of this time are reduced to what we have called economic free time. It may be that some people are in such a situation. They have a job, and they make a certain amount of money. This is used to purchase consumption goods, the enjoyment of which takes a certain time. When they have consumed these goods, people then spend the rest of their time in complete passivity. Such a mode of life, however, would seem uncommon. If people have more time left over for consumption than they think they need, most of them surely take some form of extra work. This gives them more money which they can use in consumption and thus absorb consumption time. Insofar as they do not do this, it must mean that they have reached a maximum for their consumption. The existence of any such ceiling, however, is energetically denied, at least by economists and by psychologists interested in economics.

There is no guarantee, after all, that people will devote their time off the job to entirely laudable ends. On the contrary, it is probable that many people choose to expend their increasing resources in a manner injurious to themselves and their environment. Such individuals, however, are not idle. They can be extremely busy in all sorts of mischief. This is a very real problem, but it is obviously no leisure problem, in the sense that people do not know what to do with all their time. It is a social problem. The fact that people use their money in a dangerous way does not eliminate the need for economic theory. In the same way, the fact that people sometimes use their time in dangerous ways does not mean that we do not need a theory of time allocation.

It is obviously possible also to worry over the fact that so many people occupy themselves, if not with mischief, at least with such vacuous practices as reading comics and drinking Coca-Cola. This too is something that can lead people to talk of a leisure problem. For moral, ethical, cultural, or other reasons, they cannot accept the way in which others choose to use their time. Here again; we have a problem relating not to economic free time, but to the quality of our civilization. Superficial people in the rich countries are often in a greater hurry than anyone else. They are enormously busy, even if it is sometimes difficult to see with what.

There is yet another interpretation of what leisure problem might mean. Many have expressed the fear that, as there is less demand on the individual to contribute work, we shall lose something essential to personal human value. This is an important risk, and one that we must take into consideration when assessing what higher productivity is really giving us. Here again, it is not a question of our nonworking time becoming economic free time. The underlying idea is simply that the compulsion to work confers a greater value on the individual than the freedom to consume. The problem is a psychological one.

It seems reasonable to draw the conclusion that leisure problems of a social, cultural, and psychological nature exist. But the average earner in the rich country lives nonetheless under the pressure of time. He is a member of the harried leisure class.

NOTES AND REFERENCES

The chapter quotation is from Michel Quoist, *Prayers of Life,* Logos Books, Gill and Son, Dublin and Melbourne, 1966, p. 76. Copyright 1963 by Sheed and Ward, Inc.

Walter Kerr's book *The Decline of Pleasure* was published by Simon and Schuster, New York, 1965. The quotation is from p. 39.

Two anthropological studies which explore differences in time attidues in different cultures are those of Edward T. Hall, *The Silent Language,* Doubleday, New York, 1959; and Margaret Mead (ed.), *Cultural Patterns and Technical Change,* UNESCO, Paris, 1953. These and some more such studies are discussed in Chapter II. Studies in social anthropology which, on the other hand, do not seem to devote any attention at all to time attitudes are, for instance, S. F. Nadel, *The Foundations of Social Anthropology,* Cohen & West Ltd., London, 1951; Ralph Piddington, *An Introduction to Social Anthropology,* Oliver and Boyd, London, 1950; and G. Boalt, B. Hanssen, and L. Gustafsson, *Socialantropologi,* Natur och Kultur, Stockholm, 1960. The effects of opulence on the national character have been discussed by

David M. Potter, *People of Plenty,* University of Chicago Press, Chicago & London, 1954.

As to sociological works on time budgets, the following may be mentioned: G. A. Lundberg, Mirra Komarovsky, and Mary A. McInerny, *Leisure: A Suburban Study,* Columbia University Press, New York, 1934; Pitirim A. Sorokin and Clarence Q. Berger, *Time-Budgets of Human Behavior,* Harvard University Press, Cambridge, Mass., 1939; Eric Larrabee and Rolf Meyersohn (eds.) *Mass Leisure,* The Free Press, Glencoe, Ill., 1958; Max Kaplan, *Leisure in America: A Social Inquiry,* John Wiley & Sons, New York, 1960; Sebastian de Grazia, *Of Time, Work, and Leisure* Twentieth Century Fund, New York, 1962. For further studies it is possible to explore the wealth of references in de Grazia, *Of Time.* Also Reuel Denney and Mary Lea Meyersohn, "A Preliminary Bibliography on Leisure," *American Journal of Sociology,* May 1957, pp. 602–15. A sociological work with a clear statement of time as a scarce resource exposed to the economic principles of allocation is George Soule, *What Automation Does to Human Beings,* Sidgwick and Jackson, London, 1956, Ch. 6. On the methodological problems of making time budget studies, see Nelson N. Foote, "Methods for Study of Meaning of Use of Time," in Robert W. Kleemeier (ed.), *Aging and Leisure,* Oxford University Press, New York, 1961, pp. 155–76.

The psychiatric study that discusses time problems is John Cohen, "Subjective Time," in J. T. Fraser (ed.), *The Voices of Time,* George Braziller, New York, 1966. The quotation is from p. 271. On the whole, this collection of essays on time makes fascinating reading.

For instance, John F. Due, *Intermediate Economic Analysis,* 3rd ed., Richard D. Irwin, Homewood, Ill., 1956, presents the labor-leisure time allocation theory that is standard in economic analysis. See pp. 328 ff. The statistical study relating income level and hours of work in various countries is Gordon C. Winston "An International Comparison of Income and Hours of Work," *Review of Economics and Statistics,* February 1966. The quotation is taken from p. 28. Many text books do not even bother to mention that the utility of a certain quantity of a product, say, a pound of coffee, depends upon the length of the period within which this quantity is to be consumed. See, however, Lloyd G. Reynolds, *Economics,* revised ed., Richard D. Irwin, Homewood, Ill., 1966, pp. 138–39; and J. M. Henderson and R. E. Quandt, *Microeconomic Theory,* International Student ed. McGraw-Hill and Kogakusha, New York and Tokyo, 1958, p. 9. But perhaps other text book authors find this fact both self-evident and trivial.

The three papers which do introduce time as a resource in consumption are: Roy F. Harrod, (unnamed paper) in Committee for Economic Development, *Problems of United States Economic Development,* Vol. I (mimeo), January 1958, pp. 207–13; J. Mincer, "Market Prices, Opportunity Costs, and Income Effects," in *Measurement in Economics. Studies in Mathematical Economics and Econometrics in Memory of Yehuda Grunfeld,* Stanford University Press, Stanford, 1963; Gary S. Becker, "A Theory of the Allocation of Time," *Economic Journal,* September 1965, pp. 493–517.

It may be added that the concept of "time" figures extensively in economic analysis in a completely different sense from the one in which it is being used in this essay and by these three previous authors. Time is introduced as a dimension which sets up lags and expectations, and which permits the connection of casually related factors in a noninstantaneous manner. This time is a necessary ingredient in a process analysis undertaken to study paths towards an equilibrium (or away from an equilibrium). The concept of time in this essay is not the one which is introduced to conduct dynamic analysis. Time as introduced here is a resource of individuals, like any other resource. It has to be allocated according to certain principles, and these principles may very well be handled in static or comparative static analysis. Evidently, *changes* in this allocation may, if this is found convenient, be studied, also *overtime,* i.e., within the formal framework of dynamic analysis.

The reference to Veblen's gilded leisure class alludes to arguments presented in Thorstein Veblen, *The Theory of the Leisure Class,* Viking Press, New York, 1899.

The Ancient Greek concept of "leisure" is discussed, e.g., by S. de Grazia, *Of Time,* Ch. I. For a treatment of what is the "cultural" leisure problem in the U.S. and Soviet Union, see two papers by Paul Hollander, "Leisure as An American and Soviet Value," *Social Problems,* Fall 1966, pp. 179–88, and "The Uses of Leisure," *Survey—a Journal of Soviet and East European Studies,* July 1966, pp. 40–50.

the background
of leisure

SEBASTIAN DE GRAZIA

Aristotle in the *Politics* says a curious thing. The Spartans remained secure as long as they were at war; they collapsed as soon as they acquired an empire. They did not know how to use the leisure that peace brought.[1]

In Aristotle the words "peace" and "leisure" come together often. They repeat his thesis that wars are fought to have peace, and peace is needed for leisure. Sparta trained its citizens for war. It designed its laws principally with war in mind. Leisure and peace were used to prepare for war. The Spartans made another mistake. A well-ordered state manages to secure leisure or freedom from the necessity of labor. Now the Spartans did obtain leisure, but in a wrong way. They wrung it from a system of serfdom. What leisure could there be when Helots lay in ambush waiting for a chance at their masters? The moral is plain. Sparta had not discovered the best mode of governing for a life of leisure.

Sebastian de Grazia, "The Background of Leisure," *Of Time, Work and Leisure* (New York: The Twentieth Century Fund, 1962), pp. 11–25.

[1] *Politics,* II, 1271b.

One more charge against Sparta: the men by their military life were educated to discipline, which at least tided them along in times of peace and leisure, but the women were given absolutely no education in self-control. With the men absent for long periods, the women abandoned themselves to license and luxury. Legislators like Lycurgus tried to bring them, as well as the men, within range of the law, but they opposed him and he had to abandon the attempt. The results brought misfortune to Sparta—the growth of luxuriousness, avarice, maldistribution of property, shortage of warriors, and a female population that in war caused more confusion than the enemy.

These then are the charges. A citizenry unprepared for leisure will degenerate in prosperous times. Women, too, are liable to fall on evil ways. Furthermore, leisure based on serfdom is so insecure as to be no leisure at all.

The Greeks took the question of leisure seriously. Their ideas are worth attention for they not only examined many of the problems confronting us today but asked questions we have not dared to ask ourselves. Who today would say that a nation could collapse because it didn't know how to use its leisure? Who today so predicts the downfall of the United States or of China? But Aristotle not only lived in but was preceded by a century interested in leisure. His Greece, his Athens, pulled back the curtains to offer the West an ideal.

The etymological root of *schole* meant to halt or cease, hence to have quiet or peace. Later it meant to have time to spare or, specially, time for oneself. Of the great Greeks, Aristotle was the one who most often used the word *schole*. For him life could be divided into different parts—action and leisure, war and peace. Citizens must be capable of a life of action and war, but even more able to lead a life of leisure and peace. Warlike states are safe only while they are fighting. A sword resting unused in the scabbard loses its temper. In any case it never had a temper for peace. Courage in battle is a virtue of limited use in peacetime. The legislator is to blame if he does not educate citizens to those other virtues needed for the proper use of leisure. A greater emphasis on temperance and justice should be taught them for times when they are faring exceptionally well and enjoying all that the world holds to be happiness. In war the virtues of men come forth for a united effort; in peace and prosperity men lose their temperance and justice toward one another and become overbearing. The greater the abundance of blessings that fall to men, the greater will be their need for wisdom, and wisdom is the virtue that cannot appear except in leisure.

So, the dangerous period is peace. Yet for Aristotle it was self-evident that just as a person would not want to be fighting all his life, so a state would not want to make war all the time. The end could never be war. It had to be peace. The good thing about peace was that it allowed leisure.

But what was this precious leisure? If the legislator was to provide for it, he had to know what it was. Or how was he to keep leisure in mind with regard not only to what wars are fought for, but to all problems pertaining to the state?

In some cases it seems that leisure is another word for spare or free time. For example the well-to-do, says Aristotle, if they must attend to their private affairs have little leisure for politics and absent themselves from the assembly and the courts. In common usage *schole* seems to have had this meaning. Aristotle apparently uses the same sense when he says the Spartans used their leisure to prepare for war. But one senses a different element, an ethical note, a hint that spare time when misused is not leisure. The case of the Helots who lived for one day only, the day on which they would massacre their masters, reveals that free time if shot through with fear is not leisure. Yet the clearest of the charges against Sparta is that against the women, whose time, though all free, became not leisure but license. Obviously time on one's hands is not enough to make leisure.

At one point Aristotle gives a rough equivalent of leisure. He speaks of it and then adds, "or in other words, freedom from the necessity of labor."[2] This at a glance seems similar to the modern idea of free time—time off the job—but we would be well advised to go slowly here. The differences, though mainly in the nuances of words, reflect a different world. We can note to start that free time accentuates time; it sets aside a unit of time free of the job. In Aristotle's short definition time has no role. Leisure is a condition or a state—the state of being free from the necessity to labor.

Elsewhere Aristotle mentioned not labor but action as a contrast to leisure. He spoke of the life of leisure versus the life of action. By action here he intended activities toward other persons or objects in order to effect some purpose. He was using "action" in a common meaning, but, as he often makes clear, for himself a living being can hardly be anything but active. The gods live and therefore they too are active. Though invisible, even thought moves, even pure speculation, and so does contemplation, the activity of the gods. Indeed, thoughts and those who hold them are active in the fullest measure since it is they that move persons and things to the outward, visible kind of activity.

Leisure is active, then, though not necessarily a highly visible kind of activity. But what had Aristotle against labor that he made it almost the contrary of leisure? In Greek there are two common words for labor or work.[3] One is *ponos*, which has the connotations of toil in our sense, that

---

[2] *Politics*, II, 1269a.

[3] On the etymology of words connected with leisure, such as work, labor, and activity, see Hannah Arendt, *The Human Condition*, Doubleday, Garden City, 1959. The quotation from Martial is from the *Epigrams*, X, 58. Seneca's remark about the barber and ringlets occurs in *de otio*. His paradigm for Lucilius (*Vaco, Lucili, vaco*) appears in *Epistulae*, 62, 1.

is, the sense of fatiguing, sweating, almost painful, manual effort. The other is *ascholia,* which is more like our idea of work or occupation in that it has less of the painful physical element. In origin the word really denotes the absence of leisure for its root is *schole,* before which an *a-* is placed to signify a want or a lack. It thus means un-leisure or the state of being busy or occupied. This being at unleisure, though it seems a roundabout way of putting things, may be the closest to our phrase of being occupied or at work. The Spartan women, however, were free of the necessity of working, and still they had no true leisure.

The idea of occupation here is somewhat different from ours. We come closer to it when we speak of being occupied or busy, for the noun forms, both occupation and business (originally busyness), are further away from the idea, having come to be associated with work and the job. We can now rewrite the original definition thus: Leisure is freedom from the necessity of being occupied. This includes freedom from the necessity to labor, but it could also embrace any activity one finds necessary to perform, but would fain be free of. Here again we seem to be near a modern notion of leisure, as time in which a person can do as he pleases, time, perhaps, for amusement or recreation.

We would still do well to proceed cautiously. When Aristotle uses the word occupation, he cuts out the idea of "do as one pleases." An occupation is activity pursued for a purpose. If the purpose were not necessary, the activity would not occur. Therefore no occupation can be leisure, not even the self-employer's, whose purpose is self-chosen. Nor can leisure be anything related to an occupation. Amusement (*paidia*) and recreation (*anapausis*) are necessary because of work. They are not ends in themselves. Happiness does not lie in amusements, the things children do. In the *Ethics,* Aristotle says, "To exert oneself and work for the sake of amusement seems silly and utterly childish."[4] Rather is it the reverse, that we take to amusements as relaxation. We need relaxation, for we cannot work constantly. We need amusements and recreation to restore, to re-create ourselves for our occupation. But the goal of being occupied should only be to attain leisure.

The distinguishing mark now begins to appear. Leisure is a state of being in which activity is performed for its own sake or as its own end. What Aristotle means by an end in itself or a final end he himself has demonstrated in the *Ethics:* clearly not all goals are final goals, though the chief good evidently is. Therefore, if there is only one final goal, this will be what we seek; if there are more than one, what we shall seek is the most final among them. Now that which is in itself worthy of pursuit we call more final than that pursued for the sake of something else, and that which

[4] *Ethics,* X, 1176b.

is desirable not for the sake of something else we should say is more final than things that are desired partly for themselves and partly for the sake of some other thing. And we call final without reservation that which is always desirable in itself and never for the sake of something else.

Leisure stands in the last class by itself. It is not exaggerating to say that, as Aristotle is a philosopher of happiness, he is also a philosopher of leisure. Happiness can appear only in leisure. The capacity to use leisure rightly, he repeats, is the basis of the free man's whole life.

We can better see the logic of this conception if we ask, What is one to do in leisure? To play would be impossible. Play—at least for adults— belongs to the side of occupation: it relaxes the worker. It produces not happiness but the pleasant feeling of relief from exertion and tension. "Leisure is a different matter," Aristotle holds in the *Politics.* "We think of it as having in itself intrinsic pleasure, intrinsic happiness, intrinsic felicity. Happiness of that order does not belong to occupation: it belongs to those who have leisure."[5] Occupations aim at some end as yet unat- tained; felicity is a present end and is attained by leisure in its every act and very moment. When Aristotle himself puts the question, it is clear that play is out, for he says, "With what kind of activity should we do (*skolen agein*) our leisure?" We do not *do* our leisure with play, yet we do not *do* it with work. An occupation is not taken on as an end in itself, and play for adults is needed only to relieve work. Aristotle has an answer for his question. There are two activities he cites as worthy of the name leisure —music and contemplation.

These two things are not so limited as they may seem. To understand what Aristotle meant we shall have to go back to Plato. Aristotle was his pupil for twenty years, until Plato died as a matter of fact, and often— particularly in the case of contemplation—he neglects to give an introduc- tion to a subject that Plato has already discussed fully.

But let us take music first, the subject of almost the whole of the last book of Aristotle's *Politics.* The matter at hand is education. Aristotle, we remember, was interested in education for leisure. He makes short shrift of reading and writing: they are useful for money-making, for housekeep- ing, for acquiring knowledge, and for some political activities. As for gymnastics: it fosters only the virtue of courage. Drawing: it helps men judge paintings correctly and thus buy them prudently. They are useful, these studies, but at the same time that is their defect: they are mainly useful. All branches of learning ought to be studied with a view to the proper use of leisure in cultivating the mind. Studies pursued with an eye to an occupation are to be regarded merely as a means or a matter of necessity. Now what purpose can the teaching of music have?

[5] *Politics,* VIII, 1337b.

The first argument for music is tradition, an important argument for Aristotle as for Plato. Their forefathers made music a part of education, but neither because it was necessary—it is not—nor because it was useful. We are left with its value for cultivation of the mind in leisure. It ranks as part of the culture proper to free men. Homer's lines testify that only those should be summoned to the bountiful banquet who "call with them a minstrel, to please all men with his music." Amusingly enough, Aristotle almost rejects drawing as a leisure pursuit because it may be held *useful* in saving people from mistakes in their private purchases of works of art. Later, however, he admits it because it helps develop in the young an eye observant to beauty in form and figure. He relents generally on the other subjects too, for they also *can* be pursued in a liberal spirit. But the emphasis remains on music.

Plato is just as insistent. Whoever cannot hold his place in the chorus, he asserts in the *Laws,* is not really an educated man. To hold one's place meant to be able to sing and dance at the same time. In the *Republic* he fondly recalls the ancient times when education consisted of gymnastics for the body and music for the soul. For Plato music often signified the dominion of the Muses. For the ancients it was generally restricted to the vocal and instrumental, but in both cases the word music covered a much broader field than it does now. Today we think of the Greeks as philosophers and mathematicians. We remember their scientific side. In considering their artistic side we recall their poetry, architecture, and sculpture. We forget that we see their statues without color, that culture and education in Greece were more artistic than scientific, that mathematics declined, and the arts, both literary and plastic, bowed before music. Above all, the Greeks were and wished to be musicians. Music was for them almost a synonym for culture. Music in the dance gave the beat to gymnastics; in song it carried the meter of poetry, the only form archaic literature took; and in the march, Plutarch says, "It was a majestic and terrible sight that of the Spartan army marching to the attack to the sound of the flute."[6]

Up to the sixth century B.C. Sparta was the musical capital of Greece, and by no means for martial music alone. Its magnificent calendar of holidays served up music in every refinement, admired in all Greece. It is difficult for us to realize the shame that Themistocles, the Athenian general and statesman, felt at a banquet when the lyre was passed around and he didn't know how to play it. Themistocles was a parvenu and had never received the fostering in poetry and music that Plato and Aristotle and

[6]The remark on the Spartan army's music appears in the story of Lycurgus in Plutarch's *Parallel Lives.* In his "Life of Pericles," Plutarch presents an extreme view of activity in leisure. He quotes the philosopher Antisthenes as saying in reply to a remark about an "excellent" piper, "It may be so, but he is but a wretched human being, otherwise he would not have been an excellent piper."

Pindar told of. Book learning was far from their minds. To learn to play the lyre the pupil sat face to face with the musicmaster. He did not decipher fly-specks on a sheet of paper; he followed the dexterity of the master's fingers. In the classical epoch the child went to three masters. To the original two, the masters of gymnastics and music, a third was added —the master of letters, of the reading and writing and arithmetic that Aristotle depreciatingly called useful. But this third master eventually won out over the others to become, without further qualification, "the master" or "the instructor."

As yet, in the period of Socrates, Plato, and Aristotle, the adult educational forum to which a youth aspired was the symposium, the banquet, the club of friends. Here he conversed, ate, and then drank into the evening. And to every dinner partner, one by one, passed the myrtle branch to show each that his turn had come, tortuously but inevitably, to sing his song, the *scholion,* the fundamental, lyrical, literary genre to which other arts came round in intermezzi of the lyre, the pipes, and the dance.

Leisure of *schole,* believed Newman, the student of Aristotle, meant being occupied in something desirable for its own sake—the hearing of noble music and noble poetry, intercourse with friends chosen for their own worth, and above all the exercise, alone or in company, of the speculative faculty. From what we have learned of those musicians, the Greeks, we would agree with him, though we would make explicit the *playing* of music, the *reciting* of poetry, and the *composing* of both. All these things fit the word Aristotle uses occasionally to describe the activities of leisure, namely, the cultivation of the mind (*diagoge*). He used the word leisure in at least two senses, as we have seen—one as available time, the other as absence of the necessity of being occupied. It is not immediately clear whether in talking about *diagoge* he is saying that in leisure you should cultivate your mind or that in the true state of leisure you cannot do anything but cultivate your mind.

So far I have not discussed contemplation, or what Newman described as above all the exercise of the speculative faculty. By going into this idea, we shall get a firmer grasp on what Aristotle meant by the cultivation of the mind and "freedom from necessity" in leisure, and the relation between the two. Contemplation in the Greek sense is so close to leisure that in describing one and the other repetition is inevitable. Plato first developed the idea in the *Republic.* His models were the Ionian philosophers, whose absorption in knowledge for its own sake inspired Plato's academy and Aristotle's Peripatetic school. Thales of Miletus was one of these philosophers. Plato has told us his story, of how gazing at the stars he fell into a well, and of the little maid who, standing by, laughed at the sport. The idea of contemplation itself in those days seemed to be groping for its true meaning. Our word comes from the Latin but the Latin is a translation from the Greek *theorein,* to behold, to look upon. *Theoria* was also the word for theory, and was used in the phrase "the theoretical life," which in Latin became "the contemplative life," both of which have a fast friendship with the life of leisure.

Contemplation for Plato and Aristotle was the best way of truth-finding. They prized it above all other activities. It was the only activity in which they could picture the gods. The contemplator looks upon the world and man with the calm eye of one who has no design on them. In one sense he feels himself to be close to all nature. He has not the aggressive detachment or unfeeling isolation that comes from scrutinizing men and objects with a will to exploiting them. In another sense he is truly detached because he looks on none of them with intent to manipulate or control or change, on neither man nor beast nor nature. Whoever does look on the world with design, who wishes to subdue or seduce others, to gain money, to win fame, cannot see much beyond the slice he is cutting. His aim on the world puts lenses before his eyes. He doesn't even know his sight is distorted.

When Plato describes the ideal education of those who should be the rulers of the country, he has them passing every test and trial with honors, so that finally they can "lift up the eye of the soul and fix it upon that which gives light to all things." In contemplation they can see the essence of the good and take it for their pattern. They can see things and how they fit together so well because, as rulers, they are free of all necessity to take an oblique view. They do not have the compulsion of those who must make money or win honors. Take the mechanic or anyone who has to work for his living. He is the one who must watch his job and tools and his boss, who must have relief from toil and calculate how best to sell his wares or his services, and who gets caught up in a futile flurry of activities that lead nowhere. How can he see true and carry truth forward to the outer reaches of the cosmos circled by man's eye?

Contemplation, like leisure, or being itself leisure, brings felicity. Aristotle in the *Ethics* contends that happiness extends only so far as contemplation does. Those who can contemplate are the most truly happy. Indeed, happiness must be some form of contemplation. The activity of God, surpassing all others in blessedness, must be contemplative. Those men who most cultivate the mind are most akin to the gods and therefore dearest to them. The man in contemplation is a free man. He needs nothing. Therefore nothing determines or distorts his thought. He does whatever he loves to do, and what he does is done for its own sake.

There is one more Greek philosopher whose influence on the contemplative life was great, Epicurus, but his contribution comes in better at a later stage of our study. Thus far we can see how philosophers, in an interplay of *schole* and the contemplative life, transformed a word meaning simple spare time into the classical ideal of leisure with all its sense of freedom, superiority, and learning for its own sake.

We begin to grasp how leisure is related to politics. If a man is at leisure only when he is free, the good state must exist to give him leisure. What he does in this leisure can be equated with what we today call the good life. Surprisingly few political philosophers have seen the connection between freedom and leisure as ends of the state. The prevalence of work in modern times, as we shall see, partly explains the oversight.[7] Aristotle took it for granted: the life of leisure was the only life fit for a Greek.

FROM GREECE TO ROME

The ideal of leisure went into Rome, carried there largely through the works of Plato and Aristotle and Epicurus. In Latin the word for leisure was *otium,* and as in Greece its verbal opposite was formed by a negative prefix, *negotium.* In most Roman writers the question of leisure is posed in the pendulum of *otium* and *negotium.* Leisure lured them; they sang its praises chiefly in terms of the *beata solitudo,* blessed solitude in the country. The way of conquest, of organizing and building, prefixed their thought so that even in the days of the Empire Rome found itself unable to shake off its Catonic heritage. Seneca first gave the ideal real consideration, and he almost alone among Romans carried the standard forward. Cicero, who in this matter is typical of most Roman writers, rarely if ever leaves the track of *otium/negotium.* A man is occupied—in the affairs of army, commerce, or state, whatever—and then he rests and re-creates himself. Old age itself is a peaceful well-earned rest from on-the-go of *negotium.* Aristotle would not have called this leisure. *Otium* thus conceived is not for its own but for *negotium's* sake. As Seneca conceives it, though, it comes close to the contemplation of Aristotle and Epicurus.

Seneca, who knew Cicero's world well, wrote of him that he took to leisure when he was in political difficulties or in a petulant mood at not being appreciated by his associates as he thought he deserved. Pliny makes another example: the active life is his meat but he also feels leisure's tug. Vanity and duty, both, make him a victim of the thousand-things-to-do. He winds up wishing for leisure rather than enjoying it, and worries often of how to avoid the crime of inertia (*inertiae crimen*). Pliny likes the retreat in the country for cool reflection, the charms of nature, study, the hunt, and distraction and freedom from the city's demands—for the pleasures, after all, of nobles. He advises others to alternate *otium* and *negotium:* when tired of one, take to the other. So in one of his letters, Pliny reports that

[7]One can see the lack of reflection on leisure as freedom in Mortimer J. Adler's compendium on *The Idea of Freedom,* Doubleday, Garden City, 1958.

the city is in tumultuous holiday, and that during these wild days he finds his leisure in letters, which the others in their madcap pursuits miss. Pliny's pleasure comes actually from the external things around him, his note-books and pamphlets. The sentimentalism of the atmosphere he expresses is philosophical rhetoric. Some of Martial's epigrams set a similar tone. The calm retreat by the sea, the house on the shore, the wood, the lake: with these he had had leisure to court the Muses. But greatest Rome wears him out. "Here when is a day my own?" he complains. "I am tossed on the high sea of city, and life is lost in sterile work."

Seneca sees through all the postures. He doesn't consider among the leisured the one who is a finical collector of Corinthian bronzes; or who flares up if the barber does not put his ringlets in place ("as if he were shearing a real man!"); or who gives banquets for which how diligently they tie up the tunics of pretty slave-boys, how anxiously they set out the silver plates, how carefully unhappy little lads wipe up the spittle of drunkards; or who bakes his body in the sun; or who becomes a laborious trifler over learning. It was a foible confined to the Greeks to inquire how many rowers Ulysses had, but now the passion had seized the Romans too, so that they asked such questions as, Who first induced the Romans to go on board ships? These are not the leisured, but mere busy idlers; they have only idle occupations, not leisure. Seneca touches Pliny and Martial more closely when he advises Lucilius by letter not to make bombast out of leisure. One way to make bombast is to hide out while letting everyone know you're hiding out and where. A man creates a legend about being a hermit, and the curious crowd mills around his retreat. If he wants to go into a retreat, it should not be to make people talk about him but to help him talk with himself for a change.

From thought and experience Seneca arrives at conclusions that bring him, though he was formally a Stoic, closer to Epicurus. In his essay on *The Shortness of Life* he gives examples of many busy persons, including Cicero, who seek *otium* not for itself but because they are fed up with *negotium,* who crawl up through a thousand indignities to the crowning dignity only to find that they have toiled for an inscription on a tomb. They cry out that they have been fools, and would henceforth live in leisure, but too late. All the great ones, like Augustus, long for leisure, acclaim it and prefer it to all their blessings. They can answer the prayers of mankind, yet their own prayer is for leisure. Augustus's conversation, even his correspondence with the Senate, kept reverting to his hope of leisure. Seneca concludes that the only men of leisure (*otiosi*) are those who take time for philosophy. They alone really live.

In later writings Seneca carries the theme further. From *Of Tranquillity* through *Of Leisure* to his *Letters,* the succession runs: first, a prelude to going into a life of leisure; second, the philosophical justification; third, the spirit of that life as it shines through to one who tries it. The young and the old, Seneca says, need leisure. No one can go without it. Only in leisure can one choose the model by which to direct his life. And he cites the case of Cato who threw himself into political life without realizing that liberty had already gone bad, that he was fighting only for a choice between tyrants, and that the winner could only be worse than the loser. In politics —we shall see later that the position, while different from both Stoicism and Epicureanism, yet has moved from the first toward the second—it is as if one were told the best life is to sail the seas, but then cautioned against shipwrecks and sudden storms. In reality one is being instructed not to set sail. The wise man does not launch ship on the sea of politics: the state with its tempests is too likely to wreck him. This is true for the state to which one belongs by accident of birth. That other *res publica,* the universal one that embraces gods and men alike, that houses all corners of the world, that defines citizenship by the path of the sun—*that* one we can serve even in leisure, actually serve it even better in leisure. If this universal state we dream of can nowhere be found, leisure is necessary in spite of and without the state. For the perfect state, the one thing that might have been preferred to leisure, exists nowhere. What one should aim for is to be able to say, as Seneca expresses it in a letter, "I am free, Lucilius, free, and wherever I am I am myself."

In Seneca, the thought of the Greco-Roman world converges. Four centuries, from the second until the sixth, feel the influence of his drawing together and fusing Stoic thought with Greek writings on leisure and contemplation. Poetry and prose both profit from it. The emperor Julian, the last great defender of pagan ideals, solemnly declared that whoever tries to persuade us that the philosophical life, meaning the life of leisure and contemplation, is not superior to everything else, is trying to cheat us. We have reached, indeed gone beyond, the point where the trail leads back to Plato and then goes off through Plotinus and into Christianity and monasticism. Here the contemplative element was singled out. Yet leisure, with part of itself withdrawn into monasteries, still did not quit the garden for the cloister.

The ideal has had an enormous secular influence. One current runs through the Stoics, for they lived as though they were Epicureans, and from them into Cicero and Seneca who later pass northward, penetrating as far as the English schools to put a stamp on the English and on part, but a lesser part as we shall see, of the American character as well. Another current helped form the idea of the liberal arts out of that of the general culture. Much of the tenacity of the liberal arts (they survived the barbarian invasions) and their strange attraction (they won over Theodoric who was illiterate) comes from their freedom, the liberality of having their end in themselves.

We cannot follow all the ramifications. They would commit us to a world's history of leisure and contemplation. At best we can mention only some of the various figures and periods that touched the ideal, not so much leaving it with a distinct impress as taking away some of the brilliance to which the Greeks had polished it, and forgetting some of the bitter experiences the Romans sought to drown in it.

NOTES AND REFERENCES

In spite of the importance of leisure and contemplation in ancient culture, relatively few studies on ancient civilization examine the problem with any care. Of the works that do treat it, most have passing references but do not go into the subject.

The Greek ideal of leisure is discussed by Jacob Burckhardt, *Griechische Kulturgeschichte,* Vol. III, Neunter Abschnitt, Stuttgart, 1952; Cecil Deslisle Burns, *Greek Ideals: A Study of Social Life,* Bell, London, 1917; Ernest Barker, *Reflections on Leisure,* National Council of Social Service, London, n.d.; Arnold Toynbee, *A Study of History,* Oxford U. Press, London, Vol. IX, 1954; and William A. Newman, *The Politics of Aristotle,* Clarendon Press, Oxford, 1887–1902.

Definitions of pertinent Greek concepts can be found in R. Arnou, Πράξις et θεωρία —*étude de détail sur le vocabulaire et la pensée des Ennéades de Plotin,* Paris, 1921.

A discussion of *otium* in the thought of the Church Fathers is found in Adolphe Alfred Tanquerey, *Compendio di teologia ascetica e mistica,* Rome, 1927.

Christian views in general are reviewed by J. Clark Murray, "Idleness," in *Encyclopaedia of Religion and Ethics,* James Hastings, ed., Scribner, New York, 1908–26, Vol. VIII, p. 100. A small but penetrating modern Catholic work is Joseph Pieper, *Leisure, the Basis of Culture,* tr. by Alexander Dru, Faber, London, 1952.

On contemplation, see Franz Boll, *Vita contemplativa,* Festrede zur zehnjährigen Stiftungsfeste der Heidelberger Akademie der Wissenschaften, C. Winter, Heidelberg, 1920; André M. J. Festugière, *Contemplation et vie contemplative selon Platon,* Vrin, Paris, 1936; Rodolfo Mondolfo, "Origen del ideal filosófico de la vida," *Revista de Estudios Clasicos,* U. Nacional de Cuyo, Mendoza (Argentina), I, 1–34, 1944. Alberto Grilli, *Il problema della vita contemplativa nel mondo greco-romano,* Bocca, Rome, 1953, is mainly concerned with the positions of Epicurean and Stoic philosophers on contemplation, and deals with most of their relevant passages, but traces their origin from Aristotle and the thinkers that followed him. However, the author has not realized the significance of the concept of time in the Epicurean position. Essential to the Epicurean notion of good life is the condemnation of the connection between time and human life: time is an accident of cosmic movements, whereas the time of the soul is different. The relevant passages are quoted in the booklet by Jean Fallot, *Le plaisir et la mort dans la philosophie d'Epicure,* Julliard, Paris, 1951. For the Stoic, an essential element of ethical life was the adjustment of the time of human life to cosmic time. See Victor Goldschmidt, *Le systéme stoïcien et l'idée de temps,* Vrin, Paris, 1953.

A treatment of Christian views of contemplation is found in the article "Contemplation" by Charles Baumgartner in *Dictionnaire de spiritualité ascétique et mystique, doctrine et histoire,* Marcel Viller, ed., Beauschesne, Paris, 1937–57, Vol. II, pp. 1643–2193. Contributions can be found also in Marcel Viller, *La spiritualité des premiers siècles chrétiens,* Bloud et Gay, Paris, 1930; Edward C. Butler, *Western Mysticism: the teachings of SS Augustine, Gregory and Bernard on contemplation and the contemplative life,* Constable, London, 1922; and Gustave Bardy, *La vie spirituelle d'après les pères des trois premiers siècles,* Bloud et Gay, Paris, 1935.

The following works deal with contemporary Catholic attitudes: Jacques and Raïssa Maritain, *Liturgy and Contemplation,* tr. from French by Joseph W. Evans, Kenedy, New York, 1960; Jacques Maritain, "Action et contemplation," *Revue Thomiste,* XLIII, 1937, pp. 18–50; Reginald Garrigou-Lagrange, *Christian Perfection and Contemplation,* Herder, St. Louis, 1946; Thomas Merton, *The Ascent to Truth,* Harcourt, Brace, New York, 1951, and *Bread in the Wilderness,* 1953.

Other discussions of contemplation can be found in Edward I. Watkin, *A Philosophy of Form,* Sheed & Ward, London, 1950; William James, *The Varieties of Religious Experiences,* Riverside Press, Cambridge, 1903; James H. Leuba, *The Psychological Origin and the Nature of Religion,* Constable, London, 1909; Emile Bréhier, *La philosophie en Orient,* Presses Universitaires de France, Paris, 1948; and Douglas Van Steere, *Work and Contemplation,* Harper, New York, 1957. For a notable fictional account, see Herbert Read, *The Green Child,* Eyre and Spottiswood, London, 1947.

Some helpful works on the history or culture of the various periods discussed in this chapter are: for Sumer, Samuel Kramer, *History Begins at Sumer,* Doubleday, Garden City, 1959; for Egypt, W. M. Flinders Petrie, *Social Life in Ancient Egypt,* Mifflin, Boston, 1923; for Greece, Fustel de Coulanges, *The Ancient City,* Doubleday, Garden City, n.d.; Emile Mireaux, *Daily Life in The Time of Homer,* tr. by Iris Sells, Macmillan, New York, 1959; and Alfred E. Zimmern, *The Greek Commonwealth,* Clarendon Press, Oxford, 1911; for China, Fung Yu-lan, *A History of Chinese Philosophy,* tr. by Derk Bodde, Princeton U. Press, Princeton, 1952; and Marcel Granet, *Chinese Civilization,* Knopf, New York, 1930; for India, Sarvepalli Radhakrishnan and Charles Moore, eds., *A Source Book in Indian Philosophy,* Princeton U. Press, Princeton, 1957; and Joseph Campbell, ed., *Philosophies of India,* Pantheon, New York, 1951; for Rome, Jerome Carcopino, *Daily Life in Ancient Rome,* Penguin, Harmondsworth, 1956; Edith Hamilton, *The Roman Way,* Norton, New York, 1932; and Grant Showerman, *Rome and the Romans,* Macmillan, New York, 1931; for the Middle Ages, Eileen Power, *Medieval People,* Doubleday, Garden City, 1954, and G. C. Coulton, *Medieval Panorama,* Macmillan, New York, 1946; for scholasticism, Etienne Gilson, *Reason and Revelation in the Middel Ages,* Scribner, New York, 1938. On Venice, Pompeo G. Molmenti, *Venice, Its Individual Growth from the Early Beginning to the Fall of the Republic,* tr. By Horatio F. Brown, McClurg, Chicago, 1906–08. On the transition to the Renaissance, Eugenio Garin, *Dal medioevo al rinascimento,* Sansoni, Florence, 1950. On Florence, J. Lucas-Dubreton, *La vie quotidienne à Florence au temps des Médicis,* Hachette, Paris, 1958. On Christianity and classical culture, Charles Cochrane, *Christianity and Classical Culture,* Oxford U. Press, New York, 1957, and Umberto Fracassini, *Il misticismo greco e il cristianesimo,* Il Solco, Gubbio, 1944, p. 347. On Greek and Roman education, see William Barclay, *Educational Ideals in the Ancient World,* Collins, London, 1959, and Werner Jaeger, *Paideia: The Ideals of Greek Culture,* tr. by Gilbert Highet, Oxford U. Press, New York, 1945. For the relations of Islam, Greece, and Christianity, Gustave von Grunebaum, *Medieval Islam,* U. of Chicago Press, Chicago, 1956. On Egyptian education, Pierre Montet, *Everyday Life in Egypt,* tr. by A. Maxwell-Hyslo and Margaret S. Drower, Arnold, London, 1958; for the life of the Sumerian scribe, Kramer, *History Begins at Sumer;* for the life and material of Greek and Roman writers, Moses Hadas, *Ancilla to Classical Reading,* Columbia U. Press, New York, 1954; for scribes, schools, students, and professors in the whole ancient world see Henri Marrou, *Histoire de l'éducation dans l'antiquité,* Editions du Seuil, Paris, 1948; for the Christian scholar, Elmore H. Harbison, *The Christian Scholar in the Age of the Reformation,* Scribner, New York, 1956.

chapter three

Discretionary Time: Quantitative Leisure

The most common conceptualization views leisure as *that portion of time which remains when time for work and the basic requirements for existence have been satisfied.* Leisure is discretionary or nonobligatory time, a concept which parallels the economic concept of discretionary money. Time falls into three classes: time for existence, sleeping, eating (meeting biological requirements); time for subsistence (working at one's job); and leisure (time remaining after the basic necessities of life and work requirements have been accomplished).

The concept of leisure as time free from work-related responsibilities is held by most Americans. Our society's dominant view of how time should be spent is illustrated by the industrial worker: hours to be devoured, in order to receive sustenance. Participation in the daily routine has become the goal of life itself. Americans have inherited from the time of the Industrial Revolution of the nineteenth century a sociopsychological attitude which equates individual self-worth and productivity with working. Don Fabun states that the contemporary definition of work as a normal outlet for man's energies was fostered in the sixth century.

This idea may have had its first concrete expression in the Sixth Century when St. Benedict at his monastery at Monte Cassino pasted rules for the monks. "Idleness is the enemy of the soul," begins Rule XLVIII. "And therefore, at fixed times, the brothers ought to be occupied in manual labor, and, again at fixed times, in sacred reading."

For the first time not work as such, but work for a stipulated time, became integral to Western thought. In later years we were to confuse the two, so that "putting in the time" became more important than the work. But what was new here at the beginning with the monks of Monte Cassino, was that work was good for the soul. This was the myth that has become a monster in our times; it drives even the rich to maintain the illusion that they are working, and those who do not work into an incessant apologia for being alive.

The "work" monster gained substance from the idea that the progress of a society or a culture is something like the natural progress of man; as he grows older and works harder, he accumulates more wisdom and more material things.

It is probably no accident that the idea of social progress and the sanctity of work as a means to achieve it grew into a now virtually unexamined ethic at the same time that the Industrial Revolution began to need more "workers." This kind of work was not like the work that had gone on before; it was specially oriented in space (in the factory or foundry) and structured in time (the necessity for the worker to be in a certain place, at certain times, performing certain prescribed activities).[1]

The glorification of work through industrialism led to the separation of work and leisure, and an emphasis on economically productive functions as the most significant aspects of life, with the eventual relegation of leisure to the status of "spare time." The concept of work in industrialized Western culture, typified in the United States, provides man not only with financial reward but also with self-respect. However, there is a growing awareness that the tradition of work (and thereby the modern tradition of leisure) as the moral and religious core of life is no longer so widely accepted. This has caused a corresponding erosion of the view of leisure as discretionary time, time from increased efficiency and productivity.

The autonomous craftsman, responsible for the total creation and performance of his product, has virtually disappeared from the American industrial scene. The highly specialized assembly-line nature of modern industrial work has left the individual with little opportunity to use judgment or take initiative. However, the trend away from work as a source of emotional and social satisfaction does not mean that such satisfaction is no longer important for the worker. For many workers the job continues to fill what would otherwise be a void in life. In a society where most men work, jobs continue to furnish important identity recognition, to smoothe

---

[1]Don Fabun, *The Dynamics of Change* (Englewood Cliffs, N.J.: Prentice-Hall, Inc., 1967), pp. 13–14.

the individual's routine of waking and sleeping, time on and time off the job.

Significantly, the changed attitude toward work has resulted in what Bennett Berger describes as the "problem of leisure."[2] Work has steadily lost its influence and power to command people's identification and loyalties; as they attempt to find alternative sources of moral experience, society loses an important source of normative integration. Berger suggests that the transfer to the leisure institution of functions formerly performed by the institution of work results in enormous increase in the attention devoted to the problem of leisure. The strain on the individual of this shift as a potential source of fulfillment is seen as significant because of the dramatic shift in the economy toward abundance, supported by discretionary money.

Automation has done much to free the mind and liberate man from repetitive, monotonous, and often hazardous kinds of labor in poor environments beneath the ground, in polluted atmospheres, and in unattractive settings, but it has not, to date, enhanced personal gratification. The social constraints and moral sanctions which limit our behavior have not been altered substantially to guide behavior which is free from or has relatively little relationship to work. Accordingly, many Americans are searching for ways to behave off the job.

LEISURE AS DISCRETIONARY TIME

The social patterns associated with technological changes that began in the nineteenth century were assimilated into the popular culture through twentieth century innovations. Industry has effectively incorporated many of the concepts of the Protestant Ethic into work and has even conditioned the worker in his off-work hours. The glorification of work in the Protestant Ethic has produced for most people a residual feeling of guilt toward the enjoyment of leisure. Those who assumed the separation of work ethic and leisure ethic generally face a dilemma regarding the need for a major value reorientation if the potential benefits of increased leisure are to be realized. It seems rather clear that to pose work and leisure as antithetical concepts tends to obscure the more fundamental value of personal fulfillment in all of life's endeavors.

Many people feel that the industrial and technological thrust in America has had a detrimental influence on the appreciation and fostering of leisure. To permit some response to the promise of leisure held out by our economic system, we have developed an elaborate rationalization that

[2]Bennett Berger, "The Sociology of Leisure: Some Suggestions," *Industrial Relations*, 1 (February 1962).

holds leisure to be time earned as a respite from work—time for rest and relaxation. It is to be basically *recuperative* in nature. The depreciation of leisure as justifiable only as release from work time relegates off-the-job living to second-rate status and only compounds the leisure problem.

The concept of discretionary time is central to the obvious relationship between time and leisure. Somehow most Americans believe that there is a time famine. To remove ourselves from the "rat race" is a kind of escape. The confusion of Americans in regard to the leisure problem poses interesting challenges to our social order, based largely on the economic-materialistic model perpetuated by the work ethic. Traditional ideas founded in an era of industrial expansion involve values and beliefs which are inappropriate to the spread of leisure, which threatens to overtake work as the central focus for contemporary American society. Economic growth can increase real income, but it cannot add to total time and it may even increase the demands on what little time is available.

Time, unlike purchasing power, cannot be expanded or accumulated. It may be reallocated among uses, but there is danger that it may be "saved" for lost causes or utopian dreams forever postponed. Accordingly, time can become more and more scarce compared to goods. It follows that the "price" of time can therefore rise faster than the price of goods. David Gray[3] states that such a dynamic relationship between time and goods can result in people seeking things to buy which take little time to enjoy and maintain. By viewing leisure as discretionary time, "free" time which becomes more scarce while goods become more plentiful, people tend to invest in activities which involve the purchase and consumption of goods rather than in activities which involve the commitment of time.

SUMMARY AND IMPLICATIONS

Leisure may be seen as that portion of time which remains when time for work and the basic requirements for existence have been satisfied. What is left is discretionary time, available for use according to one's desires.

The challenge to our economic system is to recognize and then implement the consequences of the changed energy flow of production and to discover new ways of looking at work and leisure and their roles in society. Applying economic analysis, Staffan Linder examines the changing uses of time.[4] He finds that contrary to expectations, economic growth has not

[3]David E. Gray, "This Alien Thing Called Leisure" (paper presented at Oregon State University, Corvallis, Oregon, 8 July 1971).

[4]Staffan B. Linder, *The Harried Leisure Class* (New York: Columbia University Press, 1970).

resulted in an abundance of free time and a leisurely life; it has, in fact, produced a scarcity of time and a more hectic life tempo. According to Linder, the scarcity of time, a result of persistent consumption needs which require man to work more and therefore cancel out increases in free time, corrupts the individual's pleasure of cultivating his mind. While de Grazia estimates that the industrial worker has gained over thirty hours of off-the-job time since 1850, he has reinvested this time into job-related activities. Linder agrees with this premise and argues that economic growth and higher standards of living mean less free time.

Linder posits a relationship between increasing goods and decreasing time in our industrial economy. As time becomes increasingly scarce, there is a need to continually reallocate time among competing goods and needs. Inevitably, values begin to change, the quality of life is altered, and we become trapped in the consumption-oriented complexities of modern living, limiting our potential self-enrichment.

According to Linder, the leisure problem is that people busy themselves with "nothingness"; that people engage in consumption to fill their "free time" with utility to show something for their toil. He suggests that people who have jobs and a certain amount of money use it to purchase consumption goods, the enjoyment of which takes time. After consuming these goods, they spend the rest of their time in complete passivity. People are not necessarily idle, but neither are they engaged in "leisure"—they simply do not know what to do with all their time. They are sociopsychologically maladapted to leisure.

The average worker lives under the pressure of time, and because he is likely to try to fill it with consumption-oriented goods, he is unable to truly engage in or comprehend leisure. Similarly, Fabun states that our society is on the threshold of a time when leisure is at last possible for most people, yet we are doing very little to prepare them for this new dimension of human life.

What happens when, as some have predicted, 2 per cent of the American population is employed in producing the necessities of life, and 98 per cent is not? How, indeed, can we hope to live meaningful lives in an "economy of abundance"? The tragedy is not, as some seem to believe, that this way of life may come about well within our lifetimes; the tragedy is that, knowing this, we are doing little or nothing to prepare ourselves or the younger generation to cope with it. When and where will we begin to chip away at the antiquated work ethic and come up with new systems and new institutions in which leisure, and not work, is the desirable and socially acceptable of man?[5]

[5]Fabun, *The Dynamics of Change*, p. 17.

The Protestant Ethic of serving God by extreme restraint, giving up pleasure through constant work, is the primary condition of human life. Leisure activities are viewed essentially as recreative and restorative, of secondary importance to the proliferation of culture. The Protestant view of leisure, dictated by Calvinist theology, led to the separation of work and leisure, placed the emphasis on economically productive functions as the most significant aspects of life, and relegated leisure to the status of free time. This view contrasts with the classical interpretation, in which leisure is concerned with life maintenance, a style of life expressing the highest values of a culture. Gray states:

> Currently our daily leisure is broken up into rather small segments—perhaps a little before work and a little at lunch time, but most is available in the late afternoon or early evening, after work and before bed. The total number of leisure hours per day—usually after four—is broken up into small increments. This limits its uses. Our weekly leisure is weekend leisure. . . . Regular personal chores reduce the time available and often jobs undone during the week are allowed to pile up on the weekend. Nevertheless, the longer period of time and the more flexible schedule which mark the weekend permit activities which would be impossible during the remainder of the week.[6]

Leisure for the contemporary American is fragmented. In primitive societies work and leisure were fused. In preindustrial feudal social orders, some differentiation of various daily tasks occurred. In the industrial order, a sharp distinction exists between work, religion, education, and leisure. Primitive cultures define man essentially as a creature of leisure—*homo ludens;* in the industrial order, man is defined as a working being, *homo faber* —work is the creator of values. In our society participation in work has almost become the goal of life. According to the discretionary-time concept of leisure, man is allowed respite from work, even fun, only after work-related responsibilities and essential life-maintenance activities have been satisfied.

[6]Gray, "This Alien Thing Called Leisure."

leisure in modern america

MARION CLAWSON and
JACK L. KNETSCH

Merely to maintain life, man must sleep, eat, and have time for some minimum personal hygiene. In order to subsist, he must work. In our modern society, this means work at a job or jobs. With the income obtained from this work, he buys goods and services produced by other men. For better lifetime subsistence, he must be trained for higher productivity, which today means he must go to school. Beyond these general categories, his time is discretionary. Leisure is largely discretionary time, to be used as one chooses.[1] It excludes existence and subsistence time, and time spent in socially or group determined activities in which the individual would prefer not to participate.

These categories are not completely watertight. Time for existence, if the latter is strictly interpreted, is fairly clear; yet time spent in eating may be for pleasure as well as existence. In subsistence, one may choose a minimum of income in order to have a maximum of leisure, or one may seek maximum income at the cost of leisure, or one may choose some intermediate position. The individual is not completely free in the modern world because the time requirements of jobs are largely group determined;

From Marion Clawson and Jack L. Knetsch, *Economics of Outdoor Recreation,* published for Resources for the Future, Inc. by The Johns Hopkins Press, 1966.

[1]Leisure is a subject which has evoked a large body of writing by those concerned with its psychological and social aspects; our concern in this book is primarily with the availability of time for outdoor recreation, and the factors affecting it. Some general references which underlie this chapter, and which in turn contain additional references, providing more consideration of the psychological and social aspects of leisure, include: Nels Anderson, *Work and Leisure* (New York: The Free Press, 1961); George Barton Cutten, *The Threat of Leisure* (New Haven: Yale University Press, 1926); Sebastian De Grazia, *Of Time, Work and Leisure* (New York: Twentieth Century Fund, 1962); Johan Huizinga, *Homo Ludens: A Study of the Play Elements in Culture* (London: Routledge and Kegan Paul, Ltd., 1949); Eric Larrabee and Rolf Meyersohn, ed., *Mass Leisure* (New York: The Free Press, 1958); Martin H. and Esther Neumeyer, *A Study of Leisure and Recreation in Their Sociological Aspects* (New York: A. S. Barnes and Co., 1949); Arthur Newton Pack, *The Challenge of Leisure* (New York: Macmillan Co., 1934); G. Ott Romney, *Off the Job Living—A Modern Concept of Recreation and Its Place in the Postwar World* (New York: A. S. Barnes and Co., 1945).

and some nonjob activities are so closely determined by social custom or pressure that little discretion is left to the normal individual. Yet many major choices are possible within discretionary time.

Discretionary time is similar to income. It is what is left after necessary obligations are met; its use connotes a large degree of purposefulness or choice. Mere idleness is not leisure, any more than lack of expenditure is use of discretionary income. This does not exclude a purposeful decision to do nothing; but it does exclude idleness which arises out of lack of something desirable to do.

Leisure time may be completely filled, or like discretionary income it may even be overcommitted. A person may wish to do so many things, or may have agreed with others to do so many things, that he either has no free time left, or is unable to meet his commitments.

A classification of time as work or leisure raises some difficulties. Broadly speaking, leisure is the time left over after sleep, necessary personal chores, and work. It is time available for doing as one likes, within the range of one's interests and abilities. But it is not synonymous with idleness. The use made of leisure—and, in fact, the distinction between leisure and idleness—depends upon the general economic situation in the society and for the individual. In many low-income societies, the bulk of the population has idle time which could be turned into leisure, given modest outlays for leisure activities, including training for them. Leisure and recreation are highly correlated, but they are not the same. Leisure is *time* of a special kind; recreation is *activity* (or inactivity) of special kinds. Recreation takes place during leisure; but not all leisure is given over to recreation. We return to recreation in more detail in the following chapter.

The way people use their leisure can shape a society as much as the way they work. Until recent decades, leisure as we define it was the privilege of the few. It is still that way in much of the world today, but meaningful leisure has become available to the bulk of the population in the United States and in the western world generally. Many students of the subject have been frightened at the prospect of mass leisure because it provides time for socially undesirable activities as well as for constructive ones. Clearly, some people have used leisure badly, often because they did not know how to put it to better use.[2]

Man's activities in the western world today extend over a long continuum, from the most unattractive drudgery to the most delightful leisure, and also from the greatest activity to the sheerest inactivity. Attractiveness or satisfaction and degree of activity are not necessarily correlated at all. The distinction between job and fun has narrowed for some parts of the

[2]James C. Charlesworth, ed., *Leisure in America: Blessing or Curse?* Monograph 4, American Academy of Political and Social Science, Philadelphia, April 1964.

population, but widened for others. Some people must today seek such physical activity as they wish at times and places other than on the job. Others find their jobs physically tiring, and look to leisure for rest. Even when they engage in a specific outdoor recreation activity, such as picnicking, people are motivated by different forces and seek different kinds of satisfactions. All of this adds to the complexity of the job for the planner or administrator of outdoor recreation.

LEISURE VERSUS WORK

By and large, leisure and work are competitors for time. If one increases, the other decreases. This is so for the individual and for society as a whole.

The number of hours of work performed by an individual worker, and thus the opportunity to balance work against leisure, is to a large extent socially determined. The nature of production and also commercial processes often preclude individual variations in working hours. The limits to which individuals must conform to the group pattern are extended in cases of those self-employed and those taking part-time work or two jobs. Individuals may join together in an attempt to modify their working hours.

It is within these limits of choice that the individual attempts to balance hours of work and hours of leisure. The choice will in part be dependent upon the wage rate he anticipates. While the desire for leisure may be great, the incentive to work longer hours lies in increased money income, and the taking of more leisure time consequently becomes a "cost." As the wage rate is raised there is no assurance of how individuals will react in their desire for more or less work. Higher wage rates *and* unchanged working hours mean higher income, and the individual is able to buy better food, more clothes, and more of other consumer goods; but a higher wage per hour would also permit the recipient to choose more leisure while maintaining total income unchanged. It depends upon the individual and his income which of these desires will dominate.

Historically, workers have been able to increase incomes and take more leisure as well, owing largely to increases in economic productivity. Over the past century, workers have taken about half of this increased productivity in more income and about half in more leisure; from 1920 to 1950, it was 60 per cent for more income and 40 per cent for more leisure.[3] Taking more leisure is certainly one of the ways we have chosen to enjoy the fruits of technological progress, and no doubt future workers will choose to work still shorter hours. More time will be taken for leisure, not so much because it improves productivity while on the job, but mostly because people get a great deal of enjoyment from it.

[3]Clark Kerr, discussion of paper entitled "The Shortening Work Week as a Component of Economic Growth: The Alternatives," by Charles D. Stewart, *American Economic Review,* Vol. 46, No. 2 (May 1956), pp. 218–23.

TIMING AND SIZE OF PIECES OF LEISURE

Time is one resource which every human has in equal measure—24 hours a day, 365 days a year, as long as he lives. But the use made of it varies greatly. The amount of leisure, in the sense we use the term, depends upon life expectancy and labor force participation, upon length of the typical workweek, upon reliance on part-time and second jobs, upon vacations and other paid time-off, and perhaps upon other factors. As far as outdoor recreation is concerned, the timing and size of pieces of leisure are as important as the total amount of leisure. Just as the possible use of land may be greatly affected by the size of the parcels into which it has been subdivided, so may the use of leisure time be equally affected by the size of the pieces. In each case, excessive subdivision may reduce a total value.

Because of improved medicine and better economic conditions generally, the life expectancy of babies born in this country has increased substantially. The average life expectancy for boy babies rose from 48 years in 1900[4] to 65.5 years in 1950; and is expected to reach 73 by the year 2000. The greatest change has been made in reduction of death rates among babies and small children, so that a larger proportion of those born live to grow up; but progress has been made in extending life at the older ages. Many students think that greater progress will be made along the latter line in the decades ahead.

In 1900, the average boy would spend about 13 years in getting educated and growing up before entering the labor force, 32 years in the labor force itself, and about 3 years in retirement. By 1950, each of these figures had risen: to 18 years becoming educated and growing up, 42 years in the labor force, and nearly 6 years in retirement. By 2000, the figures are expected to be: nearly 20 years growing up and getting educated, 45 years in the labor force, and nearly 9 years in retirement. Thus, the effect of increased longevity will continue to be felt in each of these three broad phases of the life cycle. Longer and presumably better preparation for life is possible; more working years; and at the end of life a longer period of retirement provides a major opportunity for enjoyment.

For women, the picture is somewhat similar, but more complicated.[5] The life expectancy for women is greater than for men, by about 6 years; it, too, has increased over the years, from the same general causes. But the employment pattern for women varies considerably from that for men. Girls enter the labor force in considerable numbers in the years up to 20,

---

[4]Seymour L. Wolfbein, "The Changing Length of Working Life," in Eric Larrabee and Rolf Meyersohn, eds., *Mass Leisure.*

[5]Stuart Garfinkle, "Tables of Working Life for Women, 1950," *Monthly Labor Review*, Part II, Vol. 79, No. 8 (August 1956); and Part III, Vol. 79, No. 10 (October 1956). See also U.S. President's Commission on the Status of Women, *American Women* (Washington: U.S. Government Printing Office, 1963), for a generally similar analysis.

and women enter much more slowly after that age. For women between 20 and 25 years of age, the number who leave the labor force greatly exceeds the number who enter it; marriage and childbearing take a large proportion of the total. It is at this age that marked differences begin to show up between the women who marry and those who do not, and between those whose marriages are broken by death or divorce and those remaining married. The women who do not marry before the age of 30 are likely never to marry. Most of them stay in the labor force unless ill health forces them out. Widowed and divorced women are often forced back to a job, and are likely to remain there for economic reasons. The average age of women when the last child is born is 26 years, and between 35 and 44 years of age the number of women who enter the labor force is larger than the number who leave. Those entering at this time are, for the most part, women who formerly worked and whose children are now enough older so that their family situation permits their return to work. The need for additional income or the desire for the stimulus of a job are the major reasons for their working. At older ages, women begin to leave the work force. But many married women with children will work 20 or more years during their lifetime.

Interestingly enough, the average woman who has worked spends about twice as many years in retirement, after work, as does the average man. Although historical data on work force participation are less complete for women than for men—in part because of more complicated life work histories—there is good reason to think that present trends will continue. There will almost certainly be a longer period of growing up and getting educated for the average young woman; some will work for a relatively short period, marry, raise children, and then re-enter the labor force when they still have many active years ahead; a modest number of career women will work continuously; and the number of retired women will be larger. All of this has its implications for outdoor recreation.

The typical workweek and the average workweek are not exactly the same. For instance, most workers may be working a 40 hour week, and thus this is typical. But in some occupations, workers may have either a longer or shorter week; overtime lengthens the week for some, lay-offs and operations at less than capacity shorten it for others; and paid time off the job, in vacations and for other reasons, also effects the time actually at work. Some of these differences vary according as boom or prosperity affect the demand for labor.

The average workweek has declined greatly in the past 100 years or more.[6] In 1850, the average workweek was 70 hours—about 72 hours for

[6] J. Frederic Dewhurst and Associates, *America's Needs and Resources—A New Survey* (New York: The Twentieth Century Fund, 1955); and Joseph S. Zeisel,"The Workweek in American Industry 1850–1956," in *Mass Leisure*.

agriculture and about 65 hours for all nonagricultural employment. By 1900, the average was down to 60 hours, and by 1920 to 50 hours, and today to about 40 hours. Part of the declining trend was due to the rise of nonagricultural employment, which typically has shorter working hours, but agriculture also shows a declining trend. The average has declined because typical hours per day have shortened, from 10 or 12 to 8 or less; because typical days per week have declined from 6 or 7 to 5 or less; and because of the rise of the paid time off. Declines in the average workweek have varied from industry to industry, and from occupation to occupation.

Some men and women work only part time. Students, housewives, and others may have other demands on their time which permit them to work only a portion of the week. Pay and working conditions in part-time jobs are often not attractive to workers. Moreover, there are major obstacles to a wider use of part-time workers, especially in industry. In wartime or when labor is short, employers may be driven to a greater use of part-time workers, but revert to employing full-time workers when labor conditions are normal again. In the service occupations, part-time work is more practical.

A special situation is the worker who has two or even three jobs.[7] In 1963, 3.9 million persons in the United States, out of a total labor force of about 75 million, more or less regularly had two or more jobs.[8] Nearly half of these workers were self-employed at their second job—a farm for many of them, or a small business or profession. Some types of public service, as the postal service, are characterized by second job-holding. In New York City, it has been asserted that 60 to 70 per cent of the policemen and 50 to 60 per cent of the firemen hold a second job. Most of the double jobholders are men; the highest rate is for men in the 25 to 54 year age bracket, who often have heavy financial obligations. This seems a clear case where added income is valued more highly by the worker than is added leisure.

Another major development has been the increase in the paid vacation, or, more generally, in paid time off the job. The total number of weeks of paid vacation in the nation rose from 17.5 million in 1929 to 78 million weeks in 1959; or, based upon all members of the labor force, from 0.37 week in 1929 to slightly more than 1 week in 1959 per member of the labor force[9] and has continued to rise in more recent years. However, substantial numbers of self-employed, casual, and non-unionized workers have no

---

[7]Gertrude Bancroft, "Multiple Jobholders in December 1959," *Monthly Labor Review,* Vol. 83, No. 10 (October 1960).

[8]U.S. Bureau of Labor Statistics, *Special Labor Force Report No. 29,* "Multiple Jobholders in May 1962" (1963); *Special Labor Force Report No. 39,* "Multiple Jobholders in May 1963," by R.A. Bogan (1964).

[9]Economic Report of the President, January 1960, and for earlier years.

paid vacations; this means that those with a paid vacation actually have far more time than these figures indicate. The paid vacation has long been a privilege of the managerial or upper professional employees in industry, education, and other major activities. For the hourly employees in industry, less than half had paid vacations before the war, but now almost all have them.[10] There has been a strong trend toward longer paid vacations. Length of paid vacation is often correlated with length of service with the company. In addition, hourly workers get paid vacations on holidays during the year. Nearly all workers get six such paid holidays and a substantial proportion get eight or more.[11]   Also, in some companies, workers are allowed time off with pay for various personal matters such as a trip to the doctor or for voting, or for civic activities such as jury duty. There is considerable evidence that the full-time regular employee in a unionized plant, or in one with similar employment conditions, enjoys as much paid vacation time as do the managerial employees. The situation is different for the casual worker, for the typical nonunionized worker in service activities, and for the self-employed; they typically get no paid vacations.

A number of studies have been made in the past as to the daily living, work, and leisure schedules of various classes.[12]   The typical employed male in the United States today arises between six and eight in the morning, showers and shaves, eats breakfast, and departs for work, usually with no leisure except possibly scanning the morning paper or listening to the radio. The journey to work—varying from a very few minutes to more than an hour in the largest cities for some workers—possibly averages half an hour. For those who drive in a car pool with fellow workers, visiting en route, the trip to work is at least partly leisure; for those who take public transportation and read while traveling, the ride to work has a strong leisure content. At work there are some opportunities for visiting with co-workers, perhaps during coffee breaks. Lunch, especially for business and professional men, may be a combination of business and pleasure. A journey home after work completes the working part of the day. From three to six hours is likely to remain before bedtime, for eating, necessary personal chores, and leisure. The latter may be used in one of many ways —at home or away, outdoors or in, actively or passively, at a wide variety of activities. On the weekend, maintenance of home, car, and yard, and

[10]Harold Stieglitz, *Time Off with Pay* (Studies in Personnel Policy, No. 156), National Industrial Conference Board, New York, 1957.

[11]Bureau of Labor Statistics, *Wages and Related Benefits: All Metropolitan Areas, United States and Regional Summaries, 1962–63,* Bulletin No. 1345–83, Part II.

[12]For an early study of this type, with a comprehensive bibliography of published studies up to that time see Pitirim A. Sorokin and Clarence Q. Berger, *Time budgets of Human Behavior* (Cambridge: Harvard University Press, 1939).

other chores will occupy some time. So may church and civic activities. But as much as four to twelve hours can be found for leisure pursuits on each of the two weekend days.

There are many variations in this pattern. Some men work shifts other than the normal daytime one, and therefore have entirely different daily schedules. However, for them, too, daily leisure is typically after work. The daily pattern for the child or youth going to school is roughly similar, with generally less time spent in travel, shorter hours at school than on the job, but more likelihood of homework from school than from job. The married woman has a somewhat similar schedule also, in part because the demands on her time are partly established by the activities of her family. She may arise earlier or later than the male, but usually must get her children their breakfast and get them off to school. During the day, her work schedule is more easily varied. Coffee with a neighbor may intermix leisure with work. Shopping may combine necessary household duties with pleasure. Many housewives do a considerable part of their daily work in the late afternoon, in getting dinner and in clearing up afterward, thus working later than other members of the family. For them the weekend days are similar to weekdays, and they have less additional leisure than the other members of the family.

The whole family, together or in various groupings, is likely to take an annual vacation, usually in summer, although winter vacations are becoming more common. Spring and fall vacations may become increasingly popular in the future. The vacation may be spent at home, at a mountain or shore resort, traveling, or in other ways. Children of certain age groups often go to summer camp. A major problem is to find a vacation which is reasonably enjoyable to each member of the family. For example, the man and boys may enjoy camping and fishing, while the women and girls find the outdoors a particularly inconvenient place to do necessary housework.

For most persons from ages 6 to perhaps 65 years, leisure time comes in one of three major forms: (1) daily, for the approximately 180 school days or for the approximately 240 work days, in amounts of perhaps 3 to 6 hours each day, not necessarily all continuous, after the demands for sleep, work or school, and personal chores have been met; (2) on weekends, for about 100 days a year, when work is typically absent, and the time may run as high as 12 hours per day; and (3) annually, for vacations extending over a period as long as 75 to 90 days for school children and as long as 20 to 30 days for workers, when the whole pattern of family life may be different, and oriented largely to the leisure activities. The pre-school and retired ages have different patterns, less regular and less geared to the weekly and annual cycle; to a lesser extent, so do housewives. But all members of a household are affected by the schedules of the school and working members.

NATIONAL TIME BUDGET

As far as we can ascertain, very little work has been done on a compilation of a national time budget for the United States. Certainly there is no authoritative continuous series of annual time budgets showing how total time is used for the whole nation. National money income accounts, showing how national income originates and how it is used, annually, have been in existence for several decades. Perhaps "time is money," but the statisticians have never attempted to account for time. In a sense, this is curious, for in an advanced industrial society such as the United States the real wealth is very much in the time of its members, and not merely in the dollar accounts. It is altogether possible that in the future the competition for consumers' time will be more severe than for their money. This is possibly true on TV today; it may well be true for outdoor recreation tomorrow. Money can be used to buy time-saving measures and hence money is translatable into time, within limits.

The fact that goods and services are sold in some kind of a market place, with money price tags attached, makes money national income vastly easier to estimate than a national time budget, since the use of time is so much a personal affair. However, a national time budget has been estimated for 1900, 1950, and 2000 and is shown in Table 1 and Figure 1.[13] Total time (population multiplied by hours per year) is broken down by use, including leisure, and then leisure time is further subdivided. How time is used depends in part upon the number of people in various age and activity classes, and upon what the typical person in each class does with his time. Although our information is relatively good on the first point, it is poor on the second, and our estimates are only approximately accurate.

By far the largest use of time at each period is for sleep—approximately 40 per cent of the total time is used in this way at each date. The time spent in work has declined from 13 per cent of total time in 1900 to 10 per cent in 1950, and is expected to decline further to only about 7 per cent in 2000. Only a part of this decline is due to average working hours per week; part is due to differences in participation in the labor force. Other readjustments in use of time have occurred or seem probable. For instance, the time spent in housekeeping has risen less than proportionately to the increase in total time, less than proportionately to the increase in paid work, and very much less than the rise in leisure.

[13]Mary A. Holman, "A National Time-Budget for the Year 2000," *Sociology and Social Research*, Vol. 46, No. 1 (October 1961).

Our particular concern is with leisure. It has risen greatly in absolute terms; with total time roughly doubling in each 50-year period, total hours of leisure for the whole population increased nearly threefold between 1900 and 1950 and are expected to increase 2.5 times between 1950 and 2000. Leisure time has also increased relatively, from 27 per cent of total time in 1900 to 34 per cent in 1950, with an expected further increase to 38 per cent by 2000. There have also been some changes in the distribution of leisure among its major types. Daily leisure remained a relatively constant proportion of total leisure from 1900 to 1950, but is expected to drop in relative terms by 2000 as other types of leisure increase relatively more. In contrast, weekend leisure has risen greatly in relative terms, and promises to continue to do so. Curiously enough, vacation leisure had hardly kept pace with the rise in total leisure up to 1950; a comparison to 1960, however, might show a different result as this type of leisure is expected to rise greatly in relative terms by 2000. The change in total hours of the whole population plus the changes in time distribution of leisure will mean a tenfold increase in total vacations and total retired time between 1900 and 2000.

These comparisons of 1900 and 1950 are based upon the best available estimates of what has actually happened over this period. The comparisons of what may happen between 1950 and 2000 are based upon certain assumptions as to the form of leisure in the latter year.[14] The total leisure then available is likely to be about as estimated, but of course some of it might be shifted from one category to another.

The combined influence of many more people, of more of them in leisure age groups, and of more leisure for the working ages all combine to suggest a very great increase in total leisure in the decades ahead. The effect of such changes upon outdoor recreation will continue to be very great.[15]

[14]These are discussed in Holman, "A National Time-Budget for the Year 2000."

[15]It is only fair to warn readers that not everyone accepts our findings, either as to past trends in leisure or as to outlook for the future. Those who criticize our interpretation of the past do so mostly on the grounds that other demands of our modern urban society take so much time that the increase in genuine leisure is much less than we estimate. Sebastian De Grazia, in *Of Time, Work and Leisure* (New York: Twentieth Century Fund, 1962) almost goes so far as to deny that there has been any increase in leisure. Various reviewers of an earlier draft of this manuscript think that the extent of leisure today is exaggerated. We can only reply that we think our statements are correct in terms of our definition of leisure. Those who criticize our views of the future do so on directly contrasting grounds. On the one hand, Donald Michael in *Cybernation* (Santa Barbara: Center for the Study of Democratic Institutions, 1960) and *Work and Free Time* (Philadelphia: American Recreation Foundation, 1962) and Robert Theobald in *Free Men and Free Markets* (New York: Clarkson Potter, 1963) think that science and technology will so reduce labor requirements for most types of economic enterprise that the amount of unemployed time will rise enormously more than we estimate. Taking the contrary view are various persons who think that consumers' demands for goods, plus the necessities of the international situation, will require that leisure be kept to a lower level than we have estimated, in order that more productive work be done.

Table 1 and Figure 1 present data on leisure for the whole population; this will be shared unequally among individuals. Not every individual, or at least not every individual in every year, will necessarily experience an increase in leisure over the next few decades. Professional and white-collar adult workers, during the weeks they work, may well work as long hours

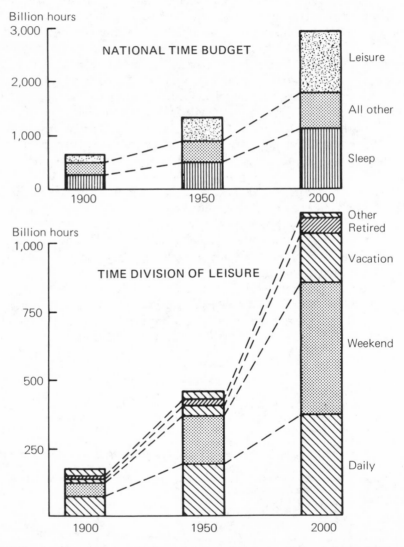

Figure 1. National time budget and time divisions of leisure, 1900, 1950, and 2000.

Table 1. National time budget and time division of leisure, 1900, 1950, and 2000

Use of Time	1900 Billion Hours	1900 Per Cent of Total Time	1900 Per Cent of Leisure Time	1950 Billion Hours	1950 Per Cent of Total Time	1950 Per Cent of Leisure Time	2000 Billion Hours	2000 Per Cent of Total Time	2000 Per Cent of Leisure Time
1. Total time for entire population	667	100		1,329	100		2,907	100	
2. Sleep	265	40		514	39		1,131	39	
3. Work	86	13		132	10		206	7	
4. School	11	2		32	2		90	3	
5. Housekeeping	61	9		68	5		93	3	
6. Preschool population, nonsleeping hours	30	4		56	4		110	4	
7. Personal care	37	6		74	6		164	6	
8. Total (items 2–7)	490	73		876	66		1,794	62	
9. Remaining hours, largely leisure	177	27	100	453	34	100	1,113	38	100
10. Daily leisure hours	72		41	189		42	375		34
11. Weekend leisure hours	50		28	179		39	483		44
12. Vacation	17		10	35		8	182		16
13. Retired	6		3	24		5	56		5
14. Other, including unaccounted	32		18	26		6	16		1

Source: Adapted from Mary A. Holman, "A National Time-Budget for the Year 2000," *Sociology and Social Research*, Vol. 46, No. 1 (October 1961).

as now; but they may enter the labor force at a later age than now is common; they may have longer paid vacations, including perhaps "sabbaticals" of several weeks duration at intervals of a few years; and they may have more years in retirement. In recent years, blue-collar workers have perhaps gained relatively more leisure than white-collar workers, as union contracts have frequently included more paid time off, as well as shorter workweeks in some instances. While the variations among individuals will be important to the persons concerned, the total demand for outdoor recreation will be affected primarily by the total volume of leisure, and very little by its distribution among individuals.

The past and prospective increases in leisure per capita are sharply at variance with the past and probable increases in real income per capita. For the 1900–1950 period, leisure per capita rose about 27 per cent, while real incomes per capita increased about 150 per cent; for the 1950–2000 period, the contrast may be still sharper—a rise of about 12 per cent in per capita leisure to be contrasted with an anticipated rise of at least 150 per cent in real income per capita. The total supply of time per person is absolutely fixed; while leisure has increased, and is expected to increase further, there are rather definite limits to the increase per person. On the other hand, real incomes per person can rise more or less indefinitely, and in fact have risen sharply in the past. The leisure-income balance is shifting toward much more income and to only slightly more leisure, each on a per capita basis. People will be under increasing incentive, and will increasingly have the means, to spend part of their larger income on making the most of their limited leisure. The vacationist will fly to his destination and rent a car, rather than spend time in driving there, for instance. It is this divergence in prospective trends of per capita real income and of per capita leisure which has led us to state that the competition for time will become more severe than the competition for leisure.

chapter four

Leisure
as a Function
of Social Class, Race,
and Occupation

CONSPICUOUS LEISURE

Leisure, particularly in the Greco-Roman concept, has been most often associated with an elite social class. In earlier, less industrialized societies, leisure was available in great quantity only to aristocrats, ruling classes, and the privileged, who were immune from labor. Thorstein Veblen demonstrates how through various periods of history, the wealthy elite have been identified through their possession of leisure.[1] Veblen's book profoundly affected social scientists, leading to a conceptualization of leisure as representing free time and social class in economics. Veblen's treatise admonishes the elitist "leisure class" for exploiting others while themselves engaging in "conspicuous consumption." This is possible because they are economically self-sufficient and can afford to be unproductive and to fill their free time with consumption of goods. Veblen's identification of the "idle rich" led to the concept of *leisure class.* Richard Kraus states:

[1]Thorstein Veblen, *The Theory of the Leisure Class* (New York: New American Library, 1953).

Veblen's major work, *The Theory of the Leisure Class,* pointed out that in Europe, during the feudal and Renaissance periods and finally the industrial age, the possession and visible use of leisure became the hallmark of the upper class. Abstention from labor became the evidence of wealth and social standing.[2]

The concept of social class views leisure as a way of life for the rich elite. Leisure and life-style orientation have become increasingly an area of concern and interest, although Veblen's interpretation of the rigid dichotomy of social class is no longer relevant. The diffusion of culture, the spread of wealth, and increases in free time for the working class have resulted in increased access for the masses to material possessions and forms of relaxation and entertainment.

Kenneth Roberts notes that as leisure "has gradually established a definite place in people's lives its autonomy from the influence of other institutions has correspondingly increased."[3] In the nineteenth and early twentieth century a person's social class was central to the pattern of his life. As leisure has become an increasingly differentiated institution and integral aspect of the social structure, activities people elect during leisure have become independent from other social roles. While class, occupational, racial, and other social determinants play an important role in determining one's leisure pattern, they have become less significant elements in advanced industrial and technological societies.

SOCIAL CLASS DIFFERENCES AND LEISURE

A number of studies have investigated class differences in the use of leisure. Many activities have been found to be correlated to class level, "particularly those in which participation requires a certain level of education; others, such as television viewing, are not distinctly related."[4] Clyde R. White,[5] Saxon Graham,[6] Joel Gerstl,[7] Leonard Reissman,[8] and Lawrence

[2]Richard Kraus, *Recreation and Leisure in Modern Society* (New York: Appleton-Century-Crofts, 1971), p. 255.

[3]Kenneth Roberts, *Leisure* (London: Longmans Green and Co., Limited, 1970), p. 91.

[4]Rolf Meyersohn, "The Sociology of Leisure in the United States: Introduction and Bibliography, 1945–1965," *Journal of Leisure Research,* 1 (Winter 1969), 56.

[5]Clyde R. White, "Social Class Differences in the Uses of Leisure," *American Journal of Sociology,* 61 (September 1955), 145–50.

[6]Saxon Graham, "Social Correlates of Adult Leisure-Time Behavior," in *Community Structure Analysis,* ed. Marvin B. Sussman (New York: Thomas Y. Crowell Co., 1959), pp. 331–54.

[7]Joel Gerstl, "Leisure, Taste, and Occupational Milieu," *Social Problems,* (Summer 1961), 56–58.

[8]Leonard Reissman, "Class, Leisure and Social Participation," *American Sociological Review,* 19 (February 1954), pp. 75–84.

C. Thomas[9] have investigated the relationship between social class differences and the uses of leisure, and have found clear distinctions among the various social class levels.

White's study analyzed the relationship between social class differences and the uses of leisure by identifying four social classes in several census tracts in Cuyahoga County, Ohio: upper-middle, lower-middle, upper-lower, and lower-lower. He identified several major categories of leisure use and grouped them under headings related to settings for leisure activity. They included: (1) public recreation facilities, (2) group-work agencies, (3) church, (4) museums, (5) libraries, (6) commercial amusements, and (7) other. He found that lower classes made much greater use of public facilities than upper classes, and the home was the most frequent setting for leisure involvement, with commercial amusements a close second. Differences between lower and upper class in leisure participation sharpened with age.

Max Kaplan[10] cautions that social class determinants are no longer effective in predicting leisure interests and needs because the diffusion of culture, increased mobility, the mass media, and rising affluence have brought varied forms of leisure within reach of almost everyone. Meyersohn also reveals that social class differences may not be as crucial as other variables.

Of greater interest are the more detailed examinations of leisure usage within educational, occupational, and income groups, such as Gerstl and Hecksher and de Grazia. These studies make clear that even though socio-economic level is an important variable, the kind of work, defined more subtly, constitutes a significant variable as well.[11]

A recent study by David A. Cunningham et al.[12] found few significant relationships between occupational groups and participation in active leisure activities. This study suggests the need for community recreation authorities to make various types of leisure opportunities available to all occupational groups.

[9]Lawrence C. Thomas, "Leisure Pursuits by Socio-Economic Strata," *Journal of Educational Sociology*, 29 (May 1956), 367–77.

[10]Max Kaplan, *Leisure in America: A Social Inquiry*, (New York: John Wiley and Sons, 1960).

[11]Meyersohn, "The Sociology of Leisure in the United States," p. 56.

[12]David A. Cunningham, Henry J. Montoye, Helen L. Metzner, and Jacob B. Keller, "Active Leisure Activities as Related to Occupation," *Journal of Leisure Research*, 2 (Spring 1970), 104–11.

OCCUPATIONAL DIFFERENCES AND LEISURE

Leisure appears to be related to people's working lives. Roberts notes that several writers have attempted to analyze the role of leisure in society and its relationship to occupational positions and the functioning of the economy. Roberts gives three essential reasons for the relationship, as revealed by various authors: (1) Marx saw that leisure offered the worker under capitalism a means whereby the labor force could rejuvenate itself; (2) subsequent writers have shown leisure to be based on values and interests generalized at work; and (3) for others, leisure offers an opportunity to compensate for the frustrations and monotony involved in work in modern industry.[13]

Occupations appear to have a strong influence on leisure, and while generalizations are often misleading, most research reveals that working classes tend to spend their leisure passively, seeking entertainment through spectator events, viewing television, or through relaxation. Middle classes are most inclined to adopt active leisure pursuits, participating and running associations, meeting and entertaining friends, or becoming involved in pursuits that demand some degree of mental or physical activity. These differences widen as people grow older and progressively adapt themselves to the patterns of their social strata.

Roberts offers seven reasons for different types of leisure pursuits among individuals of various occupations:

1. Manual occupations demand a great deal of time and energy, leaving such people unable to cultivate active leisure pursuits.
2. Manual occupations are physically arduous and therefore may result in a need to spend leisure simply relaxing or recuperating.
3. Less financially well-off persons do not have substantial incomes to invest in leisure interests outside the home and do not have discretionary money to spare for club subscriptions, trips to the theatre, sports equipment, etc.
4. White-collar families have a greater opportunity to travel abroad and this exposure may stimulate another leisure interest. Certain leisure activities appear to trigger off others.
5. Education awakens white-collar people to leisure interests outside the sphere of the manual worker.
6. A white-collar worker's job may create more opportunities for one to acquire skills that can be exploited during his leisure.
7. Leisure habits emerge as status attitudes, which are generated at work, spill over into and influence people's leisure lives.[14]

[13]Roberts, *Leisure,* pp. 23–24.
[14]Ibid., pp. 28–29.

Work has dictated to a large degree when, how, and where industrial man spent his leisure. "The rhythm of the individual's life is largely determined by the interplay between the demands made by work upon the individual and the demands that he makes upon his leisure."[15] Roberts suggests that more research on employee behavior and its relationship to various leisure interests and pursuits would be more fruitful if researchers would use the styles of life and attitudes that employees have developed outside to explain their behavior at work. The dominant work rhythm of life and leisure is no longer determined by the demands of the economy. Leisure behavior appears to have become an important influence on industrial behavior.

LEISURE AND RACE

The public provision of leisure service has traditionally been most prevalent in white middle-class communities. While the early efforts of the recreation movement in America were oriented to the needs of the urban underprivileged, this concern was basically limited to white youth. The delivery of public recreation and leisure service has been scrutinized as a result of surveys and investigations of impoverished conditions in urban communities stimulated by civil unrest during the 1960s.

Public servants have assumed that all groups of people have an equal need for recreation and that recreation is a universally voluntary experience. Oppressed racial groups, including blacks, Chicanos, Puerto Ricans, and Indians, have never been able to engage in leisure prusuits as freely as the advantaged Anglo citizen, whatever their social class or occupation, because of discriminatory practices, insufficient discretionary money, and inadequate leisure opportunities and services available in their communities.

The failure of organized public recreation and leisure service to effectively serve nonwhite Americans has recently attracted some consideration. Kraus[16] states that not until the 1960s did the recreation profession begin to give special attention to the leisure needs of the poor—especially the nonwhite poor—in urban slums. The federal government's antipoverty program, which provided funding to aid disadvantaged groups, gained impetus from a wave of urban rioting which erupted throughout the nation in 1964 and 1965. Only after these civil disturbances were the needs of inner-city residents brought forcefully to the attention of the public.

The extent to which public recreation and leisure service practices egalitarianism in providing leisure opportunities for various nonwhite ra-

[15]Ibid., p. 34.
[16]Kraus, *Recreation and Leisure in Modern Society*, p. 388.

cial groups has recently been vigorously questioned. It is generally believed that participation by nonwhites in community associations, clubs, and other cultural and leisure activities represents a significant step toward their integration into mainstream American life.

A National League of Cities study, cosponsored by the Bureau of Outdoor Recreation and Department of Interior, found that "in most cities surveyed, officials readily admitted that the needs of all population groups were not being adequately met. Only in recent years have cities begun to recognize the obligation to provide recreation for the handicapped and deprived."[17] The study revealed that recreation and leisure-service programs and facilities are considered a high-priority item among the deprived. "Residents of deprived urban neighborhoods are almost entirely dependent upon public recreation facilities, whereas residents of more affluent neighborhoods have a wide range of recreational opportunities."[18]

Although many city officials claimed that the leisure needs of disadvantaged persons are essentially the same as those of the rest of the community, studies by Shirley Jenkins[19] and Edwin J. Staley[20] document the dependency of the poor on public recreation and leisure-service facilities and programs. Jenkins and Staley conclude that the deprived, particularly nonwhite inner-city poor, require greater opportunities for leisure and cultural experiences than do the economically and socially advantaged.

James F. Murphy's study of public recreation and leisure service delivery approaches for blacks indicates that the provision of public service at the national level has had effects similar to municipal-level recreation:

1. The black community has been and is today largely isolated from the mainstream interests of American society. The relationship between the two communities, black and white, has not been one of interdependence but one of a dominant majority, dependent minority relationship.

2. The socializing function of recreation in both black and white communities has been largely to establish the legitimacy of the values, ideals and interests of the dominant majority.

3. Because the black minority has been thwarted in the pursuit of those values,

[17]Department of Urban Studies, *Recreation in the Nation's Cities: Problems and Approaches* (Washington, D.C.: National League of Cities, 1968), p. 2.

[18]Ibid.

[19]Shirley Jenkins, *Comparative Recreation Needs and Services in New York City Neighborhoods* (New York: Community Council of Greater New York, 1963).

[20]Edwin J. Staley, *An Instrument for Determining Comparative Priority of Need for Neighborhood Recreation Services in the City of Los Angeles* (Los Angeles: Recreation and Youth Services Planning Council, 1968).

ideals and interests, it was socialized to accept and did accept [that] the socializing function of recreation in the black community has been dysfunctional with regard to the real needs and interests of the black minority.[21]

The convergence of the last two perspectives has resulted in an incomplete democratization process in public recreation and leisure service. Blacks, as well as Chicanos, Puerto Ricans, Asian-Americans, and Indians, have been partially circumscribed by a society that has permitted them only limited outlets and opportunities for leisure expression. Most racial minorities have historically been barred from places of white amusement—theaters, movie houses, amusement parks, pool halls, bowling alleys, parks, and zoos—even when these were supported by public funds. Discrimination and the lack of access to public leisure facilities and programs has encouraged certain racial minorities, particularly blacks, Chinese-Americans, and Chicanos, to develop their own music, life style, dress, and sanctions for fun.

In his study of the leisure participation patterns of blacks of all ages in twenty-four suburban communities in New York, New Jersey, and Connecticut and the five boroughs of New York City, Kraus[22] found a sharp contrast between the reported recreation involvements of black and white participants in such activities as sports, cultural programs, and activities for specific age groups in public recreation, park, and school programs. Blacks dominated such sport activities as track and field, use of swimming facilities, basketball, and various forms of combative activity, particularly boxing. Blacks participated far less in activities such as tennis, golf, and archery, which have traditionally been considered white middle-class pastimes. Black children and youth were found to participate widely in the areas of music, drama, and dance. Also, black families tended to make extensive use of picnicking, fishing, and biking facilities, which are relatively inexpensive. Contrarily, they were found to make only limited use of more expensive activities, such as boating, skiing, and riflery. White participants dominated those activities that represent "upper-class" cultural tastes. In cultural programs in which blacks did become involved, activity was typically segregated. The patterns reported by Kraus were recognized by recreation directors to be characteristic both in terms of activities in which they participated and their involvement by age group.

[21]James F. Murphy, "Egalitarianism and Separatism: A History of Approaches in the Provision of Public Recreation and Leisure Service for Blacks, 1906–1972" (Ph.D. thesis, Oregon State University, 1972), p. 197.

[22]Richard Kraus, *Public Recreation and the Negro: A Study of Participation and Administrative Practices* (New York: Center for Urban Education, 1968), pp. 31–32.

Samuel Z. Klausner[23] notes some other black leisure-participation patterns:

> In the middle class, sex-homogeneous recreational activities, such as hunting by males and card-playing by females, are common. Among low-income Negroes, most recreation seems to be sex-heterogeneous. Among youth, boy-girl recreation, the drama of mating, is significant. Among all age groups, family picnicking, a type of harvest rite, seems frequent. Apparently, the association between recreation and sexuality differs across class lines.
>
> Eating rituals are an important feature of recreation in this group. Some of the activities, borrowed from other cultural groups, even take their names from the type of food consumed—beer parties, weiner roasts. The drama here may express the problem of food deprivation in everyday life.
>
> Among youth, one observes a good deal of aggressive (not necessarily hostile) behavior. This drama has to do, in part, with the establishment of dominance—submission relations. . . . Also, one observes behavior in which the self is tested against some natural barrier; the meaning of this activity, on the psychological level, relates to the seeking of stress. Stress-seeking is not class-bound, but it is probably differentially distributed among classes.

Klausner's inferences of the leisure traits of blacks, particularly in the low-income population, indicate that the black community is not homogeneous. Significantly, the meaning of leisure for blacks and other subordinated minority groups may reveal the life problems played out by these groups during their free time. Typically, blacks, Puerto Ricans, Chicanos, Indians, and Asian-Americans grow up in environments characterized by isolation, constriction, and rejection. They live in encapsulated communities which shelter and, at the same time, separate them from the wider society. Tensions and opposing forces bear heavily on them from within and without their communities. The environment of the poor, particularly of deprived racial minority groups, tend to influence the development and support of recreation and leisure efforts, and to evoke participation patterns characteristic of the particular milieu. According to Moore,[24] the problem of adequate social development of many of the nation's poor is compounded by their inadequate leisure potential.

1. Coping with sustenance difficulties produces a pragmatic orientation; goals tend to be short term and abilities to defer gratification are limited. Thus,

[23] *A Program for Outdoor Recreation Research,* Publication number 1727, National Academy of Sciences, Washington, D.C. 1969.

[24] Velva Moore, "Recreation Leadership with Socioculturally Handicapped Clientele," in *Recreation and Leisure Service for the Disadvantaged,* ed. John A. Nesbitt, Paul D. Brown, and James F. Murphy (Philadelphia: Lea & Febiger, 1970), p. 167.

leisure rewards must be relatively immediate and concrete; and they must accompany income security, or else futility is reiterated.

2. Restricted childhood play experiences—a possible characteristic of low-income areas—implies an underdeveloped recreation repertoire. The disadvantaged population seldom has the opportunity to gain leisure "know-how" in the realms of the dominant society's positively sanctioned leisure and play activities.

3. Disadvantaged neighborhoods are distinguished by their lack of recreation services—whether they be public, semi-public, private, nonprofit or commercial.

4. Disadvantaged populations, though often residentially mobile within their own neighborhoods, infrequently travel outside this context on their own volition. This may be due to deficiencies in transportation, income, knowledge and/or self-confidence: this factor considerably lessens the extent and degree of potential recreation experience and resources.

5. Cultural differences may be the source of leisure habits that are inappropriate to the urban setting, or contradictory to values and norms of the larger society.

6. Minority membership may deter participation in available leisure activities because of social pressures and discrimination by other groups of the society.

SUMMARY AND IMPLICATIONS

Although sharp contrasts in leisure behavior and interests have been documented among different social class, occupational, and racial groups, we expect that a lessening of distinct leisure class differences will occur. Some of the major reasons for this expected decline are: (1) the population as a whole is growing more affluent, which will increase the range of activities available to an ever-widening section of the community; (2) growth of mass leisure industries and mass media will spread similar tastes (diffuse culture) and opportunities, resulting in more people's using leisure in similar ways; and (3) the volume of free time that people have has expanded, resulting in increased opportunities for people to develop autonomous leisure interests.

A number of studies comparing blue-collar and white-collar leisure interests and patterns report similar findings. Essentially, most reveal that the blue-collar worker differs from the white-collar worker in reading fewer books and periodicals; attending fewer movies, lectures, concerts, and theatres; and displaying less interest in artistic and musical pursuits; while spending more time watching television, working on cars, traveling for pleasure, playing cards, fishing, and frequenting bars. The amount of free time devoted by the blue-collar worker to associational life—belonging to formal organizations—has been minimal. When they do belong to organizations, blue-collar workers tend to participate in lodge, veterans', or labor union groups. Milton M. Gordon and Charles A. Anderson[25] summarize blue-collar leisure, as portrayed in the literature:

> It appears to flow quite naturally from what are held to be the basic themes of the stable working-class subculture: a desire for stability and security and an unwillingness to take social and economic risks which could disrupt the old security found in a group of solidary familiars, an anti-intellectualism which aspires for the understood result and the concrete, and a person-centeredness.

Studies indicate that social class may no longer be so significant to leisure interests and behaviors, and that certain social indicators, including race, economics, education, and environment, may be more important factors in determining leisure orientation and preference. This is particularly true of socially deprived racial minority groups whose monotonously restricted environments produce apathy and insufficient novel and diverse stimuli to generate satisfactory intrinsically motivated leisure behavior patterns.

[25]Milton M. Gordon and Charles A. Anderson, "The Blue-Collar Worker at Leisure," in *Blue-Collar World: Studies of the American Worker,* ed. Arthur B. Shostak and William Gomberg (Englewood Cliffs, N.J.: Prentice-Hall, Inc., 1964), p. 411.

kinds of leisure
and their meaning today

STANLEY PARKER

This is the age of increasing leisure, we are constantly told. But what *kind* of leisure? There are many ways of filling free time, ways which amount to a complex 'machinery of amusement', all the parts of which *look* different while probably performing in many cases the same function to the individual. And what of society itself—does it have an interest in the enjoyment of its leisure-seekers in any way comparable to its interest in the productivity of its workers? In a parallel exercise to that undertaken in the previous chapter we may look at the research findings on both the use of leisure time and the meaning attached to leisure.

SOCIAL AND INDIVIDUAL FUNCTIONS
OF LEISURE

Leisure has functions in the life of an individual, and its experience by individuals and groups has functions for the society in which they live. We may consider first how leisure serves society. It does this in three main ways: it helps people to learn how to play their part in society; it helps them to achieve societal or collective aims; and it helps the society to keep together.[1] These functions apply to groups as well as to the wider society.

The word sociologists have for describing the process by which people learn how to play their part in society is 'socialization'. It starts in childhood but continues into adult life as people have to learn how to cope with

From Stanley R. Parker, *The Future of Work and Leisure* (New York: Praeger Publishers, Inc., 1971, pp. 55–63. By permission of Praeger Publishers, Inc. and MacGibbon & Kee Ltd.

[1]These social purposes may be compared with the 'functional problems of social systems' put forward by Talcott Parsons and his associates—pattern maintenance and tension management, adaptation, goal attainment and integration. See E. Gross, 'A Functional Approach to Leisure Analysis', *Social Problems,* Summer, 1961.

new situations and to fit in—more or less—with what is expected of them. Leisure in the form of play and story-telling is used as a technique for teaching young children and reconciling them to school work. Leisure in the form of horseplay and initiation ceremonies often helps to socialize young workers into their jobs.

The work essential to society is aided by the recreational function of leisure. After a certain point work results in fatigue and often in boredom. With the intention of increasing productivity, some firms allow their workers more breaks than are strictly necessary for physiological purposes. Other firms encourage their workers to take 'wholesome recreation' off the job (the whole subject of industrial recreation will be dealt with in the next chapter). In another sense, industry needs the consuming time of workers as much as it needs their producing time. Businessmen in the 'leisure industries' are interested in making leisure serve economic purposes by encouraging people to buy leisure goods and to pay for leisure services. But a trade unionist, Mr E. S. Williams, made the following remarks in seconding a motion on reduced working hours and increased holidays:

> I would draw attention of the Congress to the need for our Movement to intensify its efforts among workpeople to ensure their full understanding of the need for adequate rest and leisure periods as essentials in the modern world of speed, speed and more speed. Intensification of effort over shorter working periods must be accompanied not only by longer rest and leisure periods but also by a full appreciation among our people of the need for them to use such leisure time in the pursuit of relaxation of their physical and mental processes which are of such importance in the modern industrial world.[2]

It is not suggested that the views of Mr Williams are typical of trade unionists—his subordination of leisure to the needs of industry is more typical of the nineteenth-century cult of work than of the twentieth century cult of leisure. But old ideas die hard. Also under the heading of societal aims there is the motivation that leisure may provide for work. Acquiring expensive leisure objects such as boats or caravans may only be possible through extra work (in the form either of overtime or a second job), and the prospects of a life of total leisure may be the motive for certain types of gambling, such as the big football pools.

Finally, leisure may contribute to the integration of society by promoting solidarity. At work, people may behave in leisure-like ways, such as 'horsing around', which help them to feel a sense of belonging together. Play and sporting activities serve as focal points of group identification. This raises the question of the degree of organization that is permissible

[2]Report of Trades Union Congress, 1965, p. 413.

in leisure activities. There is a paradox in planning for the use of what is supposed to be an uncommitted part of one's life. Since, however, the provision of leisure opportunities and the spread of ideas about how leisure time should be spent are largely functions of society, there is no guarantee that the absence of planning would increase the individual's choice of leisure opportunities. We shall return to this subject in the final chapter.

The state's attitude to the use of leisure by its citizens reflects both its function as an integrative institution and the shared values of those it controls. All states in the modern industrial world need to exercise at least a minimal control over the leisure activities of individuals. Some types of leisure behaviour or the provision of leisure facilities are defined as illegal, and the 'leisure industries' are subject to the same general laws which control other enterprises. Beyond this, the attitude of the state to the use of leisure may vary both with its degree of economic development and with the political views of the electorate. Countries such as China, having only recently embarked on the road to industrialization, require their citizens to render additional service to the state in their free time, to engage in organized physical culture for greater work efficiency, and to use entertainment, music, literature and art to reinforce the state's economic objectives. Russia, becoming like America in many economic if not social respects, dilutes a utilitarian approach to leisure with a liberal dose of concern for the development of the individual: 'Two major themes permeate the official discussion of leisure. One is the interdependence of leisure and work, that is, the contribution which well-spent leisure can make to efficiency at work; the other is the relationship between leisure and the "all-round development of the personality".'[3] In America and Britain government as such tends not to attempt to influence leisure activities, although the big business of commercialized leisure imposes its own standards of conformity.

Turning now to the functions of leisure for the individual, these can be classified on the basis of observed behaviour. An important classification is that of Dumazedier, who believes that leisure has three main functions of relaxation, entertainment, and personal development.[4] Relaxation provides recovery from fatigue, and repairs the physical and nervous damage wrought by the tensions of daily pressures, and particularly by those of the job. Entertainment provides relief from boredom—a break from daily routine. It has a strong element of escape—*realistic* in the form of a change of place or style (trips, sports), and involving *fantasy* in the form of identification and projection (cinema, the novel, etc.). In their extreme form these

[3] P. Hollander, 'The Uses of Leisure', *Survey*, July 1966.
[4] J. Dumazedier, *Toward a Society of Leisure*, London: Collier-Macmillan, 1967, pp. 14–17.

active and passive entertainment functions of leisure may be compared respectively with the 'compensatory' and 'spillover' hypotheses of Harold Wilensky, the former involving 'explosive compensation for the deadening rhythms of factory life' and the latter referring to the situation where mental stultification produced by work permeates leisure.[5]

Dumazedier's third function of leisure—personal development—'serves to liberate the individual from the daily automatism of thought and action. It permits a broader, readier social participation on the one hand, and on the other, a willing cultivation of the physical and mental self over and above utilitarian considerations of job or practical advancement. It may even lead to discovering new forms of voluntary learning for the rest of one's life and induce an entirely new kind of creative attitude.' Dumazedier observes that the three functions are interdependent and exist in varying degrees in everyone's life. They may coexist in a single leisure situation or may be exercised in turn.

Less comprehensive assessments of the roles of leisure may be fitted into the Dumazedier classification. One example is William Faunce's statement that 'leisure may be recuperative in the sense that time is spent relaxing from the job completed and preparing for the job forthcoming or it may be actively spent in the sense of physical or emotional involvement in an activity. . . . Leisure time may serve as a relief from boredom or as an escape from involvement.'[6] A. Giddens's remarks on the two major psychological functions of play noted are slightly different ways of talking about relaxation and personal development: cathartic (dissipating tension accumulated in other spheres) and ego-expansion (satisfactions of achievement and self-realization which are frustrated elsewhere).[7]

The type of work experience does not enable us to predict actual leisure behaviour, but it does enable us to predict what sort of function may be served for the individual by leisure behaviour. Those who want excitement, as well as those who want quiet, may only be searching for compensations for the kind of working life they have. For example, excitement may be sought in leisure because most of one's working life is dull; and the duller it is, the cruder the excitement that is satisfying. In the preface to a study of pigeon cultivation among French miners, Georges Friedmann pointed out that leisure does more than merely offer a compensation for the technique of work. It brings professional compensations for work with a limited horizon, emotional compensations for the crudity of social relations in a mass of people, and social compensations through the success

[5]H. Wilensky, 'Work, Careers and Social Integration', *International Social Science Journal*, No. 4, 1960.

[6]W. A. Faunce, 'Automation and Leisure', in H. B. Jacobson and J. S. Roucek (eds.), *Automation and Society*, New York: Philosophical Library, 1959.

[7]A. Giddens, 'Notes on the Concept of Play and Leisure', *Sociological Review*, Mar. 1964.

which this leisure-time activity can provide. After quoting this study, Dumazedier and Latouche observe that, far from being a compensation, leisure is more often only an extension of occupational life.[8] They refer to a study by Louchet showing that there is a tendency for the most frustrating leisure to be associated with the most frustrating work.

THE USE OF LEISURE BY OCCUPATIONAL GROUPS

How much leisure time people have and the ways in which they use it depend to a large extent on how much of their time and energies they invest in their jobs. Few studies have been made of the duration of leisure time for various occupational groups, no doubt partly because of the difficulty of defining leisure time. In the American suburban study by Lundberg and his associates in the early 1930s the average leisure time of male white-collar workers was reported as 438 minutes per day and that of executives as 401 minutes, but this included eating time.[9] Without giving figures, Harold Wilensky deduces from the comparative lengths of work weeks and work obligations that professionals, executives, officials and proprietors have less leisure time than the 'masses'.[10] In Poland the daily estimated time spent as leisure was 3.5 hours for workers in manufacturing industries, 2 hours for railwaymen, 3 hours for clerks, teachers and engineers and 2 hours for scientists and physicians.[11] It was noted that railwaymen read newspapers and even books during their working time, so their total time for leisure activities probably does not constitute an exception of Wilensky's broad generalisation.

Many more studies have been made of *types* of leisure behaviour in different occupational groups. The first national recreation survey in Britain showed that 'the higher the income level, occupational class and educational status of contacts, the greater the number of pursuits they mentioned for their weekend before interview, and the greater the importance of the "active" compared with the "passive" recreations. In short, those with the highest socio-economic status not only do more things, but do more active things. . . .'[12] A Government Social Survey report gave

[8]J. Dumazedier and N. Latouche, 'Work and Leisure in French Sociology', *Industrial Relations,* Feb. 1962.

[9]G. A. Lundberg *et al., Leisure—A Suburban Study,* New York: Columbia University Press, 1934, pp. 100–101.

[10]H. L. Wilensky, 'The Uneven Distribution of Leisure', *Social Problems,* Summer. 1961.

[11]H. Strzeminska, 'Socio-Professional Structure and Time-Budgets', report to Sixth World Congress of Sociology, Evian, 1966, pp. 7–8, 13–14.

[12]British Travel Association—University of Keele, *Pilot National Recreation Survey—Report No. 1,* July 1967.

similar findings: employers, managers and professional people watched only half as much television, but participated nearly twice as often in physical recreation, as semi-skilled and unskilled manual workers.[13] The *choice* of recreation also varies among occupational groups. Among employers and managers eighteen per cent play golf, compared with less than five per cent in the manual groups. Soccer is predominantly the game of manual workers, while cricket is more popular among the non-manual. Income is not a factor in this last choice, because participation in the two games costs about the same. Soccer is on the whole a rougher and tougher game than cricket and may fit in better with a manual worker's idea of what is a manly sport. It is also a sport requiring closer co-operation between members of a team, reflecting more the content of working-class occupations than of individualistic middle-class occupations.

Various American studies confirm the conclusion that occupation is related to certain preferred ways of spending leisure. For example, Joel Gerstl found that college professors spent less time with their children and around the home and less time on sport and non-professional organizations than did either admen or dentists.[14] Instead the professors tended to have 'work in leisure' by reading around their subject. Saxon Graham concluded that the proportion of professional workers participating in strenuous exercise was nearly twice that of unskilled workers.[15]

Other studies have been made in terms of wider class or status groups, which may reveal some occupational differences while obscuring others. According to R. Clyde White, the upper middle class more often use libraries and have home diversions and lecture-study groups, while the two lowest classes more often use parks and playgrounds, 'community chest' organizations, churches, museums and community entertainment.[16] Leonard Reissman found that those in higher class positions were more active and diverse in their social participation than those in lower classes and that the middle class tended to dominate the organizational activity of the community.[17] Alfred Clarke concluded that 'spectatoritis' occurred most often at the middle level of occupational prestige and that craft interest tended to vary inversely with prestige level.[18]

[13]K. K. Sillitoe, *Planning for Leisure*, London: H.M.S.O., 1969, p. 50.

[14]J. E. Gerstl, 'Leisure Taste and Occupational Milieu', *Social Problems*, Summer 1961.

[15]S. Graham, 'Social Correlates of Adult Leisure-Time Behaviour', in M. B. Sussman (ed.), *Community Structure and Analysis*, New York: Crowell, 1959, p. 347.

[16]R. C. White, 'Social Class Differences in the Use of Leisure', *American Journal of Sociology*, Sept. 1955.

[17]L. Reissman, 'Class, Leisure and Social Participation', *American Sociological Review*, Feb. 1954.

[18]A. C. Clarke, 'The Use of Leisure and its Relation to Levels of Occupational Prestige', *American Sociological Review*, June 1956.

A study has been made of the leisure activities of a group of workers on rotating shifts, whose hours of work fall at all times of the day or night, during the week and at week-ends.[19] As compared with day workers, the rotating shift workers in this sample tended to belong to fewer organizations and to go to meetings less often, and had fewer activities in which participation can occur only at specific times. Activities, like visiting, that can occur at different times were less affected, and those that can occur at any time, like indoor work and hobbies, were increased.

THE MEANING OF LEISURE

'The meaning of leisure in a given civilization depends on the meaning given to work. . . . What the individual demands of leisure depends on what he has and has not found in his work, and on what the education he has received has made him.'[20] These propositions by Raymond Aron are consistent with such impressions and evidence as we have but they can scarcely be said to have been adequately researched.

Most of the reported research on subjective meanings of leisure has been carried out by Robert Havighurst and his associates. They did not use type of occupation as a specific variable, but some clues to the meaning of leisure for occupational groups can be gained from the analysis of social class groups. In a study of the leisure activities of a sample of middle-aged people in Kansas City, Havighurst concluded that different age, sex and social class groups can derive similar values from their leisure, even though its content is different.[21] A comparative study was carried out in New Zealand, and leisure was found to have about the same meaning in the two countries. The principal meanings (defined as felt satisfactions or reasons for carrying on a particular leisure activity) in order of frequency were: just for the pleasure of doing it, a welcome change from work, brings contact with friends, gives new experience, makes the time pass, and gives the feeling of being creative.[22] Certain differences according to sex and social class were found: for example, the 'creative' meaning was more often expressed by women, and working-class people tended to stress the 'makes time pass' meaning.[23]

[19]E. H. Blakelock, 'A Durkheimian Approach to Some Temporal Problems of Leisure', *Social Problems*, Summer 1961.

[20]R. Aron, 'On Leisure in Industrial Societies', in J. Brooks *et al., The One and the Many: the Individual in the Modern World*, New York: Harper and Row, 1962, pp. 157, 171.

[21]R. J. Havighurst, 'The Leisure Activities of the Middle Aged', *American Journal of Sociology*, Sept. 1957.

[22]M. N. Donald and R. J. Havighurst, 'The Meanings of Leisure', *Social Forces*, May 1959.

[23]R. J. Havighurst, 'The Nature and Values of Meaningful Free-Time Activity', in R. W. Kleemeier (ed.), *Aging and Leisure*, New York: Oxford University Press, 1961.

Havighurst agrees with Aron that most of the meanings of leisure are also the meanings of work. People in talking about their work say that they get all the satisfactions from work that they might get from leisure except that of a change from work. In comparing these meanings Havighurst states a general principle of the *equivalence of work and play:* to a considerable extent people can get the same satisfactions from leisure as from work. There are, of course, limitations to this principle. For instance, a person who has found friends at work and who values sociability with these friends may have very little further need for sociability during his leisure time. But when he retires he may find sociability in a non-work setting and thus substitute leisure for work satisfactorily, provided the other positive meanings that work had for him can also be continued by substitute activities. Happy retirement depends on the previous life a person has led, as well as on the physical and social conditions in which he finds himself at this point in his life.

In a further report Havighurst and Feigenbaum related leisure activity to social role performance.[24] They distinguished two general patterns of life-style and leisure; community-centred and home-centred. They noted that these two patterns appeared to be equally accessible to middle-class people but that working-class people were rarely community-centred. In about five per cent of cases life-style and leisure style were not in close relation: these were people who invested most of their energy in work or in home and children, with little time and inclination for leisure. Another six per cent had a high level of leisure activity, but were dissatisfied or inadequate workers, parents or spouses who attempted to compensate with a high leisure performance.

In this chapter we have considered the functions, activities and meanings involved in leisure. Three general conclusions emerge. First, the functions which leisure has for the structure and pattern of society are related to those apparent in the lives of its individual members. Secondly, ways of spending leisure time tend to vary with the demands and satisfactions of the occupation. And thirdly, the meanings found in leisure and the attachment to home or community appear to be different for sex and social class groups.

[24]R. J. Havighurst and K. Feigenbaum, 'Leisure and Life-Style', *American Journal of Sociology,* Jan. 1959.

chapter five

Leisure as a Form of Activity

Leisure can be viewed as *nonwork behavior in which people engage during free time.* The leisure experience, viewed from this perspective, recognizes an *ecological* relationship between various elements of the leisure service delivery system: the leisure service agency, participant(s), and the social and physical environment. The experience is best understood by recognizing the relationship between the various components involved in the delivery of leisure service.

Leisure experience, in a behavioral context, includes all the potential nonwork opportunities available to people and "stresses that leisure is voluntary activity carried on in free time, in sharp contrast with work, which is required, is utilitarian, and is rewarded in economic terms."[1] Leisure behavior, however, must be recognized as an expression of the individual's total self; cognitive, affective, and motor domains are potentially engaged. E. William Niepoth[2] suggests that the perceptions of the individual engaging in leisure are the basis for his response. Behavior is inferred; to understand its meaning, we must assume its reference.

[1]Richard Kraus, *Recreation and Leisure in Modern Society* (New York: Appleton-Century-Crofts, 1971), p. 256.

[2]James F. Murphy, John G. Williams, E. William Niepoth, and Paul D. Brown, *Leisure Service Delivery System: A Modern Perspective* (Philadelphia: Lea & Febiger, 1973).

Niepoth suggests that leisure services are those activities which, through the creation and/or manipulation of human and physical environments, provide opportunities for the expression of a wide variety of recreational behavior. Behavior is goal-directed. The leisure experience, then, is a direct result of goal-seeking. The degree of success or failure of an individual engaging in leisure behavior will influence his decision to continue, modify, or terminate participation. Leisure service delivery, viewed from an activity perspective, must seemingly be based on a commitment to provide opportunities for people which encourage and facilitate, individually and collectively, their engaging in leisure behavior.

FUNCTIONS OF LEISURE

According to Joffre Dumazedier,[3] leisure fulfills three functions: relaxation, entertainment, and personal development. Relaxation "provides the individual recovery from fatigue," entertainment "spells deliverance from boredom," and personal development "serves to liberate the individual from the daily automatism of thought and action." To Dumazedier, "Leisure is activity—apart from the obligations of work, family, and society—to which the individual turns at will, for either relaxation, diversion, or broadening his individual and his spontaneous social participation, the free exercise of his creative capacity."[4]

To permit some response to the desire for leisure and the promise of leisure held out by our economic system, we have developed an elaborate rationalization of leisure as a respite from work that provides rest and relaxation. It is recuperative in nature. Leisure, viewed as activity, gained significance with the Industrial Revolution, according to Bennett Berger. He states that the glorification of work through industrialism led to the separation of work and leisure, resulting in an emphasis on economically productive functions as the most significant aspects of life, with the eventual relegation of leisure to the status of spare time. Accordingly, time which was separate from work—off-the-job living—came to be vulnerable to the "ministrations of the Devil . . . unless it were used productively to restore or refresh the organism for its primary purpose, work, or for unambiguously 'wholesome' purposes such as prayer, Bible reading, . . ."[5] and so on.

At one time religion (the word means "to bind together") was very much linked to leisure. The relationship is derived from the need for

[3]Joffre Dumazedier, *Toward a Society of Leisure* (New York: The Free Press, 1967), p. 14.
[4]Ibid., pp. 16–17.
[5]Bennett Berger, "The Sociology of Leisure: Some Suggestions," *Industrial Relations*, 1 (February 1962), 25.

integration, integrity, and wholeness once found in earlier forms of religion. Essentially, the concept of a spiritual and leisure life was splintered with the rise of industrialism. The concept of work in industrialized Western culture, typified by the United States, provides man not only with financial reward but also with self-respect. However, this tradition of work as the moral and religious core of life is no longer so widely accepted. This has caused a corresponding erosion of the concept of leisure as discretionary time, earned from increased industrial efficiency and productivity. "Instead of being responsible for turning out an entire product, as in the case of the old-time craftsman, the modern industrial worker rarely has a sense of total creation or individual responsibility for performance."[6]

The highly specialized assembly-line nature of modern industrial work has left the individual with little opportunity to use his judgment or take initiative. However, the trend away from work as a source of emotional and social satisfaction does not mean that such satisfaction is no longer important for the worker. For many workers, jobs continue to fill what would otherwise be a void.

> In such a situation we may expect . . . the transfer of functions formerly performed by the institutions of work to the "leisure institutions," and this, it seems to me, is precisely the significance of the enormous increase in attention which the problem of leisure has received in recent years.[7]

People derive from work benefits such as role, status, sense of striving, feeling of self-worth, productivity, competence, and achievement. We now experience pressures to alter the status of work (decreases in the work week, earlier retirement, longer life span, greater affluence, increased mobility) and to replace it with some other form of activity. The problem of leisure is a problem of finding, in the norms (expectations of behavior) which exercise constraint in specific situations, new values which will command moral identity. It seems rather fruitless for a leisure ethic to survive a work-oriented society (especially after its decline) if leisure patterns are a reflection only of worker frustration and groping. "The problem of leisure is exacerbated when men are asked to use their free time for activities beyond their means or for activities whose value they do not recognize."[8]

Berger believes that when the necessary values (traditional and new) are present for the diffusion of a leisure ethic, the problem of leisure will have been alleviated. The task is to discover what these values are and the

[6]Kraus, *Recreation and Leisure in Modern Society*, p. 304.
[7]Berger, "The Sociology of Leisure," p. 36.
[8]Ibid., 36–37.

pattern of activity through which they are sought. There is little question that the prevailing moral value of the Protestant work ethic, while slowly losing importance, has bound men's use of free time and effectively constrained their leisure. The moral system must provide satisfaction so that people can be free to pursue their goals.

LEISURE LIFE STYLES

While particular leisure activities are somewhat useful in analyzing behavior, greater consideration is being given to the total life style of the participant. Additionally, participant observation studies are often misleading in revealing the sociopsychological predispositions and significance of particular leisure activities. Rolf Meyersohn states that

> . . . since the values underlying participation in any particular leisure activity are not readily apparent from the study of activities themselves, it is very difficult to document the shift in values that might occur as a result of shifts in residence or even in social status.
>
> Leisure activities have no built-in gratificational or symbolic limits, and, much as children can make toys out of virtually any artifact, so adults can attach symbolic meaning to virtually any leisure activity. The status symbols and social significance of particular leisure activities are not immutable. Thus, the discoveries of correlations of participation in particular leisure activities with social class or occupation are perhaps more valuable to our understanding of the meaning of the class than they are toward our understanding of the meaning of leisure.[9]

With the proliferation of a diversity of subcultures in American society, the term *life style* has become an important social indicator for determining leisure interests; it is based on such factors as cultural heritage, family life, education, income, and occupation. Saul D. Feldman and Gerald W. Thielbar provide a further understanding of the meaning of life style:[10]

1. Life style is a group phenomenon. *A person's life style is not a unique or individual pattern of behavior; it is influenced by his participation in various social groups and by his relationships with significant others. We can predict a person's life style with reasonable accuracy from certain social and demographic characteristics. . . . The life style of a hairdresser differs from that of a college professor. And*

[9]Rolf Meyersohn, "The Sociology of Leisure in the United States: Introduction and Bibliography, 1945–1965," *Journal of Leisure Research*, 1 (Winter 1969), 57.

[10]From *Life Styles: Diversity in American Society*, Saul D. Feldman and Gerald W. Thielbar, pp. 1–3. Copyright © 1972 by Little, Brown and Company (Inc.). Reprinted by permission.

that the life style of a man who is concerned with his reputation in the community is different from that of a man who has rejected the values of society.

2. Life style pervades many aspects of life. *Knowing how an individual behaves in one area of his life may allow us to predict how he will act in other areas. . . . People whose self-rated political leanings are "left" or liberal will more likely attend an art film than conservative or middle-of-the-road individuals.*

3. Life style implies a central life interest. *In American society, many things may be of central interest to a person: work, ethnic heritage, politics, lineage, children, avocational interests, and others. A distinct life style is evident when a single activity or interest pervades a person's other interests and unrelated activities—a drug addict is an extreme example.*

4. Life styles differ according to sociologically relevant variables. . . . *Life styles in America vary according to age, sex, ethnicity, religion, and more.*

The concept of life style provides a more complete perspective of the leisure participant, since various groups in American culture are characterized at the same time by both great uniformity and great diversity. Certain behavior patterns are often observed without regard to their relation to life style.

Merely to know that both executives and skilled workers engage in leisure-time activities is not to understand their leisure behavior. More important is their leisure activities relate to their central life interests. Recreation for an executive may mean a temporary escape from work (so that he can function better when he returns to the office) or may serve as an informal setting for business contacts. For a skilled worker, recreation may serve as a family-centered activity. Thus leisure activities for executives may be integrated with their central life interest of career and for skilled workers with their central life interest of family.[11]

SUMMARY AND IMPLICATIONS

Robert J. Havighurst[12] believes that life style, a reflection of personality, values, attitudes, and aspirations, is a more influential leisure activity determinant than the variables of age, sex, and social class. Life style attributes, hard to use as a basis for planning leisure offerings, are indicative of the way individuals respond to activities and represent the satisfactions they derive from such participation. Viewing leisure activity from a

[11]Ibid., p. 46.

[12]Robert J. Havighurst and Kenneth Feigenbaum, "Leisure and Life Style," *American Journal of Sociology*, 64 (January 1959), 396–405.

life style perspective, one sees that the similarities and/or differences in personal response among individuals cut across age, sex, social class, and education in determining suitable leisure experiences for people. Noel P. Gist and Sylvia F. Fava state:

> An urban upper middle class man, middle-aged, with a college education, may have in common with a working class man, also middle aged, but with scant education, the capacity to participate enthusiastically in leisure-time activity, deriving much enjoyment from it, because such activity meets their personality needs.[13]

From a sociopsychological perspective, in Havighurst's view, it is not the differences in form and content of leisure activity that matter, but the *subjective experiences* of the participants, either as active recreationists or as passive spectators.

Patterns of leisure, like other forms of expression and behavior, are aspects of daily life. Leisure behavior, when viewed as life style, cannot be understood unless a total investigation is made of an individual's daily life activities, showing the interrelatedness of all his behavioral patterns. Is there a modal or typical leisure life style pattern? According to Don Martindale,[14] the American life style is represented in white Anglo-Saxon Protestants and their New England ancestors; David Riesman[15] suggests that American life style is best expressed by middle-American, middle-majority consumption patterns. However, American society embraces several ethnic groups, including blacks, Chicanos, Jews, and Indians. Recognizing this dilemma, Feldman and Thielbar pose the following questions in response to the process of America's cultural destiny—whether we intend to support cultural pluralism (the process of preserving separate ethnic life styles) or Anglo-conformity (the process by which groups disappear by conforming to the white Anglo-Saxon standard):

> Is the accepted American life style symbolized by being a member of one of the many groups that make up the ethnic mix in America and maintaining an ethnic life style? Or is the accepted American style that of conforming to the middle-majority life style?[16]

[13]Noel P. Gist and Sylvia F. Fava, *Urban Society*, 5th ed. (New York: Thomas Y. Crowell Co., 1964), p. 426.

[14]Don Martindale, *Community, Character and Civilization* (New York: The Free Press, 1963), pp. 291–360.

[15]David Riesman, "Some Questions About the Study of American Character in the Twentieth Century," *The Annals*, 370 (March 1967), 36–47.

[16]Feldman and Thielbar, *Life Styles: Diversity in American Society*, p. 273.

Cultural pluralism is present when an ethnic minority seeks acceptance within a society through group conformity in those areas where this is felt to be necessary to the national well-being, yet simultaneously maintains its native cultural traits in other areas that are not felt to be so essential. Pluralism implies that a group seeks toleration for its differences, the idea being that various cultures can flourish peacefully side by side in the same society—a pattern acceptable to the dominant culture.

Leisure, viewed as activity, represents all potential nonwork opportunities available to people and is generally recognized as fulfilling three functions: relaxation, entertainment, and personal development. Because leisure behavior invovles the total self, a fully developed comprehension of the individual's personality, attitudes, aspirations, and background is necessary before adequate delivery of leisure service can occur. The wide variance of possible activity patterns in any one community seemingly requires an altered perspective of viewing nonwork behavior.

The rhythm of life and leisure. The rhythm of life in our society has traditionally been based around the organization of work. The organization of leisure opportunities is geared primarily to this dominant rhythm of life. Not every person fits society's rhythm. "Outsiders" cut off from the normal rhythm find it difficult to enjoy a normal style of leisure, a fact which emphasizes the extent to which the leisure of the vast majority of people is geared to a common rhythm. The outsiders may be the unemployed, the retired, hippies, blacks, Chicanos, and others whose jobs necessitate unusual hours. Their conditions of employment, cultural traditions, and other ethnic factors render them incapable of enjoying leisure. Roberts states, "Enjoying leisure in modern society is conditioned upon having a job because, without work, a person's normal rhythm of life and his approach to the daily routine is undermined, and participation in normal forms of recreation and social relationships becomes impossible."[17]

Abnormal rhythms of life force the individual into being responsible for his allegedly deviant behavior. Most Americans' life style is governed by the dominant rhythm, and the deviants—hippies, lower-class blacks, retired people, and so on—are for some reason cut off from this rhythm. It is likely that the size of these groups of outsiders will increase, because the proportion of elderly people in society is expected to increase, shift work is expected to become increasingly common, acceptance of divergent subcultural groups is becoming more prevalent, and growing alienation will frustrate people no longer gaining moral strength from the repetitive tasks of assembly-line work. Society must find a way of integrating outsiders into normal leisure activities.

[17]Kenneth Roberts *Leisure* (London: Longmans Green and Co., Limited, 1970), p. 13.

Mass culture: unity or diversity?   Leisure service agencies must identify the most discernible behavior patterns and values related to subcultural life as manifested by outsiders to make their life styles and images more acceptable to those who influence professional recreation policy, affecting the ability of such outsiders to realize aspirations sought through recreation experiences.

The dysfunction between means and ends has led to a generation and cultural gap in values and goals between youth and their elders, blacks and the dominant white majority, women and men, and so on. Youth have taken positions, for example, of economic and emotional liberation as a basis for experimentation. A mass culture can absorb an incredible variety of values and life styles, but America has been reluctant to do so. Youth are attempting to demonstrate to adults the dynamics by which a mass culture functions—characterized by experimentation and continual change.

Affluent Americans have done precisely what they set out to do: they have liberated their children. They have given them the economic, techno-logical, and psychological basis for self-determination. Values and atti-tudes valid in the past, acquired during the wars and the pursuit of economic security, are no longer valid when applied to today's youth. Adults see in their children the things they wanted for themselves: free-dom of self-expression, an experimental attitude toward life, a deep moral commitment, and an openness to new and different life styles. The forces of affluence and technology have reinforced the ability of many young people to achieve an experimental approach to life. A new public life philosophy appears to be necessary, as the past value system is largely inappropriate when applied to many of today's behavioral expressions, as exemplified by various subcultures. Youth, blacks, and women tenaciously refuse to adapt to white middle-class standards of behavior and control of the system with an outdated code of values.

Leisure has become the part of life to which people attach an increas-ingly greater interest and importance. Work no longer provides all the moral justification it once did; therefore it is paramount that leisure service agencies give people satisfying and rewarding experiences so that they may achieve a sense of identity and worth.

leisure and life-style

ROBERT J. HAVIGHURST and
KENNETH FEIGENBAUM

ABSTRACT

The Kansas City Study of Adult Life, studying the social role performance of people aged forty to seventy, gave ratings of performance on various social roles. When leisure activity was related to the pattern of social role performance (called "life-style"), four general life-styles were found: community-centered, home-centered high, home-centered medium, and low level, the adjectives for altitude referring to level of social role performance. The most successful life-styles, judged by the level of role performance, involved patterns of leisure which were active and similar rather than contrasting with the other social roles. Middle-class people may be community-centered or home-centered in life-style and in leisure, but working-class people are either home-centered or generally low in social role and leisure performance.

Leisure has generally but vaguely been seen as a source of satisfaction and even of delight. In a society in which most people had to work, and to work hard and long, leisure was scarce and was regarded either as a reward to be earned by work and to be enjoyed because one had worked so hard for it or as a good thing conferred by inherited wealth or by marriage to wealth.

With the coming of more leisure in the lives of the common people, not all the rosy promises have been realized. Some people have found themselves with more leisure than they really wanted. The values of increased leisure to welfare and the quality of living of society as a whole have been seriously questioned. It is clear that modern leisure is not an unmixed blessing. This suggests the desirability of studying the uses that people make of their leisure, what satisfactions they get out of it, and how it fits into the rest of their lives.

Robert J. Havighurst and Kenneth Feigenbaum, "Leisure and Life Style," *American Journal of Sociology*, LXIV (January 1959), 396–405. Reprinted by permission of The University of Chicago Press.

Using the concept of "life-style" to describe a person's characteristic way of filling and combining the various social roles he is called on to play, we may see how leisure fits into it. To do so, the Kansas City Study of Adult Life interviewed a sample of men and women aged from forty to seventy to get an account of the way the person spent his time and the significance to him of his major social roles—those of parent, spouse, homemaker, worker, citizen, friend, club or association member, and user of leisure time. About a quarter of the interview was devoted to leisure. The individual was asked about his favorite leisure activities, what they meant to him, why he liked them, whom he did them with, as well as a number of questions about vacations, reading, television, radio, and movies, and what he did around the house.

On the basis of this interview, ratings were made of the competence of the individual in his social roles. Rating scales were devised to represent the general American expectations or definitions of these roles.[1] The rating scale for user of leisure time follows:

a) High (8–9).—Spends enough time at some leisure activity to be rather well known among his associates in this respect. But it is not so much the amount of leisure activity as its quality which gives him a high rating. He has one or more pursuits for which he gets public recognition and appreciation and which give him a real sense of accomplishment.

Chooses his leisure activities autonomously, not merely to be in style. Gets from leisure the feeling of being creative, of novel and interesting experience, sheer pleasure, prestige, friendship, and of being of service.

b) Above average (6–7).—Has four to five leisure activities. Leisure time is somewhat patterned, indicating that he has planned his life to provide for the satisfaction of the needs met through these activities.

Leisure interests show some variety. Displays real enthusiasm for one or two —talks about them in such a way as to indicate that he has put considerable energy into acquiring proficiency or the requisite understanding and skills and prides himself on it.

c) Medium (4–5).—Has two or three leisure activities which he does habitually and enjoys mildly—reading, television, radio, watching sports, handwork, etc. May do one of these things well or quite enthusiastically, but not more than one. Gets definite sense of well-being and is seldom bored with leisure.

Leisure activities are somewhat stereotyped; they do not have a great deal of variety.

d) Below average (2–3).—

(1) Tends to take the line of least resistance in leisure time. Needs to be stimulated. Looks for time-fillers.

May have one fairly strong interest but is content with this one which brings him some sense of enjoyment. Leisure time is usually spent in passive spectatorship. *Or:*

---

[1]For the other role-performance scales and for the pattern analysis mentioned later see Robert J. Havighurst, "The Social Competence of Middle-aged People," *Genetic Psychology Monographs,* LVI (1957), 297–395.

(2) May have very little spare time. What time he has is taken up with activities related to his job or profession or with work around the house viewed as obligatory and not as a pastime.

e)Low (0–1).—

(1) Apathetic. Does nothing and makes no attempt to find outside interests. *Or:*

(2) Tries anxiously to find interesting things to do and fails to find them. Is bored by leisure and hurries back to work. Dislikes vacations and cannot relax.

Not only was the person's use of leisure time rated according to the foregoing scale but the objective significance of his favorite activities was evaluated according to a set of nineteen variables,[2] of which the most useful appear to be: autonomy of other-direction; creativity; enjoyment; development of talent; instrumentation or expressiveness; relation of leisure to work; gregariousness or solitude; service or pleasure; status and prestige; relaxation; ego integration or role diffusion; new experience or repetition; vitality or apathy; and expansion or constriction of interests.

The results of the several methods of studying leisure were related to one another and to a set of social and personal variables, including age, sex, social class, personal adjustment, and manifest complexity of life. The interrelations are summarized in Table 1.

Table 1. Leisure, personality, and social variables

	Sex	Age	Social Class	Personal Adjustment	Manifest Complexity	Social Mobility	Content	Significance	Meaning
Content	+++	+++	+++	+	++	++	....	+++	+++
Objective significance	+	+	++	+++	+++	++	+++	......	+++
Subjective meaning	+	–	+	+	+	+	+++	+++	......

+ = a small degree of relationship (not more than two or three of the content or significance or meaning variables are reliably related to a social or personal variable)

++ = a fair degree of relationship

+++ = a high degree of relationship (more than half of the leisure variables are reliably related to a social or personal variable)

[2]In addition, two other aspects of the person's favorite leisure activities were studied: (1) the *content* of the favorite leisure activities (eleven categories of content) and (2) the *subjective meanings* of the favorite leisure activities (a set of twelve statements of the kinds of satisfaction a person might get from a leisure activity, from which the respondent picked the meanings most applicable to his favorite activities). For details concerning the significance, content, and meaning studies see Robert J. Havighurst, "The Leisure Activities of the Middle-aged," *American Journal of Sociology*, LXIII (September, 1957), 152–62; Marjorie N. Donald and Robert J. Havighurst, "The Meanings of Leisure" (MS).

The procedure in studying life-style was based upon the use of the scores for performance in the eight social roles previously mentioned. A life-style was defined as a pattern of role-performance scores shared by a group of people.

Life-styles in this sense were discovered among the 234 persons in the Social Role Sample of the Kansas City Study of Adult Life. There were actually twenty-seven specific patterns, or life-styles, each characterizing from 8 to 34 members, with some people belonging to two or more. The specific patterns were grouped into four major groups, using broader criteria for membership in a group than in a pattern, and these four groups may be regarded provisionally as life-style groups. Their characteristic role-performance scores are shown in Figure 1. The names given to the life-style groups, and a brief description of each, follow:

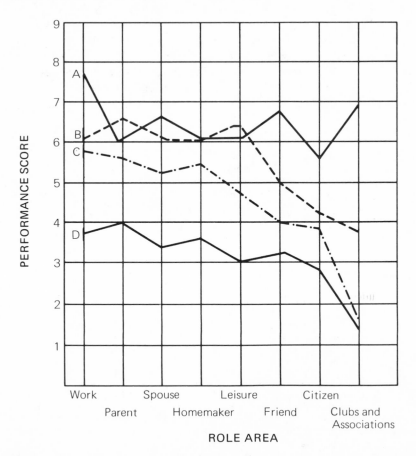

Figure 1. Life-styles of middle-aged people: *A,* community-centered; *B,* home-centered high; *C,* home-centered medium; *D,* low level.

A. *Community-centered.*—This is a pattern of uniformly high performance scores in all eight social roles. It is called "community-centered" for the sake of contrast with the following group, though the performance scores in the community roles of citizen, club or association member, and friend are not higher than those in the family areas but about the same. The social class distribution of these people in the Kansas City Metropolitan Area is shown in Table 2.

Table 2. Social class distribution of life-styles

(Per Cent)

Social Class	Sex	Community-centered	Home-centered High	Home-centered Medium	Low Level	Ungrouped	Total Group
U & UM	M	7	3	1	0	2	13
	F	6	3	3	0	1	13
LM	M	8	11	10	3	1	33
	F	5	4	17	3	4	33
UL	M	4	8	18	8	2	40
	F	2	5	23	7	3	40
LL	M	0	0	6	7	1	14
	F	1	0	5	7	1	14
Total group	M	19	22	35	18	6	100
	F	14	12	48	17	9	100

Note.—The actual distribution of individuals in the Study Sample was the basis for this table, but the figures have been adjusted to fit the true social class distribution of adults in the Kansas City Metropolitan Area, as determined by Richard Coleman (unpublished working paper in the files of the Committee on Human Development). Since some people fell into two groups, they were assigned to the particular groups which they fitted most closely.

B. *Home-centered high.*—These people have performance scores in the roles of parent, spouse, homemaker, worker, and user of leisure time which are about the same as those of the community-centered, but they fall far below the latter in the roles of friend, citizen, and club or association member. These people and the community-centered group have the highest personal adjustment scores and the highest scores on a rating of manifest complexity of life-style.

C. *Home-centered medium.*—These people have a family-centered pattern, though below that of the home-centered high group in role-performance scores.

D. *Low level.*—This is a pattern of generally low role-performance scores, with the family and work roles somewhat above the external roles. This group has very low scores on personal adjustment and on complexity.

We shall first answer the question, "What are the 'leisure styles' of the four life-styles?" By "leisure style" we mean the Gestalt formed when one observes an individual's kinds and number of activities.

The community-centered style of leisure emphasizes activities engaged in away from home. The individual uses entertainment institutions, such as the theater or the concert, or social institutions, such as the country club, Rotary, chamber of commerce, Red Cross, etc., as the context for a major part of it, either jointly by the members of a family or individually. On the basis of the significance ratings people employing the community-centered style of leisure tend to be more autonomous, that is, to "choose activity with purpose and regard for its function in one's personal life" and to engage in activities in which there was some element of novelty. They are more instrumental and more inclined to "play a game or participate in an activity for some goal beyond the game or activity (philanthropic activity, etc.)." "Benefit for society" was given quite often as the motive.

Community-centeredness is the favorite leisure style of upper-middle-class people. being successful in business or a profession induces them to join business and social organizations where they interact with each other to form wider circles of social and business contacts. Membership in the country club is part of their proper and accepted style of living. The community-centered individuals also tend not to have young children at home, which allows freedom for outside activity.

In contrast, the people who enjoy the home-centered style of leisure engage in most of it around their residence. This style is strongest in lower-middle- and upper-lower-class individuals and falls off in the lower-class, where family values lose some importance and the few pastimes become sex-differentiated, the men going fishing alone or to the bar or poolroom with the "boys."

Leisure activities are engaged in jointly by the members of the family for the majority of the home-centered, whether it be a church outing, a fishing trip, or watching television. Sex-differentiated activities, such as sewing and embroidering for the women and carpentry and "fixing around the house" for the men, still allow for conversation and interaction between spouses. Friendship and sociability are cultivated by visits from neighbors rather than through any membership other than in the church or perhaps a fraternal organization. For some people the family-centered style was not one of choice but of necessity, owing to the presence of young children.

A number of activities such as fishing and traveling during vacations were common to both leisure styles, with some differentiation as to the manner of them. In the community-centered style travel consists of going to resorts and sightseeing, while for the people engaged in home-centered leisure travel consists of a car trip to relatives in other cities. For the upper-lower-class members of the home-centered style travel may be quite circumscribed; one spoke of "taking a trolley trip to see the city."

In spite of the relationship between life-style and social class position, there were people whose life-styles did not correspond with their class positions, as would be expected in a society with a considerable degree of social mobility. From Table 2 it appears that some 10 per cent of the population may have patterns above their class level and 5 per cent below it.

This scheme of leisure activities can be further comprehended by consulting Figure 2. Each of the concentric circles contains examples of the type of activities engaged in by the subjects making up the sample. The center of the concentric circles is common living in the home, the other radiating circles representing the physical and psychological distances of activities from it. The "activity radius" of the community-centered group is much greater than that of the home-centered group, whose leisure activities never transcend circle *8,* and are usually no broader than the kind of activities listed in circle *6.* In graphic form this illustrates the socially and spatially restricted nature of the leisure of the home-centered.

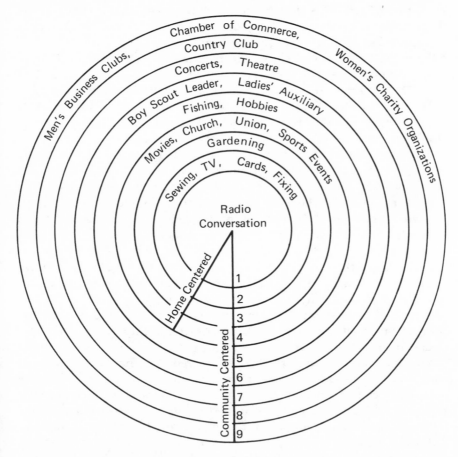

Figure 2. The circles of leisure.

Two examples, one of a community-centered man with a high rating as a user of leisure and the other of a high leisure home-centered man, may further the reader's image of the difference between the two styles of leisure.

Mr. X is a fifty-year-old executive vice-president of a bank, with a pattern of leisure activities which is the prototype of the community-centered style of leisure. He is president of one country club, a member of another, a Shriner, and a member of the executive council of a national Boy's Club movement and of a number of charity organizations. Mr. X's favorite leisure activity is to go on trips during his vacation, to New York City to see the Broadway theater, and to see exhibitions of modern art. He is active in encouraging the local art museum to acquire examples of modern art. He enjoys playing golf once or twice a week at the country club, playing cards, painting his garage, and entertaining business people both at home and at the club. He does not own a television set, preferring the good music on the radio. He goes with his wife to the movies and to all the musical comedies that come to Kansas City. As for friends, Mr. X calls ten to twelve couples "close." He met them through various activities: "My business connections here at the bank, civic clubs, church, etc." With his wife he goes out to eat once a week and entertains other couples.

In contrast to Mr. X, Mr. Y, a fifty-eight-year-old social worker, is an example of an individual who employs the home-centered style of leisure. His favorite activity is gardening, in which he spends one-half hour to an hour a day during the growing season. Mr. Y's hobby is model railroading, which he engages in with his wife in the basement of his home. He also does some woodworking and woodcarving and manual work around the home. Once in a while he reads historical fiction. The television set plays for two hours an evening, showing sport events, quiz shows, and plays. With his wife he reads, plays cards, does model railroading, and takes walks. Living in a neighborhood of younger adults, he claims that he has few friends and that a large part of his time is spent taking care of the two children of his son. Mr. Y's "going out" consists only of movies (with wife) and American Legion meetings once a month.

From this one can see that both in number and in kind of activities engaged in outside the home the "leisure complexity" of Mr. X is far greater than that of Mr. Y.

The differences between the home-centered high, home-centered medium, and low-level life-styles as far as leisure is concerned are mainly those between high, medium, and low ratings on the scale of competence as a user of leisure. A higher role performance is associated with the following significance variables: autonomy, creativity, getting strong pleasure from the activity, instrumental, high energy input, ego integration, vitality, and expansion of interests and activities.

Have those whose leisure is home-centered different personalities from the community-centered? Or is the difference caused by some external factor, such as residence in a suburb versus residence in an apartment area in the center of the city, or having several young children versus having one or none? It has been suggested by David Riesman[3] and by Margaret Mead,[4] among others, that the trend toward suburban living and the trend toward larger numbers of children are making for values and leisure activities that are more home- and family-centered.

Riesman speaks of "suburban styles of life and thought" and stresses the suburban constriction of leisure to the family and the living-room–garden–television set, at the expense of theater, concert hall, downtown meetings, country clubs, and heterogeneous social groups. Margaret Mead says that the generation which has married since the war is much more concerned with home and family life than earlier generations and is busy trying to turn home life into "a self-rewarding delight."

To explore the differences between home-centered and community-centered people, we compared a community-centered group with a similar number of home-centered people, equating the groups for age and socioeconomic status. There was no difference between the two groups in the proportions of suburban dwellers and the proportions who lived in single-family houses with gardens and recreation rooms. However, the home-centered had more children living at home. This suggests that the presence of children in the home, together with the desire to have children and to have a home-centered life, are more influential than the actual physical location of one's house in determining leisure style. It should be borne in mind, however, that Kansas City does not have many apartment dwellings for upper-middle-class people near the city's center.

The foregoing facts point to the conclusion that the personality, more than the situation, determines the leisure style.

For each of these life-style groups there are some people with relatively high leisure performance scores and some with relatively low scores. By comparing these two subgroups, it is possible to compare the leisure characteristics of people with high and with low leisure scores within a life-style. However, the range of leisure performance scores within a life-style is relatively small.

Within the community-centered life-style group there is one pattern with seventeen members which consists of people with relatively high leisure scores, and another group of nine people with somewhat lower

[3]David Riesman, "The Suburban Dislocation," *Annals of the American Academy of Political and Social Science,* CCCXIV (November, 1957), 123–46.

[4]Margaret Mead, "The Patterns of Leisure in Contemporary American Culture," *Annals of the American Academy of Political and Social Science,* CCCXIII (September, 1957), 11–15.

scores. The individuals of the higher leisure pattern show more creativity and more autonomy in their leisure and a sense of vitality in it. The individuals of the lower leisure pattern are less enthusiastic and speak of pastimes as something of a burden; they join the country club because it is expected that they do so, but they do not enjoy it intrinsically. Business activity dominates the lives of some; they claim that they have relatively little leisure time and that they had more in the past when they were not so busy. The low leisure individuals with the community-centered life-style engage in the same kinds of activities as the high but are not so active in them and do not engage in as many.

In the home-centered high group the individuals with the higher leisure pattern are more creative than those in the lower leisure group (wood-working versus watching television), and they are more instrumental in their activities, being members of PTA and church service groups, being leaders in Boy Scout work, etc. In the home-centered medium group the same differences appear between those of the higher and those of lower leisure.

In general, within a life-style group which is large enough to permit some variation in leisure-role performance scores, those with higher leisure scores are more autonomous, more creative,,more instrumental, and more vital in their use of leisure.

It has been assumed up to this point that there was a close correlation between personal adjustment and performance in the leisure role. The correlation coefficient is .32 for men and .33 for women, with socioeconomic status partialed out. Clearly, there are some exceptions to this rule. Study of these exceptions may teach us something more about the value of leisure.

Accordingly, we selected the cases which showed most markedly a high adjustment–low leisure performance combination and those who combined low adjustment with high leisure performance. There were nine of the former and twelve of the latter in the sample of 234 people. The criterion for the high adjustment–low leisure combination was an adjustment score of 6 or above on the ten-point adjustment scale and a score of 5 or below on the ten-point leisure performance scale. The criterion for the low adjustment–high leisure group was an adjustment score of 4.5 or below and a leisure score of 6 or above.

The content of the leisure and the significance ratings of the leisure activities of the low leisure–high adjustment people were similar to the general pattern of people with low leisure and low adjustment scores. There are low significance ratings as to the autonomy of the leisure activity, the creativity expressed in it, some apathy with respect to the activity and either a decline in leisure interests or no expansion of interests.

These are people who get along very well with little or no leisure. They show a great deal of vitality in the instrumental activities of life. The men are busy with their jobs and the women with their children, allowing little time for leisure and restricting them to leisure activities near home. Six out of the nine in the group are females and follow this pattern. Their leisure activities are centered either at home, where they sew, watch television, and take care of the children, or in the church. The relationship between the spouses is good, and there is a general feeling of contentment and emotional security. It is this basically which accounts for the high adjustment scores of the group.

The group of individuals with high leisure scores and low adjustment tend as a whole to be maladjusted socially or occupationally and attempt to get through leisure what they cannot get in the other roles. They use their leisure as a compensation to make up for their deficiencies and to give their life some meaning.

The men in the group, often alienated from work, from spouse, or from the "community," attempt to adjust to this alienation by engaging in leisure activities where they invest a lot of energy and through which they can enjoy themselves and see themselves as socially acceptable. One is a factory manager. He finds no satisfaction in this position but rather pictures himself as an intellectual and therefore spends a great deal of time reading. A second, an amateur pilot, directs his leisure away from a home where some emotional difficulties exist. Another man was trained as an engineer and has shifted over the years from one job to another, finally going into a business with his wife, which he does not enjoy. Like the factory manager, he pictures himself as a scholar and spends his leisure time reading oriental history. One of the men is a light-skinned Negro, cut off socially from both the white and the Negro community, who engages in leisure activities that he can perform alone or with his family, such as hunting and fishing—activities which do not put him in social contact with others.

The women in the group have difficulty in relating to their husbands and are emotionally insecure; there are degrees of feelings of unwantedness and not being loved. They concentrate their energies into a single activity which they engage in alone and where they can achieve a great deal of proficiency, such as sewing, embroidery, or petitpoint, or in church activities where they can spend time with the "women" and achieve the feeling of "doing something worthwhile."

CONCLUSIONS

1. The most successful life-styles, as judged by the level of role-performance scores, have concomitant patterns of leisure activity. The communi-

ty-centered life-style includes a leisure pattern which spreads from the home out through a variety of community circles. On the other hand, a successful home-centered life-style contains a home-centered leisure pattern. These successful leisure patterns tend to be autonomous, creative, instrumental, vital, and ego integrative, whether they be community-centered or home-centered.

The lower-level life-styles are lower in performance in roles external to the home than in the home roles. They also have lower-level leisure styles, with lower scores on the values listed in the preceding paragraph.

2. The two major types of leisure style, the community-centered and the home-centered, appear to be equally accessible to middle-class people, but rarely are working-class people community-centered. An individual with a large family of children is more likely to be home-centered. However, his place of residence—whether in a suburb, single-family home, or city apartment—does not seem to affect his leisure style to any great degree. The personality of the individual appears to find its own leisure style.

3. There are a few exceptional cases where the life-style and the leisure style are not in close relation. One group of such cases consists of about 5 per cent of adults. They are people with little or no leisure activity who have a successful life-style and good personal adjustment. These men and women generally invest most of their energy in work or in home and children, with little time and inclination for leisure.

Another group consists of about 6 per cent of adults. They have a high level of leisure activity but are dissatisfied or inadequate workers or parents or spouses who attempt to compensate with a high leisure performance.

leisure
and the social system

JOFFRE DUMAZEDIER

WHAT IS LEISURE?

First, let us examine the major components of a phenomenon which already in so many ways has affected daily work, family life, our entire culture. Obviously, for Marx or Ricardo there was no leisure to observe in the life of the worker of their day. It took the rise of the huge industrial plant to banish forever the old seasonal rhythms of rural labor relieved by games and religious days. Following the long hours of daily work, as described above, there was left just that little respite Marx referred to as reproduction of the labor force: The ideology mirrored the reality of that period. In our own day, the respite has been replaced by a complexity of pursuits of every kind, not pertaining to required activity or to family and social obligation. We have among us a third order of activity, distinct from the job of production, distinct from social obligation, but raising new problems for both of them, and constituting a revolutionary element within our social culture.

The sociologists of work, and particularly Georges Friedmann, were the first to point out the importance of hobbies, fads, and so on.[1] But hobby can mean everything and nothing. It includes useless activities and worthwhile activities, whether positive or negative for society, for culture, for the individual. Collecting cigar bands is a hobby, as is research in mechanics. Playing football, joining a gym, being a comic-strip fan or Shakespearean drama buff—all of these are hobbies. The American sociologist Eric Larrabee,[2] taking exception to the confusion surrounding the concept,

[1]Georges Friedmann, *Problemes humains du machinisere industriel,* Paris, Gallimord, 1955.

[2]E. Larrabee, "What's Happening to Hobbies," in *Mass Leisure,* The Free Press, New York, 1958.

has noted that some serious writers even include "doing nothing" as a hobby. . . . This notion of hobby, more amusing than helpful, cannot help us discover the secret of this third order of activity.

But if we go further, we may run into a dual pitfall, two opposing temptations that risk imprisoning the young and complex reality before us into an overschematized definition. The great theorizers of the nineteenth century all had more or less of an inkling of the advent of leisure; but none foresaw the ambiguities. All of them fell into the intellectualist error. For Marx, leisure meant "room for human development"; for Pierre Joseph Proudhon, "time for free engagement"; for Auguste Comte, the possibility of developing a "popular astronomy." Finally, Engels claimed the reduction in hours of work as "giving all enough free time to participate in the common interests of society." Such identification of leisure with popular education apparently still prevails in the Soviet Union. Here in France, a certain trend toward "permanent education" reflects a similar conception.

Inversely, the majority of American sociologists have concentrated on analyzing the various forms recreation takes. Many writers have tended to reduce leisure to "an activity freely pursued and without pay, which brings an immediate satisfaction." A critique outlining the various definitions given by American sociology up to the year 1958 has been published by Aline Ripert.[3] It was only recently that researchers such as David Riesman,[4] R. J. Havighurst,[5] M. Kaplan, and H. Wilensky analyzed the complex of leisure as part of the sum total of determinants of our daily lives. In France, we still have only partial ideas, arbitrary and confused, the most deplorable example being the famed "sundries" entry in the household budget.

If you look in Littré (1869), you read that leisure is a "time remaining at one's disposal after work," a definition M. Hatzfel and James Darmsteter, fifty-seven years later, were content to copy. Not until 1930, did Augé, in his dictionary, add a new meaning: "amusements, occupations, which one can turn to freely in the time not taken up with regular work." Littré's "time" has become "amusements, occupations," and Michel Augé no longer says that leisure follows after one's "occupations" but after "regular work."

The change in words, however slight, signifies a change in habits; under our very eyes, a profound transformation has taken place with respect to the role of leisure in the life of ordinary people. An exhaustive inquiry

[3]Aline Ripert, Les Sciences sociales du loisir aux U.S.A., 1960, document dactylographié.

[4]Riesman, David, The Lonely Crowd: A Study of the Changing American Character, New Haven, Yale P. 1950, and Individualism Reconsidered and Other Essays, New York, The Free Press, 1954.

[5]Havighurst, R. J., and Feigenbaum, K., "Leisure and Life-Style," in American Journal of Sociology, 64, 4 (January 1959), 396–404.

conducted in 1953 among workers and salaried employees as to what leisure represented to them made possible refinement of the dictionary definition. Though the majority still referred to leisure as "time," already more than a fourth called it an "activity" and none gave it the passive definition of a "state" (Littré's first definition). Practically all of 819 persons interviewed at random in the cities of the North, of the South and the East, and of the West and Paris, defined leisure by *opposition* to the cares and concerns of daily life called by Augé "regular work." These daily concerns were described mainly by three different expressions: "routine tasks, monotonous and repetitious," "daily chores," "necessities and obligations"—the last used almost as frequently as the other two together.

Under this third category 60 per cent of the respondents stressed the obligations of their job as primordial, although others were mentioned with varying frequency, such as family and social obligations, which, however, we cannot pause here to analyze. For the moment we shall simply give a list of activities indisputably contrasted to the notion of leisure:

1. The job.
2. Supplementary work or occasional odd jobs.
3. Domestic tasks (housework, and the strictly utilitarian aspects of animal care, miscellaneous chores, gardening).
4. Care of the person (meals, bathing and dressing, sleep).
5. Family rituals and ceremonies, social or religious. Obligations (visits, anniversaries, political meetings, church duties).
6. Necessary study (for study circles, for school or professional examinations).

We see now how wrong, how dangerously misleading it would be, to define leisure by contrast merely to one's gainful occupation, and if most economists and sociologists so define it, they are evidently seduced by the overtheoretical formula of the three eights—eight hours' work, eight hours' sleep, eight hours' leisure. Briefly, and most emphatically, contemporary leisure is defined by contrast not just to one's job, but to all of the ordinary necessities and obligations of existence, and it must be remembered that they who have and use leisure regard it as part of the dialectic of daily living, where all elements operate and interoperate. In and of itself, leisure means little; it might almost be said of it what Henri Wallon has said of play, which to some extent is part of leisure: "Play is, probably, a break away from the disciplines and the tasks which are imposed on every man by the practical necessities of his existence, the concern for his condition and his person; but far from being the negation of these, it presupposes them."

THE THREE FUNCTIONS OF LEISURE

However it functions, leisure is first and foremost liberation and pleasure, and it was so indicated by the respondents to the 1953 inquiry. Their
replies fall into three categories, corresponding as we see it, to the three
major functions of leisure: relaxation, entertainment, personal development.

Relaxation provides recovery from fatigue; leisure repairs the physical
and nervous damage wrought by the tensions of daily pressures, and
particularly pressures of the job. True, the need of physical effort on the
job has largely disappeared, but it is still a fact that the production tempo,
the complexity of the industrial setup, the long distances in the large urban
centers to and from work—all have increased the worker's need for rest
and quiet, for idleness and the aimless small pastimes. Such need is felt
even more, according to investigations by Dr. P. R. Bize, among executives
and top personnel in industry, 85 per cent of whom reported they were
overworked.[6] Concern with the recuperative function of leisure ought to
lead to broadening the study of fatigue and proneness to fatigue among
all classes of workers, heretofore restricted in France to simple observations
on the job. A new trend in this direction is discernible. Dr. Stafford A. Metz
has instigated medicosocial studies to explore relations between the
rhythms of work and the rhythms of leisure. More and more, such studies
call for collaboration between the experts in the psychology of work and
those in the psychosociology of leisure.

Entertainment is the second function of leisure. If relaxation gives recovery from fatigue, entertainment spells deliverance from boredom.
Friedmann has pointed time and time again to the woeful effect of the
monotony of fragmented tasks on the personality of the worker. Henri
Lefebvre has analyzed modern man's alienations as they result in a sense
of loss and lead to an impulse to break away from the daily atmosphere.[7]
The break away might take the form of an infraction of juridical or moral
law in any field—and thus suggest socially pathological elements. Or,
going in the opposite direction, it could become a balance, a way of bearing
up under the disciplines and constraints demanded by society. From this
might follow a search after a life of compensation, or an escape into
diversions of a different world, sometimes directly opposed, in fact, to the
everyday world. If escape is realistic, it may lead to a change of place or
pace or style (trips, games, sports); it may, on the other hand, head toward
the fantasy of identification and projection (cinema, theater, the novel)—

[6]Bize, Dr. P.-R., and Goguelin, P., *Le Surmenage des dirigeants, causes et remèdes,* Paris, éd.
de l'Enterprise moderne.
[7]Lefebvre, Henri, *Critique de la vie quotidienne,* Paris, l'Arche, 1958.

the resort to the imaginary life, for the satisfaction of what, since E. T. A. Hoffman and Feodor Dostoevski, has come to be known as one's imaginary self.[8]

This was the function of leisure—diversion, in an absolute sense— called up in the minds of the greatest number of respondents to the 1957 inquiry.

Finally, we come to the development of the personality. Here leisure serves to liberate the individual from the daily automatism of thought and action. It permits a broader, readier social participation on the one hand, and on the other, a willing cultivation of the physical and mental self over and above utilitarian considerations of job or practical advancement. It opens fresh possibilities for joining willingly with other people in recreational, cultural, and social group activities. It gives time for the pursuit of voluntary development of skills acquired at school but always in danger of being outdistanced by the continuous and complex growth of society. It encourages a positive attitude toward the use of sources of information, old and new (press, movies, radio, television).

It may even lead to discovering new forms of voluntary learning for the rest of one's life and induce an entirely new kind of creative attitude. And so, released from workaday obligations, the individual has the time to sustain new disciplines freely chosen by him with a view to the unfolding of a new personal and social life-style. This use of leisure for the cultivation of personality, not so common as simple entertainment, is of prime importance to the popular culture generally.

The three functions are interdependent, closely linked even when in opposition. They exist in varying degrees in everyone's life, no matter what his situation. They may co-exist or follow one after the other and in a single leisure-situation, they may be exercised in turn or simultaneously, and often they overlap so closely as to be indistinguishable. In actuality, any one of the three is not so much the more commonly present as the more dominant.

Leisure is activity—apart from the obligations of work, family, and society— to which the individual turns at will, for either relaxation, diversion, or broadening his knowledge and his spontaneous social participation, the free exercise of his creative capacity.

THE CULTURE OF DAILY EXPERIENCE

The interrelatedness among the functions of leisure, and of leisure to the obligations of daily life, increasingly determines participation, passive or

[8]Morin, Edgar, *Le Cinema ou l'homme imaginaire,* Paris, éd. de Minuit, 1958.

active, in social and cultural affairs. All this affects the culture of daily experience of our general society. We may safely ignore the theories that explain relations between culture and society in the abstract: One and all, they have come down from a period when the phenomena we are concerned with were not widespread, and we are bound to re-examine all such theories, if we are to move toward a concrete sociology of the leisure both real and possible under our democratic industrial civilization. We say *all*, whether their postulates be democratic or aristocratic, individualist or collectivist, whether they stem from Karl Mannheim or Ortega y Gasset, from Arnold Toynbee or G. V. Plekhanov. For a theory of culture to be cogent, it must correspond not only to a complex of values, but also to the way these values are lived, by all classes and categories of people. Today it is leisure, as an ideal and in practice, that more and more conditions our culture of daily experience.

The creative elite, the educators, and the activists who try to shape thinking and actions know quite well the added difficulty of so persuading the masses of the value of an idea that it becomes a force. . . . But evenings, weekends, and vacations have their own quota of "idea-forces." The serious civic and political indifference that we see among the masses may *not*, after all, be caused solely by lack of enthusiasm or by incompetence on the part of their social and cultural leaders—as we would be led to believe reading the innumerable confessions, and stereotyped self-examinations that line the route of these leaders' failures. Can we be sure that a new leadership could solve these problems? We may venture the hypothesis that, since the entry onto the scene of all those frivolities we call leisure activities, some profound and ambiguous changes have been wrought in people's souls, of every class.

THE NEW HOMO FABER

We have seen that time off in a given work period may not be used entirely for leisure. Friedmann is quite right in speaking tentatively and with caution of "nonwork." Twenty-five per cent of the workers at Annecy, for example, had a second occupation or did additional work, outside their regular overtime; this, if not legal, was, at any rate, regarded as obligatory. One of economic need? Perhaps, but an economic need less likely stemming from any necessity than from a new lifestyle. In countries where the standard of living is higher than in France, time off from one's regular job is used mainly for doing other paid work. In the city of Akron, Ohio, when the rubber industry reduced its work week to thirty-two hours, almost half the salaried workers (40 per cent) took on supplementary jobs, and 17 per cent worked openly at a second occupation. "Less work, less leisure."[9]

Psychological and economic motivations probably are interwoven. Everywhere, apart from the extra time spent in paid work, there is a growing range of manual occupations, half labor of love, half utilitarian, carried on in the family garden or workshop. Leisure—or not leisure? We saw that at Annecy, 60 per cent of the workers regard such activities as part of leisure, against 25 per cent who consider them obligatory tasks, and 15 per cent who think them something of both. According to a national poll conducted in selected areas by the IFOP (French Institute of Public Opinion), executives cultivate their gardens in larger numbers than workers, 44 per cent as against 36 per cent. Here is an activity part practical, part nonpractical, so to speak, in varying proportions; the two parts overlap, but one belongs in the category of obligation, the other, to leisure. We designate these as semileisure activities.[10] In our French city, the nonpractical aspect exceeds the practical; but in such economically less-developed countries as Poland or Yugoslavia, the reverse is probably true. Also, among us these semileisure pursuits consume about half the total leisure time; and everyone knows the "do-it-yourself" vogue in the country even more industrialized than ours. In the very midst of a civilization governed by the division of labor with its attendant social patterns, leisure develops among the gainfully employed, especially in the working class, attitudes typical of the artisan and the peasant, which incline them increasingly toward a kind of work different from their gainful employment. Leisure has indeed fostered the rise of a new *homo faber*, far more independent than the old one vis-à-vis his job in the production process. This, for him, has increasingly narrowed down to making a living, simply a way of earning one's bread, and already for some, of earning one's leisure. Thus a new kind of manual labor, non paid and individual, has asserted its value in the life-culture; it could, by its creative import, redress the monotony of the fragmented tasks of the industrial process, in administration and production. From all this, a new philosophy may come which would put manual labor into its proper place in a civilization based on labor. The handicrafts and modest creations of all sorts we see displayed in shops bespeak a possible use of manual work in the culture of the people—perhaps here is a germ of some kind of renewal for the culture as a whole. However, our new Sunday painters for the most part become totally engrossed in their gardening or puttering. In response to inquiry by Chombart de Lauwe,

[9]Swados, Harvey, "Less Work, Less Leisure," in *Mass Leisure.*

[10]This composite whole in which two different elements interpenetrate one another without becoming fused, overlap without mixing, corresponds to the type of relationship brought to lights by modern science under the name of mutual dialectical implication." (G. G.)

some Paris workmen reported they spend five or six whole hours a day at it! And if such men make good fathers and husbands (though Patachou says in her song that it may not be so lucky for a woman to have a Jack who's a jack of all trades—"*un bonheur d'avoir un mari bricoleur*"), they are unconcerned with what goes on outside their private lives. These are citizens limited by the fact that political, social, and cultural questions do not bother them. All around them are the mass media, from which they derive no benefit. They choose to be isolated, strike attitudes of craftsmen withdrawn within themselves, almost as if they lived in a time without press or movies, and where there is neither division of labor nor class struggle. These highly important facts ought not to be underestimated by sociologists of recreation or of education for leisure.

THE NEW HOMO LUDENS

Around the midnineteenth century, traditional games and feast days, either civic or religious, were an important part of the worker's life. We know the range of these celebrations, from gay and fanciful to brutal, through the vivid reportage of Agricol Perdiguier. In our own day, amusements have been extracted from their ritual context, and have multiplied, diversified, achieved proportions in our kind of society unforseeable by the social philosophers of the nineteenth century. Incitement to amusements and contests is uninterrupted, no longer dependent on the ritual occasion or communal celebration, but stimulated daily by radio, newspaper, magazine, and store advertising. This tends to be true even in the Soviet Union, where organs of radio and press are altogether restrained by the doctrinal preaching from higher up.

As for gambling, it is foolish to consider the exigencies of poverty as responsible for it among the masses; it is an upper-class amusement they have seized for themselves as they have seized travel and sports. Betting on the horses is no longer the exclusive privilege of the idle rich at the hippodrome at Longchamps—not since the *Pari Mutuel Urbain* came in, which in 1949 registered more than 280 millions (new francs) in bets, four times the amount spent that year by the General Administration of Youth and Sports for their total activities. Some other amusements, which began around the eighteen eighties as the exclusive province of bourgeois youth, have been democratized, have become active games of "educational value" —sports. Aldous Huxley even goes so far as to see sports as the dominant characteristic of our time. But, alongside the amateurs in action, what about the yelling, banner-waving spectators, the fans who never have played a game in their lives? In a city like Vienne (France), studies have shown, more than a third, closer to half, of the entire population are sports fans, including workers, salaried employees, executives, and professionals. The figures for the year 1947 show that 40 per cent of all Frenchmen regularly follow sports, 35 per cent being "vaguely" interested in the Tour de France bicycle races.

But to go further: This universal bent toward a life of play is something even worse in the larger sense that Caillois gives to it.[11] This play life is to one's serious life a kind of "secondary reality," with its own potent influence on everyday attitudes. It is disengaged from all obligation, set into predetermined limits of time and space, regulated, fictitious, "attended by a special awareness of being a secondary reality, or out-and-out unreality in relation to one's ordinary life." But shall we not say the same of vacations, for example, when we play for a time at being rich or primitive —something utterly at variance with out everyday lives? In the same way, we may characterize many of the activities that one by one have appeared among us in the past hundred years.

What are the consequences of all this for our life-culture? Johann Huizinga, in his classic *Homo Ludens,* notes that play has but a feeble role in the serious culture we inherited from the Hebrew-Greco-Latin tradition as watered down by the scholastics.[12] In our own cultural development, competitive games, for example, play nowhere near the part they had in Pindar's time. Nevertheless, games of every kind, serious or frivolous, hold a large place in the life-culture of millions of workers. Play is no longer, as Freud saw it, the badge of the child's world, but has become a necessity, through leisure, in the people's culture. It could indeed work a profound change in academic and avant-garde culture, could inject its own poesy and lightness into the social scene and into efforts toward social involvement.

It could, on the other hand, as Lefebvre fears, engender disaffection for modest daily life, push escape into absolute diversion in the sense of rejection of all cultural efforts and indifference to all social responsibility. Play life opens wide, only to shut out any life of commitment.

THE NEW MAN OF IMAGINATION

Shortly after the publication of Marx's *Communist Manifesto,* a major inquiry, lasting two years, was instituted into the question of the selection of popular books and the literature offered for sale by wandering peddlers. Directing the inquiry was young Charles Nisard, and while one may take

[11]IFOP, *Sondages* 46–48, *Jardinage.*

[12]Huizinga, J., *Homo ludens, A Study of the Play-Element in Culture,* Kegan Paul, London, 1949.

a cautionary view of his testimony, his documentation is impressive. He presents in two large tomes an objective analysis of the contents of the booklets that had the greatest circulation among the ordinary folk of the towns and countryside.

We learn[13] that the comparatively limited number of works of a "moralizing and edifying" nature was nowhere near the number of the occult sciences; humor ("two hundred anecdotes about drunks to give you the hiccups"); parodies of religious discourse; fiction-biographies; dream almanacs "intended especially for our feminine readers" and, above all, the romances of Mme. Cottin Amelie de Mansfield, "a romance of delirious love in which the exaltation of the senses mingles with that of the sentiments"; and also "the adventures of a great lady" (1849), a book full of "an ignorance of the human heart which I would call primitive and an abandonment of all moral sense far surpassing the worst smut writers." In addition, there was the *Le Secretaire des Amants* and *Choix de Lettres d'Amour.* The counsels these offer, remarks Nisard, "are base, I do not hesitate to call them infamous. . . . This daring dirty little book has certainly seen more editions than the best book ever issued since books began."

Yet Nisard refused to include a similar analysis of the two-penny romances which were such an essential part of the peddler's crude pack. Who read these? ". . . these serials, this printed stuff, these dramas were available to the most modest purse and in the hands of every young worker. What the last century's depravity produced in beastly ordure and rottenness, our own modern tale-spinners have exceeded"—so wrote the editor of the working-class journal *L'Atelier.* If this would seem dwelling unduly on Nisard, it is because his inquiry showed to what extent half the ordinary people of France who could read at all devoured this type of easy fiction. The popular taste for fiction was not born with the movies; it would be more correct to say that the orientation of the movies toward its fictive character corresponded to profound popular taste. One cannot overstress the point that the working-class culture of 1848, so much admired by Edouard Dolleans and Georges Duveau, could hardly have embraced any but a very small minority of the most advanced and the self-educated.

The growing demand for fiction stimulated by a growing leisure is now satisfied on a scale unprecedented since the discovery of printing, sound, and, of course, moving pictures. In the face of this demand, the influence of George Meliès was not long in passing that of Louis Lumière. The movies provide an unequaled means of "visualizing dreams." And television, so perfectly adapted to the direct reporting of vital events, has been swamped with fiction. Fiction, too, is the main ingredient of the fifteen

[13]Nisard, Charles, *Histoire des livres populaires ou de la littérature du colportage depuis le XV*ᵉ *siècle jusqu'à l'établissement de la commission d'examen des livres du colportage,* Paris, Amyot, 1864, 2 vol.

million copies of the weekly magazines catering to women.[14] Novels constitute almost half of all book production, and about 80 per cent of the books borrowed from public libraries. Still, they are not the same kind as in the time of Marx and Nisard. Contrary to accepted opinion, and despite the commonplaceness of most of what passes for works of art (an informed public opinion judges 90 per cent of such productions in literature and the movies to be "junk"), popular taste is improving. One must here record an ambiguity in the kind of fiction that feeds the leisure time of the masses.

In their culture of daily experience, the satisfactions of the imagination play a much bigger role than in school or university culture. If the latter is to respond more fully to the needs of our time, it must undergo a transformation. It has also been pointed out, by Edgar Morin, for one, that most of our prevalent ideologies are overrationalistic—fail to take sufficiently into account the imaginary man. "We must reintegrate the imaginary with the reality of man."[15] On the other hand, the mechanisms of projection and identification encouraged by current fiction can drug the critical, discriminating powers of mind. The imagination may get out of line and confusion result between the real world and the world of fantasy in which the personality is lost in the careers of the stars. Real life gives way to a proxy, where the pleasure of fiction, instead of simply offering an agreeable dream, deflects the person from all action or misleads him into maladjusted activity. Fantasy poses the same danger we have seen in the more real amusements: The personality may be seduced away form the actual world into a mythic one, to become no more than a refugee, an exile who has lost all desire to act along with his fellow men.

THE NEW HOMO SAPIENS

As much as for recreation, leisure provides time to acquire knowledge for its own sake. Only a century ago, not even a newspaper found its way into the homes of workers. Around 1846, the famous journal *L'Atelier*, published by workers for workers, had, at most, a thousand subscribers—and it was a monthly. Workmen bought few newspapers because they were too expensive. Now, of course, a daily paper is part of the domestic scene of the great majority; every day a half-hour or an hour is spent relaxing with it. Almost the whole of the city population (Annecy) reads a weekly, and more than half read at least two. In addition, a good half of this same public reviews the weekend newsreels at the movies, and 93 per cent state that they listen regularly to the radio news. A poll taken by

[14]*Echo de la presse et de la publicité,* 1958 edition.
[15]Morin, *Le Cinéma ou l'homme imaginaire.*

the INSEE (Institut National de Statistiques Economiques et Sociales) in 1953 showed that 77 per cent of the radio listening public desire "as much or more" news and information programs. Once, working people were isolated in their districts and work was their culture. They lived a life of withdrawal, turned in on themselves. Today, leisure time has stimulated a greater need which is both fulfilled and extended still futher by the development of the rotary press, with reduced cost of papers and magazines, and by revolutionary techniques in visual presentation. Digests, of every kind and quality, have had a great success. In all milieux of the population, the taste for nonfiction is growing, especially for biographies and travel books, as shown by publishing figures and library statistics.

For the majority of readers, especially in the provinces, the daily paper is a veritable book, with its editorials, reportage, feature articles, special departments, games and puzzles. Fifty per cent of the readers of such dailies, according to IFOP, follow political events, domestic and foreign, regularly, and about 38 per cent read general reportage and informative articles. A part of the public devotes some leisure time to a more intensive pursuit, self-directed but still systematic, of questions that hold some particular interest for them. In Annecy, about half the heads of families do this, and 40 per cent would gladly accept a paid study-leave of twelve days to improve their knowledge or aptitudes in various fields. In order of preference chosen interests are problems having to do with the job, general culture, scientific and technical matters, economic, social, and political questions, and, finally, preparation for assuming responsibility in their organizations. We may count about 10 per cent of urban workers and salaried employees as self-taught students, who spend a good deal of their leisure hours in their chosen subjects of study. In Paris, alone, they have at their disposal twenty-five schools offering accelerated general courses —this apart from the ordinary grades and technical and trade union training.

Leisure to study is the precondition for this "ongoing culture," which becomes more and more necessary in our complex and swift-moving civilization. It may be that this seeking after knowledge serious in content but attractive in presentation will one day bring about some very notable changes in the mass media of television and periodicals and centers for education beyond ordinary schooling. Leisure to study holds out the possibility for new directions of the mind at each new turn of our civilization. On the other hand, the pursuit of an agreeable knowledge can too readily be limited in kind. If she appears on the front page, Princess Margaret, all by herself, can be the reason for doubling the number of copies in one issue of a magazine like *Point de Vue—Images du Monde*. An IFOP poll on reading the daily paper revealed that local news was most popular, 86 per cent of readers regularly following reports of births, deaths, celebrations, parties. ... All this abundant local subject matter could be made the basis for an economic, social, political, or esthetic culture. This possibility has gone neglected in the editorial offices of our daily press. After local items, the most popular reading matter is the ads (65 per cent) and miscellaneous news (57 per cent). If not isolated, this kind of reading could be profitable in and of itself. Alone it can scarcely lead to the broadening and deepening of knowledge a modern citizen ought to have if he wishes to keep abreast. To be sure, against a swelling tide of print about national and international, political and economic, social and literary questions, the reader is submerged, unable to absorb and assimilate most of it. He finds himself resorting to what Paul Lazarsfeld has called opinion guides, those who read and listen for him and give him the gist of the matter.

A reader who strives to do his own reading of serious subjects may soon find that the clutter of general ideas and statistics have left but superficial traces in his mind, and he is tempted to revert to the miscellany of news easier to assimilate. For, despite the advances made by our journals in the presentation of difficult questions, the public's capacity to understand and assimilate has still not developed to meet the needs of any genuine democracy. It has been pointed out by A. Varagnac that if the public now has the time to keep up with what is going on, it still lacks the capacity to develop—to acquire the kind of real knowledge that traditional culture stands for.[16] Hence, it is open to question whether the plethora of information and accompanying discussion has not resulted in an ersatz activity in all areas. If discussion in one's free time has pleasurably broadened, it at the same time risks taking the place of, rather than preparing for or supplementing, active participation in community life. The inflation of the information received, given or exchanged, can create an illusion that much social good has been done, when in fact there has been only a good deal said.

THE NEW HOMO SOCIUS

Our leisure has also nurtured new forms of sociability, new groupings unknown to the last century. In the course of his inquiries at Reims, and at Lille and Mulhouse, Villermé failed to come across any recreational or cultural association, but only mutualist societies more or less political in character. On the other hand, everywhere he was struck by the great role of the café in the life of the workers. Reading his detailed and moving reports, one begins to understand the fierce campaigns waged by the staff at *L'Atelier* and by Perdiguier against working-class drunkenness. Villermé notes: "It is not uncommon to see the workers of the Lille factory working only three days a week and drinking away the remaining four, and," he

[16]Varagnac, A., *Civilisations traditionnelles et genres de vie,* Paris, Albin Michel, 1948.

adds, "this was true even before the rise of the factories." At Reims, "in a working-class quarter that makes up a third of the town, the majority of the best paid laborers work only during the latter half of the week and pass the first half in orgies. Two thirds of the men and a fourth of the women inhabiting certain streets are frequently drunk." And he concludes: "For the worker, everything becomes, so to speak, an excuse for going to the café. He goes there to rejoice when happy, and to forget when beset by domestic worries. The café is where he runs up debts, or pays them if he can, where he transacts business, forms friendships, and even where he gives his daughter in marriage."

Cafés today are still an important place of leisure for everybody and particularly for workers. Yet, contrary to what most Frenchmen imagine, acute drunkenness is probably declining compared with its widespread prevalence in the past century.[17] To be sure, the scourge is still with us, and less to be tolerated than ever. What has increased is the sense of shame it arouses—the country cannot be too zealous in getting rid of this particular affliction. It is fantastic that 40 per cent of all road accidents should be caused by drunken driving (official figure for 1958), that deaths from delirium and cirrhosis of the liver exceed ten thousand a year, and that the national expenditure on alcoholic beverages should far surpass, in France, the sum spent on education and housing combined. True, intoxication is no longer the same status symbol it once was among youth. Within a century, according to Duveau, there has been a substantial decline, relative to the total population, in the number of shops selling cheap liquor for consumption on the premises and in the number of customers.[18] A study by INED (Institut National d'Etudes Démographiques) in 1960 showed that 16 per cent of the French people visit a café once a week or more. Actually, the great change is qualitative; the atmosphere of the café has been modernized, games of all sorts are played, and the cabarets of ill-repute are kept down to a limited number. The police are fully aware that here criminals or juvenile delinquents prepare their newest exploits. But, of course, all cafés are not hangouts for hoodlums; most are places for a community expression of the many activities permitted by increased leisure.

According to our inquiry at Annecy,[19] reasons for going to a café are, in order of preference: be with friends; social meetings with colleagues or

[17]Villermé (3). See also G. Duveau, *Villes et campagnes*, A. Colin, 1954.

[18]Georges Duveau, *La vie ouvriére sous le second Empire*, Paris, 1946. See also, Solly Ledermann, *Alcool, Alcoolisme, Alcoolisation*, INED, cahier 29, 1956. In his statistics on liquor outlets, S. Ledermann includes carry-out stores, groceries, and the like. His figures are thus different from Duveau's. From 1954 to 1960, the number of liquor outlets has decreased by 20 per cent (260,000 to 160,000) INSEE, 1960.

[19]Five per cent random sample among heads of families.

clients; family outings; some conversation after work; talk things over after a get-together; attend a show or match of some kind. These cover about 80 per cent of all reasons given.[20]

But newest of the social forms developed under the new leisure is the group for recreation or education. These organizations, regulated largely by the law of 1901 (which was not made for them), have proliferated right along with industrial and urban expansion. They are not tied to the needs of the job, as are the unions and professional associations, or to the demands of a practical politics or religion, as are the parties or the church groups. They are geared first and foremost to the pursuit of leisure. Most of them are, in principle, open to everybody, regardless of background, class, or education. Around 1930, in the American town he called Yankee City, the sociologist Lloyd Warner counted about four hundred active organizations among the fifteen thousand inhabitants; today a little over 35 per cent of all Americans are estimated to be members of some group. We have no figures for France as a whole, but in 1957, the town of Annecy counted two hundred active organizations, with more than one out of every two heads of family belonging to one or more than one. Thus, while trade unions, political parties, and religious action societies could claim hardly 25 per cent of the total membership of all Annecy organizations, 75 per cent belonged to clubs for leisure, most of them for the following purposes, in order of popularity: fishing, sports, outdoor life, bowling, music, and various cultural activities. Those from a working-class background, though on the whole rather less well organized, still have their own fishing, bowling, and music clubs; and about a third of the workers belong to clubs that include members of other classes and social milieux.

Here again, we find a characteristic ambiguity in the culture of daily experience. These leisure organizations provide for the locality the sociocultural ferment studied and advocated by Kurt Lewin.[21] Within the framework of the organization, the higher-ups attempt to engage the less well educated in free discussion, while eschewing propaganda. The clubs act as effective intermediaries between remote sources of information and the local public, and help raise the cultural level by democratizing knowledge and practicing mutual education. But not always. Too often, such recreational clubs withdraw into their narrower interests and close themselves to outside influences; they are totally indifferent to the idea of taking part in any general cultural life around them. A sports club of this kind, Georges Magnane has remarked, creates "retarded children playing under careful supervision."

[20]Cf. Joffre Dumazedier and Annette Suffert, *Les fonctions sociales et culturelles des cafés dans la vie urbaine,* report to the Higher Study Committee on Alcoholism, 68 pp., 1961.

[21]Lewin, K., *Psychologie dynamique,* Paris, PUF, 1959.

In principle, one may say that the organizations of all kinds, taken as a whole, provide a framework for salutary exchanges between individuals of different social status and education. There is, unquestionably, a general trend of all leisure organizations toward a unified life-style. But, of course, cultural organizations, as such, are dominated by intellectuals, teachers, the élite personnel of all areas—in short, the middle classes. In the minority, workers are never completely at home. Social stratification, if not actively, at least passively resists the organized pressure against it. Finally, we may ask: What influence do all these organizations for leisure (whether sports or travel, whether of musicians or intellectuals) have on participation in the business community or in trade unions, or civic and political organizations. We may say that the leisure organizations furnish a kind of model for these other organizations: the latter are beginning to imitate the activity of the former—holiday celebrations, outdoor excursions, games, reunions. ... Nevertheless, in the actual operation of our liberal social system, this new *homo socius,* it is to be feared, may come to regard his membership in the leisure groups he has chosen as the only connection he needs with community life. Everything points to a tendency of these leisure clubs to set up marginal, self-contained societies, a kind of new utopianism based not, as in the nineteenth century, on work, but on leisure. And such societies spring into existence despite, not because of, the class structure. They are not concerned with the future, only with the present. They tend to divert a part of the social potential generated in the field of production and the tensions of the clashing relations toward a semireal, semi-imaginary sphere, "where man may escape his humanity and quietly shed his real self."[22]

Will leisure be the new opium of the people? The movement to lead the worker "from alienation to enjoyment" would then be contradicted by a force leading away from enjoyment of leisure back to alienation in work. The worker would be content to sell his labor as a commodity for the sake of simply enjoying the proceeds of his sale in the time away from his job. Is that all he will want? Will he leave it to someone else, to his spokesmen, to win a maximum wage for him? Though a product of the historical process, leisure is being lived, in effect, as if it were a value outside history. The man of leisure tends to be ungrateful for any past, indifferent to any future. To be sure, this is not an attitude which makes a conscientious citizen. It is this aspect of the life-culture of the masses that calls for placing leisure in its historical perspective and in its present technical, economic, and social context so that we may the better understand what forces operate, or could operate, upon it or because of it.

---

[22]Cf., in the same sense, a remark by Jean-Paul Sartre about the ambiguous role of mediator played by associations, according to the first results of our Annecy inquiry, in *Critique de la raison dialectique,* NRF, 1960, p. 50.

chapter six

Anti-Utilitarian Leisure

Charles Reich[1] states that a quiet revolution in America, originating with the individual, seeks to reject the present impersonal, plastic, desensitizing advanced technological state of affairs that has existed since the turn of the century in the United States. This new sense of emerging reality, dubbed by Reich "Consciousness III," repudiates earlier patterns and values and represents personal liberation and the primacy of pleasurable, natural, humanistic, and sensory experiences.

The concepts embodied in Consciousness III stimulate reflection about some of the elements associated with today's youth. They include a concern for the preservation and restoration of the natural environment, spiritual values and ceremonial rituals, self-fulfillment, and a sense of community. The yearning among many youths to determine their life style and evolve a pattern of behavior which will integrate work, leisure, and family life represents a desire for a return to preindustrial society, in which art, ritual, ceremony, and spiritual and work endeavors were combined into a simple, dynamic, and often meaningful life pattern.

Walter Kerr[2] articulates a conception of leisure which attempts to analyze why Americans are unhappy, alienated, and groping for purpose and

[1]Charles Reich, *The Greening of America* (New York: Random House, Inc., 1970).
[2]Walter Kerr, *The Decline of Pleasure* (New York: Simon & Schuster, Inc., 1962).

meaning when they live in a dream-come-true age of leisure and have an abundance of things to fill that leisure. Kerr's conception of leisure embraces Reich's basic points; it *accents joy, encourages self-expression, and rejects the work ethic and utilitarianism* as the only sources of value in our society. According to the anti-utilitarian concept of leisure, the Protestant work ethic (the philosophy of utility) has blinded us to the art of being open to joy and engaging in activities that have no useful end. The anti-utilitarian concept suggests that leisure is a state of mind that is a worthy end in itself. Man must learn to rejuvenate his inner self and add the dimension of *pleasure* to his life to make sense of technocracy's antagonistic influences.

Like Kerr, John Farina[3] sees leisure as a personal response consisting of activities not directly related to utilitarianism except insofar as they may promote self-realization. Farina values the classical concept of leisure; by examining Maslow's hierarchy of needs,[4] Farina attempts to provide a contemporary conceptualization of the classical Aristotelian model of leisure. Farina, like Kerr, rejects the notion that leisure activities must be dictated primarily by mechanical time. His conceptualization reflects a more personal, psychological time reference, in which the essence of leisure is self-expression through activity, whether it be intellectual, spiritual, or physical, in which the individual strives toward his full potential as a human being.

LEISURE AND THE COUNTERCULTURE

The counterculture is a separate way of life, an alternative to the dominant, technologically-based society. Its development in America was inspired by a generation of largely affluent, white middle-class youth who rejected American industrial growth and expansion in favor of a less hectic, yet difficult way of life. Advocates of the counterculture have tired of the direction of the technocratic social order, built around quantification, in which the emotional element of man is said to have been severed from his body and he is oriented solely toward efficiency. The meaning of life in the technocratic order is to serve the bureaucracy and its various functions. Every phase of life is expected to conform to the demands of a society strongly influenced by science and technology.

Bureaucratic values become the central values of life, and the criteria for beauty change to suit the efficient, functional, technical process of the bureaucracy. Residing within the dominant American society provides

[3]John Farina, "Toward a Philosophy of Leisure," *Convergence,* 2 (1969), 14–16.

[4]A. H. Maslow, "A Theory of Human Motivation," *Psychological Review,* 50 (July 1943), 370–96.

only limited joy if one's expectations do not coincide with the outcomes of societal involvement. Therefore, disenchanted youth have sought purpose and meaning through an alternative culture designed to provide the desired outcomes and rewards unavailable in a conforming, highly routinized technological society. The fascination of the counterculture for some appears to be the chance to build new institutions, to develop different values, and to rekindle a humanistic spirit in small community living arrangements.

An alternative society seeks to incorporate many of the values purported to be virtuous in modern technological society, but subordinated by the massive effects of cybernation. Some of these values include the benefits of quantitative leisure, a byproduct of industrialism. In the contemporary interpretation, leisure has often been equated with discretionary time reaped when mechanization shortened the work week, standardized function, and freed the laborer to enjoy weekends, vacations, retirement, and a multiplicity of social benefits made possible by aggressive unions. This interpretation is consistent with the already accepted time reference which holds leisure to be time free from existence and work obligations. This view is distinguished from the classical-humanistic tradition of leisure (which, according to Sebastian de Grazia, is largely missing from contemporary American society), which holds leisure to be a state of being, having nothing to do with mechanical clock time. Classical leisure is a state of being free from obligation and necessity; it can occur whenever one feels that it exists. Contemporary leisure behavior can occur only in a set time period.

Neither the classical nor the dominant contemporary interpretation of leisure fits the domain of the counterculture. While traces of both forms of leisure are found in communal living, the counterculture more nearly represents a view of leisure as a *total life form.* Traces of anti-utilitarianism appear in communal living, although the counterculture may actually represent a *synthesis* of the classical and discretionary-time concepts of leisure: the classical concept of leisure as an end in itself, and the discretionary-time concept that leisure is earned and replenishes workers during free time when the work necessary for maintaining life is finished.

Some opponents of the counterculture claim that brief experiments in communal living merely represented hedonistic, frivolous youth indulging in drugs, engaged in free love, and serving no useful, productive purpose for society. Advocates of the counterculture suggest that it provides a new, holistic definition of leisure (to be discussed in more detail in Chapter 8) as a construct of elements including a full range of human possibilities from loafing to engagement in highly creative tasks.

The counterculture is an adaptation of the dominant society, a microsystem which reflects ideas, forms, art, and technology representative of a simpler, decelerated work-oriented era. The fruits of labor are intended to be rekindled, and the attitudes that often do not accompany discretionary time blocks—retirement, vacations, and weekends—are to be integrated into the total way of life. The fragmentation and systematization of contemporary American society has led some people to reorient their lives by adapting values and beliefs to fit a social structure which gleans the benefits of work and leisure by synthesizing them into a *coordinative* life form.

Our efforts to understand and interpret leisure have been based on a mechanical time-oriented value system. Participants in the counterculture seem to want merely to alter the organizational structures which result from and support the dominant value system. The social structure ultimately devised for the embryonic counterculture may be simply an extension of the dominant American technological system. In essence, counterculturists seek simply to create new life-style patterns or ways to exhibit them. However, it appears that work and leisure will stem from the dominant beliefs about life and the way it is to be actualized. The coordinative life pattern of the counterculture may represent an adaptive way to express work and leisure behavior in a postindustrial society, including various life-style options and diverse and flexible living patterns.

At present, the life style of the counterculture does not appear to manifest a reformulated social system. The hard life of rural communal living is actually structurally opposed to leisure, making it time earned from work. While many advocates of the counterculture have found physical security with peers who will tolerate freaking out, pandhandling, loose living arrangements, and so on, their leisure seems predicated on the condition that the dominant culture has made their "freedom" possible. Organization is a time-oriented value, and its components of interdependency and deferred gains are antithetical to those who live for the moment in a more permissive, neoprimitive psychological time reference.

The pattern of leisure manifest in the counterculture is not so discernible in the dominant society. Many members of the counterculture reject the equation of leisure with unobligatory functions in favor of a more anti-utilitarian view, holding leisure to be a condition or state of mind beginning in the consciousness of the human being—whether he be at work or free from obligation. This view may be a new holistic conception of leisure expression, characterized by integration of thought and feeling molded into a total life form.

SEARCH FOR A QUALITATIVE LIFE

Most Americans already have access to extensive amounts of free time as a result of a shortened work week, longer vacation periods, earlier retirement, and the like. However, while we would expect most members of the community to have an abundance of unobligated time at their disposal and to live a leisurely life, we observe on the contrary a scarcity of free time and a more hectic life tempo. The scarcity of time results from persistent consumption pressures requiring men to work overtime or to moonlight. The pressures of a highly industrialized nation and the work ethic have diminished the value of leisure to spare time, time to be used by the industrial worker to recuperate from a hard week's toil. Such time often must be filled with utility to justify its worth.

A *qualitative* leisure option portends a significant alteration of the present value orientation of most Americans, if a leisure ethic is to be appropriately integrated into the culture. To some young people, such a drastic restructuring of the American social order appears impossible to achieve. Our patterns of relations, roles we automatically assume, and functions that we perform would all have to be altered. The development of communal villages in rural areas throughout America seem to be part of an attempt by counterculture advocates to break away from the constraints of the dominant social order. The creation of the counterculture provides an opportunity to unite the values of personal work fulfillment and contemplation into an integrated experience. It also provides an opportunity to select individual work schedules and allows for the spontaneous execution of personal desires at the moment they occur.

SUMMARY AND IMPLICATIONS

The separation of work and leisure in modern industrial American society has meant that people have had to relinquish some opportunity for personal expression to satisfy family subsistence needs. Greater value has been placed on the sanctity of work, diminishing leisure to spare time status. The work ethic—a quantitative, utilitarian view of man's purpose in life—has negated purposeless expression as a viable activity.

For some members of the counterculture every investment of human energy does not have to produce a useful result. The Protestant work ethic which permeates all facets of American life is rejected by people who wish to permit the investment of self in pursuits that promise no more than the expression of self. This does not necessarily mean that pleasure and joy have to be distinguished from work, simply that leisure can be considered a state of mind that is a worthy end in itself and that appears in various life forms, work or play.

The attractiveness of the counterculture is that it offers a vision of what the dominant society may become in the next thirty years, if the traditional clock time orientation of industrial society is discarded in favor of a more permissive, psychological time reference. Leisure in the counterculture appears to provide a freer, more permissive life orientation. Human instincts dictate a more natural, rhythmic relationship between work, play, and rest and do not necessarily enslave man to clock time, but rather instill a motivation for an unscheduled time reference.

The existence of anti-utilitarian leisure appears to have been a natural result of materialistic technology. As America has moved into a post-scarce economy, an age of automated abundance, man's lower-level needs (as defined by Maslow) for food, clothing, and shelter are more easily satisfied. A generation of affluent middle- and upper-class youth have rejected work demands and openly sought self-actualization through purposeless play.

The evolution of a counterculture underscores the yearning for a simpler, intrinsically rewarding way of life in which one may engage in work and leisure without efficiency ratings, production quotas, and other external standards for performance. Work and nonwork activity may be pursued purely for the pleasure of the experience.

The new life form of some members of the counterculture provides the dominant society with a possible new leisure option amenable to a postindustrial society. By viewing leisure as a range of possible feelings and activities, from low-brow to high-brow, man may be free to choose how he will use his leisure. The rigid framework which presently prescribes engaging in leisure during discretionary time allows only small, bunched time segments in which to enjoy family and personal interests. In a society which may be almost exclusively oriented to leisure, sufficient options spending time appear to be a sociopsychological necessity.

toward a philosophy of leisure

JOHN FARINA

Leisure is not time. Nor is it work, recreation, or any other form of activity. Aristotle's notion of a condition or state of being is a relevant point of departure in developing the concept. Interestingly, practically all writers on the subject take Aristotle as the point of departure in discussing leisure but seldom seem to move from that point. The Aristotelian notion of the condition of being free from the necessity to labor has perhaps not been critically examined in the light of modern scholarship. As a result, the idea of leisurely labor has usually been omitted as a potential occupation of leisure. Further, the compulsively neurotic pursuit of free-time activity is difficult to exclude from leisure as derived from Aristotle.

Freedom and necessity have usually been identified as the critical terms in Aristotle's statement. Freedom in relation to leisure has been discussed in relation to freedom to work or not to work, freedom to choose from a range of behavior, freedom of opportunity to pursue any of a wide range of activities, and freedom to occupy rather than use time. An additional dimension is the capacity to make choices.

The second critical variable, "necessity," has usually been discussed in the original Aristotelian sense, that is, necessity to labor. Yet necessity or need is surely a concept that influences freedom in many areas as vital as labor. Necessity presumably reflects need. While labor may in fact have some instrumental value in meeting basic human needs, it has not usually been classed as a basic need.

Much has been written about human needs, and a wide variety of need systems is described in the literature of social science. Most frequently reference is made to the needs of affection, belonging, achievement, recog-

John Farina, "Toward a Philosophy of Leisure," *Convergence, An International Journal of Adult Education,* II, 4 (1969), 14–16.

151

nition, and new experience. This classification has proven useful for recreation program-planning. Thus encouragement is given to social activities, small group activities, clubs, competitive and cooperative programs, and to some extent to adventurous activities.

Yet there is some feeling that such programs and the rationales on which they are based are incomplete in terms of any philosophic position vis-à-vis what is wanted for people. To some extent those giving leadership to free-time activities recite these five basic needs like a catechism and relate them to planning in an almost mechanistic manner only ritualistically related to maximizing the full individual potential of people.

A different approach to human need was developed by Maslow and first set forth in his book *Motivation and Personality* in 1954. Maslow rejects the notion of any sense of equity between needs, and has conceptualized a hierarchy of need sets. His scheme is sufficiently general to encompass most other theories about human needs. In Maslow's view, needs at lower levels in the hierarchy must first be relatively well satisfied before the individual is free to address himself to the attainment of satisfaction of higher level needs. For example, man no sooner satisfies his physiological needs, which are at the bottom of the hierarchy, when, as Maslow puts it, "at once other (and higher) needs emerge and these, rather than physiological hungers, dominate the organism and when these in turn are satisfied, again new (and still higher) needs emerge and so on. This is what we mean by saying that the basic human needs are organized into a hierarchy of prepotency."

The idea of prepotency is central to Maslow's hierarchical ordering of needs, and is basic to the concept of leisure as presented herein. Needs at lower levels are more basic and have greater power than those at high levels. Hence lower level needs must be relatively well satisfied, on a continuing basis, before the individual is free to concentrate his resources on achieving satisfaction of higher-level needs. If a lower-level need is frustrated, for example, if safety is threatened, the individual temporarily abandons his pursuit of higher-level needs until his safety is relatively well assured.

Maslow's classification of five prepotent need sets is as follows:

1. Physiological Needs: These include hunger, thirst, sex, activity, rest, homeostasis, and bodily integrity. These are needs which once relatively well satisfied free the individual to address himself to the next set of needs.
2. The Safety Needs: In this group are the need for orderliness, justice, consistency, routine, predictability, limits, and physical safety. Adult expression of these needs is evidenced by interest in job security, savings accounts, and various insurance plans covering a variety of life's exigencies.
3. The Belongingness and Love Needs: These needs emerge after both the physiological and safety needs are fairly well satisfied. They include the need

to love and be loved, the need for friendship, interpersonal relationships, and a sense of identity with a group.

4. The Esteem Needs: There are two sets of esteem needs, self-esteem and the esteem of others. The former refers to the need for strength, achievement, adequacy, mastery, competence, and independence; the latter refers to prestige, reputation, status, dominance, recognition, attention, and appreciation.

5. The Need for Self-Actualization: The emergence of this need usually depends upon the prior satisfaction of the needs at the four lower levels. It is the need for self-fulfillment, the need "to become everything that one is capable of becoming."

When Maslow speaks of the satisfaction of self-actualization needs, he assumes this will be without exploitation or sacrifice of others. Rather the satisfaction of such needs is likely to enhance the possibility of others' self-actualization.

Maslow's hierarchy of needs has particular significance to the concept of leisure. Indeed, self-actualization could be considered as the end or goal of leisure. Maslow's scheme, however, also offers an explanation for the wide range of activities and motivations that have been attributed to leisure.

If we accept the notion of prepotency and the idea of different levels of need, then we can re-state the Aristotelian definition of leisure. Leisure is the state or condition of being free from the urgent demands of lower level needs. Here, the category of lower level needs includes the first four levels or all levels except self-actualization. If one is functioning at the level of self-actualization, then one can literally play at, or challenge, the lower level needs. Such play or challenge represents leisure activity. For example, the physiological needs of hunger, thirst, sex, and activity, when not faced with the urgency of unsatisfied need, find expression in the activities of the gourmet, the connoisseur, the Don Juan, and the athlete. Safety needs such as orderliness, justice, physical safety, and predictability may be challenged by gambling, mountaineering, parachuting, and white collar crime. Esteem needs may manifest themselves in sports, arts and letters, intellectual output, idiosyncratic behavior, and voluntary service. Love and belonging needs may motivate membership in clubs, associations, and various teams and interest groups.

The state or condition of leisure then refers to freedom from the demands of lower echelon needs. Activity in leisure is not primarily dictated by time—time is not used but rather is occupied. Leisure then is possible during what is generally considered work time. An indicator of leisure during work time is the unhurried nature of activity reflecting freedom from demands or compulsions. The lack of hustle, bustle, and urgency in leisure activity is recognized in the general usage of the term "leisurely."

Obviously such a concept as leisure was redundant during the industrial age. It was the private privilege of a small economic elite. Leisure was viewed as a reward for work, rather than work being simply of instrumental value in the attainment of leisure. No longer, however, can any class be identified by virtue of the fact that it alone has leisure. The post-industrial age is potentially an age of mass leisure.

Mass leisure, however, may represent an unfortunate choice of terms. For leisure is personal and consists of activities not directly related to utilitarianism except insofar as they may promote self-realization. The essence of the concept is being free to express oneself through activity (be it intellectual, spiritual, or physical) in order to strive toward one's full potential as a human being.

the decline of pleasure

WALTER KERR

One of the first great adult dreams of the twentieth century was the dream of leisure. The nineteenth century, in its rush to colonize and to supply, to industrialize and to market, left the laborer, the bookkeeper, and even the man who was known as the boss with very little time to enjoy his achievements. The working day was long: most men were up at dawn, if not well before it, and most men plodded home in the dark, to eat, to discuss with their wives the price of pork, and to get to bed early enough to be able to rise again. Work was virtually uninterrupted: carpenters brought their lunches with them and ate them on planking while a foreman stood by silently urging them back to their awls; no bookkeepers took coffee breaks; few employers permitted themselves festive two-hour lunches—preceded by Martinis—in fashionable restaurants. Wives washed their own dishes, baked their own bread, sewed clothes for the children, made patchwork quilts, walked to market, entertained very rarely and then most modestly, saw little of their husbands and shared interests not at all, and were glad enough to fall exhausted into bed at the necessary hour. Of sweatshops, child labor, and the nose to the grindstone we have all heard enough. "We never sleep" and "the sun never sets" were phrases coined in the period.

In due time the conscience of the world was aroused. Children were snatched from their shoe-blacking benches and sent off to the schoolhouse and the sunshine. Bertha, the sewing-machine girl, joined a union and found herself with a two-week paid vacation in the Catskills. The carpenter began work an hour later, stopped work an hour earlier, demanded Saturday afternoon for himself and then Saturday morning as well. The boss, perhaps the last to surrender his prerogative of unceasing labor, discovered not only the two-hour lunch but the five o'clock cocktail, the Friday night flight to his farm in Connecticut, and the fact of Florida. Wives demanded not only the vote but the right to play bridge: some other arrangement would have to be made about the bread, the dishes, and the darning.

A dream stirred. What had been the point of all the work if no one was ever going to derive any pleasure from it? The very purpose of work was to create occasions for ease. The moment had come now to seize them: the world was well mechanized, the money could be made during a five-day week, gracious living required only that we stop, breathe, smile, and buy appliances. Might we, given just a bit more ingenuity and a few more years, never have to work again? In his 1932 film, *À Nous la Liberté*, René Clair showed us just what we had in mind: the factories were able to run themselves and the men who had once manned them were free forever; we saw these exuberant souls, fishing on a riverbank, their bread and cheese beside them, singing the livelong day. As M. Clair simultaneously mirrored and mocked our vision we may have grinned at the absurdity of the image. But it is clear today that, absurd or no, we did not give it up.

Everyone knows how far we have pushed the promise. The forty-hour week is no longer accepted as ideal; Boris Pregel, past president of the New York Academy of Sciences, has predicted that it will soon be reduced to twenty. Even now, no bookkeeper need stay after twilight; IBM machines are swift to the touch. The junior executive can afford to commute; the world will not fall apart if he appears shortly before ten. From four o'clock onward the highways are anthills of Chevrolets and Buicks, employers and employees jostling one another in the race to the suburban back yard and a cool glass of beer or to the exurban terrace with its twist of lemon peel in an appropriate drink. Lunch hours are comfortable at all levels, and at some they are invitations to indolence. A month in Europe is a gleam in many a wage earner's eye; trips to Canada, to Mexico, and to Disneyland are commonplace.

Domestic duties need detain no one. Dishes may be left to the dishwasher. Clothes may be passed into a machine that will wash them and dry them in a single cycle. Should any of the clothes need pressing, an electric mangle will do the job swiftly and effortlessly; because so many clothes are being made of materials that fall into shape without coaxing, there is less and less work for the mangle to do. A disposal unit will crush and carry off the garbage. Toasters, knife sharpeners, electric ranges, electric frying pans, and Waring Blendors nestle beside one another on easy-to-clean counters, each of them reducing in its own efficient way the time a wife must spend in her kitchen. Shopping need be done no more than once a month: an intelligently-stocked freezing unit will carry a family comfortably for four or five weeks. The hours that have now been spared to the housewife need never be passed in discomfort; air conditioning will see to it that her leisure is unruffled.

The homebound husband and the chore-free wife are at liberty to enjoy their release in a variety of ways. They may elect for solitude, but they are not bound to it, as their relatively immobile forebears so often were. Friends may be summoned or reached: the telephone will do one in an instant and the automobile the other in a pleasant half hour. No one need be starved for conversation or for the companionship of kindred spirits. If one prefers physical to intellectual pleasures, there are bowling alleys within walking distance, golf courses within driving distance, and boats of all sizes for those who live within fifty or sixty miles of a lake or the seacoast.

When he does choose solitude rather than company, the twentieth-century man discovers that nearly every form of delight yet devised has been built snugly into his home. He has very little call, for instance, to hie himself to a public library: the masterpieces of the past and the best sellers of the present are available to him in paperback reprints so inexpensive as to make everyman's bookshelf a potential Bodleian. Everything from Aristotle to Agatha Christie is at his finger tips. Should his taste turn from reading to the contemplation of color and form, he knows perfectly well that he is in easy possession of that "museum without walls" André Malraux promised him in *The Voices of Silence*. Grünewald, Picasso, and the contents of the Louvre are handsomely at hand as they have never been before—in reproductions that may be hung in his rooms and changed as frequently as he likes, in substantial volumes whose color plates have been made with an exacting fidelity to the originals. Should he be willing to settle for a lessened fidelity and some reduction in size, he can have the best of Goya for thirty-five cents. No treasure is kept from him behind the portals of the Prado.

In another mood he has but to snap on the television set to see and hear Leonard Bernstein conducting the Philharmonic, Agnes De Mille arranging a new dance, Sean O'Casey chatting informally about the glories of his back garden, Mary Martin or Ethel Merman or Fred Astaire or Gene Kelly romping through the materials that have made Broadway glow brightest. He can relax with *Oedipus Rex* or *The Maltese Falcon,* more or less as he likes.

If Bernstein's selections on a given Sunday afternoon do not happen to be the selections best suited to the state of his mind and nerves, he has no difficulty in suiting himself. The record cabinet is well stocked, *The Emperor Concerto* has become his for merely joining a cut-rate club, and the automatic changer on his phonograph assures him of what has been called "uninterrupted listening pleasure." Nor need he discommode himself should his fancy shift from one kind of melody to another. If it is verse he wants, verse he can have: poets will read their poems for him on another set of records, as actors will act Shakespeare and Goldsmith and Sheridan and Shaw at the drop of a needle. The resources of the lecture platform, the concert hall, the Broadway stage, the best-stocked library, and the range of galleries from the Uffizi to the Museum of Modern Art are at his leisurely beck and loving call.

The twentieth century has not only realized, within reason, its dream of leisure time but has also supplied the riches with which to fill it.

It will be obvious at once that not all of the treasures vouchsafed to modern man are being put to extensive use, and it is not my point at the moment to bewail the fact that neither *Oedipus Rex* nor the Philharmonic has ever been found among the "top ten" on a television rating log.

Recordings of Shostakovich's Fifth Symphony probably do not sell as well as the "Dance Party" records of Lawrence Welk. Indeed, there is a serious fear in some quarters that the same mass methods that have made Dante and Debussy available to everyone have ended in producing a mass culture that does not know Dante except as an admirer of Beatrice and that does not know Debussy except as a strain on a sound track for a Warner Brothers film. The term *kitsch* has come into almost deafening use among critics. *Kitsch* is composed of "popular, commercial art and literature with their chromeotypes, magazine covers, illustrations, ads, slick and pulp fiction, comics, Tin Pan Alley music, tap dancing, Hollywood movies, etc., etc." It is, as Clement Greenberg points out in *Mass Culture,* "a product of the industrial revolution which urbanized the masses of western Europe and America and established what is called universal literacy." A universal love of quality has not followed directly upon universal opportunity. Let us acknowledge the fact and not—just now—dwell on it.

Before asking what twentieth-century man has done with the treasures bestowed upon him, it may be proper to phrase a more fundamental question: What has he done with the time bestowed upon him?

I would like to consider, briefly, a man I know. This man lives in the suburbs, earns a satisfactory salary in an investment house, is educated and intelligent, gets along well with his wife and three children, has his evenings and Saturdays and Sundays at his disposal, and possesses many of the machines invented to assure him of leisure and pleasure. For a while, several years ago, he developed a surprising habit; perhaps I should say he developed a habit that is not at all uncommon among twentieth-century middle-to-upper-class men but that was surprising at the time to his family. Three or four times a year, in a rhythm too erratic to be easily understood, he would lose himself for a long weekend in a succession of bars. These periods of escape did not seem to be related to domestic crises or office tensions; they did not spill over into Monday mornings but were cut off sharply and quite soon enough to enable him to return to work; the classic symptoms of an incipient alcoholism—self-pity, indifference to family, fear of faltering in a career—were nowhere in evidence. The problem was not acute, but a problem existed.

The problem was ultimately solved, as it is now so often solved, by the purchase of one more machine for the home. This man bought himself a power saw and installed it in his basement. Certain supplementary tools were added a little later. With his new equipment, the essentially responsible husband and father transformed a rather dingy room that had been used for laundering into a pine-paneled breakfast nook, which is both charming and useful. Having completed the task, he transferred his attention to an unfinished attic, gradually turning it into a cheerful hideaway for the children to use whenever one of their rooms is pre-empted by house guests. During the coming spring he intends to devote his free evenings to the construction of an outdoor terrace, with access from the dining room, so that the summer may be made pleasanter with frequent cook-outs.

There are two things to be said about his present condition. One is that the drinking bouts have ceased. Nor is there anything in his eye to suggest that the old impulse is apt to erupt again; his activity is not feverish; the strange destructive strain that led him headlong to liquor has been assimilated and in a sense exhausted by his new interest. The second thing to be said is that he does not look particularly well. He seems tired.

It is not unreasonable that he should be tired. He is now working five days at the office and two days and five nights at home. Where his nineteenth-century ancestor worked sixty hours a week, he works approximately seventy-one. It is difficult to say whether the lines in his face are deeper on Friday night or Monday morning. Still, he goes on, content to have been rescued from his aberration.

What released him from his aberration was renewed labor. I cannot say precisely how typical this man is of twentieth-century Americans in general. I have been able to watch him, and a few dozen like him, but my range of observation is limited by the circumstances of my own life. It is clear to me, however, that the therapy of the power saw is a specific in more cases than I am acquainted with. If I am to judge by the advertisements I read in newspapers, by the helpful articles I read in magazines, and by the acres of equipment I see in hardware-store windows, the "do-it-your-self" command is nearly a national specific. Across America men seem not only willing but eager to install their own plumbing, wire their own kitch-ens, bevel their own bookshelves, assemble their own hi-fi sets, tile their own lavatories, stain their own porch furniture, steel-trim their own lino-leum counters, and, when all else is done, hook their own rugs. Indeed, manufacturers of formerly ready-made objects have estimated the situa-tion so shrewdly that they no longer go to the expense of assembling their tables, benches, cribs, and Christmas rocking horses at the factory but pass them on to the purchasers in shards, certain that every man has the time, the tools, and the desire to put these things together.

It is also clear to me that the "do-it-yourself" movement is unrelated to any urge toward economy. It is not the refuge of the impoverished man who must make with his hands what he cannot afford to pay others to make for him. An impoverished man could not afford the tools, for one thing. Add to the cost of the tools the cost of mistakes, plus a decent accounting of the man's time in terms of his earning power, and the final object will prove, in nine cases out of ten, more expensive than its profes-sionally-made counterpart.

There are, I must conclude, other men with leisure-hour problems. The problems may vary, in kind and intensity: liquor is not the only solace for an intolerably empty day or the only menace to be met by an intensified labor. But whatever peculiar coloring the individual difficulty takes on, a single cathartic seems effective in our time: work. I find, too, that the flight from leisure to labor is not confined to the longish weekend we were once so proud of.

Great critical sport has been made, in recent years, of the "business lunch." On New York's Madison Avenue and in Chicago's Loop, in Scran-ton's Hotel Casey or in any town's equivalent of the old Kiwanis Club, executives of greater or lesser rank are known to meet over Martinis, ryes, or beers, chef's salad or *Bratwurst,* to nurture, and then to consolidate, deals. Because such conferences constitute a continuation of the working day, the costs of liquor, food, cigars, and other *divertissements* are charged to the expense accounts of the participating companies: each firm is ex-pected to pay for work done in its interest. The United States Government, through its Bureau of Internal Revenue, has recognized the validity of the situation. These meetings represent, of course, the twentieth-century dream of the longish, relaxed lunch period, or what is left of that dream. There are those who smile slyly and intimate that, no matter what expla-nations are given on the expense-account vouchers, the business lunch is devoted to something less than business, that it is a rationalized break from the sales charts and a chance to down a few drinks that will keep the rest of the afternoon from becoming too strenuous. I am not sure that I share this cynicism. I have been in business offices on a number of occasions when an executive's lunch date was unexpectedly called off. On none of these occasions did the executive first sigh with regret and then hopefully cast about for a friendly soul to replace his lost guest and keep him casual company in a restaurant for the next hour or two. In each instance the executive ordered up a sandwich from a nearby delicatessen and ate it absently while he went on working.

The selection of leisure-time friends and party guests on a calculated basis has come in for its share of kidding, too. In 1958 a national magazine ran a cartoon that was intelligible both as humor and as realistic social criticism to almost everyone: an upper-middle-class woman was saying brightly to several of her peers, "We're going to enlarge our circle of friends to include some people we like."

We are also wryly familiar with the party assembled in such a way as to make certain that its costs may legitimately be entered as professional expenses, against taxes. One bright-eyed guest arriving late at a thoroughly successful party I recently attended whisked off her wrap, glanced at the fifteen or twenty familiar faces turned cheerfully in her direction, and caroled winningly, "Oh, the annual deductible!" The fact that the thought of party-giving tends to fill the twentieth-century hostess with apprehension and that the party itself, so far from relaxing her, builds up a tension that requires a week's recuperation thereafter is equally plain. Three days after the successful party I have just mentioned the man of the house was rushed to the hospital for an emergency appendectomy. His wife, our Sunday hostess, called a friend on the telephone, her voice filled with grievous distress. "In one week," she cried, "the party—and now this!"

Generally, the tendency to confine one's friendships to business acquaintances and to make up guest lists for parties on the basis of professional obligation and possible professional advancement is regarded as one of the more unattractive and self-seeking strains in the contemporary American psyche. This is status-seeking, we are told, when it is not appalling snobbery. Once again, I suspect that we are not being quite fair to a conscientious and hard-pressed society. It is an entirely legitimate practice to select one's friends on the basis of a community of interests. What is odd, to me, is that twentieth-century man seems able to find, and to share, a community of interests only among the working community. If he wants to go bowling, he does not call to his eldest son to join him on the spur of the moment or go off alone in some confidence that he will find a congenial partner at the alleys; he joins the interoffice bowling league. If he rather likes a Friday evening of living-room conversation, he does not look among his neighbors for the best conversationalists; he looks for the best conversationalists among his professional colleagues.

I think that there is a certain innocence in the pattern. The man who behaves in this way is not necessarily a crudely calculating man or a greedy one. He is very likely aware that on Friday night he is entitled to some pleasure, that he has an incontrovertible right to make himself comfortable. And he is comfortable only when he is talking shop.

. . .

Once I had begun to notice how my pleasure was invariably postponed until my work required it, I also paid attention to the quality of that pleasure and to my conduct while pursuing it. I was, I soon realized, racing to get through, though there was no absolute deadline over me. I was making frequent marginal notes, rather more than I should ever need for a report. I was assuaging a powerful feeling that I was cheating in reading Stevenson at all by insisting on the urgency and necessity of the task. I was indulging myself in something for which there was neither time nor rational justification, and I was able to endure my truancy only by keeping firmly in mind its value as profitable labor. When a friend sees me with a book in my hand and reaches to read the title as friends often do, I always feel an urge to explain to him how I happen to be reading this particular book. I have caught myself laughing off a copy of *Northanger Abbey* as apologetically as the hostess who has nothing but her own company to offer. I am acquainted with only one commuter who reads Shakespeare on the way to Wall Street; and he speaks of his habit so often and so exuberantly that I know he feels a fool.

We are all of us compelled to read for profit, party for contacts, lunch for contracts, bowl for unity, drive for mileage, gamble for charity, go out for the evening for the greater glory of the municipality, and stay home for the weekend to rebuild the house. Minutes, hours, and days have been spared us. The prospect of filling them with the pleasures for which they were spared us has somehow come to seem meaningless, meaningless enough to drive some of us to drink and some of us to doctors and all of us to the satisfactions of an insatiate industry.

In a contrary and perhaps rather cruel way the twentieth century has relieved us of labor without at the same time relieving us of the conviction that only labor is meaningful.

Although we assume ourselves to be a people possessed of unusual opportunities for leisure, we are actually occupied in more and more work. Although we assume our children to be coddled and play-mad, they are actually more interested in work than we are. The situation is strange and, in some ways, frightening.

I do not think that my friend with the power saw is about to revert to his drinking. He is likely to remain sober, and industrious, until the day he dies. But I shall not be surprised if that day comes sooner than he has a right to expect. He is engaged in the therapy that kills.

It is customary to explain the hypertensions and the heart attacks that bedevil the contemporary American male by pointing to the abnormal pace and the abnormal work pressures of twentieth-century life as though that pace and those work pressures had been established by someone other than the man himself. We imagine some blind, mindless, mechanized force in whose grip we all are, and whose thrust we are unable to resist. But what force should this be in a society that has provided more time for relaxation than any other? Isn't it odd that a century which should, by all rights, be the most leisurely in all history is also known to be, and condemned for being, the fastest? Who has set this pace, if not the fellow who has insisted upon maintaining its tempo during all the hours when his office doors are locked?

Work-minded as we have become, we are not yet wholly unaware of a world that exists, or was meant to exist, apart from work. We have, for instance, a memory of pleasure; fragments of idle and delighted hours freely squandered when we were younger come back now and then to haunt us, and when Robert Paul Smith writes a brief evocation of childhood called *Where Did You Go? Out. What Did You Do? Nothing* an ounce of nostalgia stirs in all of us. We are vaguely aware that an uncorrupted pleasure awaits us somewhere, if we can only learn to forgive ourselves for taking it; we sense that the taking is both possible and desirable. We even suppress a sigh as we reach for our hammer and nails by telling ourselves that the work we do today is done in the interests of a pleasure postponed: when we have finished the terrace and the barbecue pit we shall have the unalloyed delight of a carefree cookout. The cookout, too, will be corrupted when it comes by being made the occasion of shoptalk with colleagues, but no matter; a promise remains half alive and we may sooner or later find some way of realizing it.

It is probable that our very awareness of the existence of pleasures that we are either postponing or denying ourselves adds to the tensions induced by unrelieved labor. We feel guilty when we take our pleasure, because there is so much work we might do. We feel guilty when we work so hard, because our lives may depend upon pausing for pleasure. The two guilts are incompatible, and we suffer further from the head of steam their mutual abrasiveness builds up. Still, there is always hope of resolving the dilemma; the life line may be badly snarled, but it has not been permanently cut.

What disturbs me most about our admirable children is that the life line, the thread of release, the promise of a pleasure that is not in itself labor, seems never to have existed for them. They are not only accomplished in their command of what is useful but are also content with it. They will not have my memory of a foolish and useless and all-consuming passion; they do not want it. They will, I must conclude, grow to manhood without a nagging acquaintance with a possible alternative to their pursuits; they have not been interested in making such an acquaintance. They will have single, rather than divided, minds, and the unquestioning simplicity of their lives may release them from feelings of guilt. But, given the sudden descent of a dark night of the soul, they will have no place to go.

It is almost as though the twentieth century had been engaged in a long struggle to produce a new kind of man—a man whose sole concern should be his useful work—and, in our children, had successfully accomplished the mutation.

Though they do not know it yet, I know that my children will one day come to a paralyzing moment in which everything they have loved is robbed of its flesh, a moment in which the circle of light that has long surrounded an object flickers sickeningly and its dimensions collapse like a retractable tin cup. For one of them a column of figures will straggle down a page in mocking unintelligibility, defiant. For another geology will turn to so much carefully sifted dust.

What will the robin do then, poor thing?

. . .

Instead of berating the man who works all of the time, we should pause to salute him. He is devoting himself without interruption to an activity that has always been possessed of great dignity. "In the morning," wrote Marcus Aurelius, "when thou risest unwillingly let this thought be present —I am rising to the work of a human being."

The human being who is profitably busy can respect himself: in addition to what he is doing for the welfare of his immediate family, he is giving his own private nudge to the national economy and he may even, in certain circumstances, be contributing to the increase of knowledge that is so imperative if the economy is to grow and the nation to survive. He may, in one sense, be enjoying himself as he makes these creative movements. If he is not enjoying himself freely, as Huck Finn might have enjoyed himself now and then on the raft, and if he is conscious of being constricted by his time-tables and weighed down by his tools, he can take a considerable satisfaction in the size of his accomplishment. Even when the accomplishment does not seem altogether stable, or the satisfaction deeply personal, there is an impersonal glory to be derived from serving—in Bentham's phrase—the greatest good of the greatest number. For one human being to devote his days and his nights to the hoped-for happiness of all other human beings is by no means despicable.

Furthermore, the time in which we live seems to offer no alternative. History races ahead of us just now: continents are unexpectedly roused from their sleep, the earth's population suddenly promises to run wild, the moon has been touched and not by us, a rival political system is in the ascendancy, the very globe on which we work may be rocked from its orbit. This is not, we sensibly feel, the moment for idleness. Small matter that some of us have quite enough to eat for the moment and are even worrying about eating too much; without instant, constant, and massive labor at all practical and theoretical levels each bite we eat may be the last we are granted.

Plato spoke for us. "What will be the manner of life," he asked in the seventh book of his *Laws*, "among men who may be supposed to have their food and clothing provided for them in moderation and who have entrusted the practice of the [crafts] to others, and whose husbandry . . . brings them a return sufficient for men living temperately? . . . To men whose lives are thus ordered, is there no work remaining to be done which is necessary and fitting, but shall each one of them live fattening like a beast?

"Such a life is neither just nor honourable," he answered, "nor can he who lives it fail of meeting his due; and the due reward of the idle fatted beast is that he should be torn in pieces by some other valiant beast whose fatness is worn down by brave deeds and toil."

We do have a clear and intelligent fear that "some other valiant beast" may, even as we fret, be working harder and more efficiently than we are; only by doubling our labor can we hope to catch up. "Night and day are not long enough," Plato warned us for the necessary work of nourishing the body and educating the soul, "and therefore to this end all freemen ought to arrange the way in which they will spend their time during the whole course of the day, from morning till evening and from evening till the morning of the next sunrise." Toil around the clock is called for; we cannot even be sure that so much single-mindedness, and so much dedication, will turn the trick.

Our total absorption in work, then, is justified on several counts: work is worthy of a man, it is satisfying to a man, it is the unavoidable duty of a man in times like these. There may be only one thing to be said against our generous willingness to undertake the labors of Hercules and Sisyphus together without rest or regret; there is always the danger that unrelaxed pressure on a tool may break the tool, in which case the work will not get done.

We need not concern ourselves long with the most obvious aspect of this danger: the chance that the man at the wheel will crumple, losing control of his muscular power, his nervous responses, and the wheel. We know that such catastrophes do occur and that no death-wish need be involved. I once talked for a few minutes, on the steps of a sanitarium, with a man who had been a bookkeeper: he was pleasant, he seemed calm and coherent, and he explained that one morning the column of figures he was accustomed to working with had simply meant nothing to him; though he was normal enough in every other way, the significance of numbers had fled from him.

This silent and invisible rebellion sometimes becomes noisy and visible. The newspapers will always let us know when the president of a railroad has blown out his brains or a high government official has hurled himself through a window, just as the gossips will keep us informed of the prominent playwright's latest visit to a mental institution. "Crack-up" is a slang term that has made itself quickly and intelligibly at home in the twentieth-century vocabulary.

But the backlash that is forceful enough to lead to self-destruction or even partial incapacity is relatively rare. The human intellect is incredibly resilient, even stronger and more resilient than the physical constitution that houses it. We have had, and will have again, prodigies of industry whose fibers never fray. We have had damaged constitutions whose disabilities seemed to liberate, rather than imprison, the minds they played host to. We have had spectacular evidence of the human animal's recuperative powers: after all, John Stuart Mill was once more in possession of his energies after a mere two years and perhaps wiser for the experience. Unlike machines, men can be repaired from within. And when they cannot be satisfactorily repaired, they can be replaced: society is prodigal at throwing up reserves, and nature itself is not instantly dismayed at the lemming-like loss of vast numbers who have overtaxed their private resources. For a very long time, there are more where the last battalions came from. Men break down, and the experience is privately, sometimes publicly, painful; but the likelihood that a great many men will break down at a moment of great crisis is encouragingly remote.

The most obvious danger is not necessarily the greatest. The abrupt disintegration of a few, for instance, would not be half so alarming as the progressive disillusion of the many, as a steady loss of faith in the hearts of men standing firmly at their tasks. Damage done to the constitution is not so irreparable as damage done to the will; nervous exhaustion is not so serious as the exhaustion of personality.

Is there any sign that the perpetual pursuit of a very real profit may produce such a secondary, and insidious, infection? I think so. The contemporary evidence seems to suggest that something other than an occasional crack-up threatens us, that we are more widely menaced by a near-universal ennui, an ennui rooted in a contradiction. Even as we hurl ourselves feverishly into more and more work, we are quietly aware of a stirring nausea, of a faintly sickening distaste for the work we must do, the world we must do it in, and the selves we must live with while we are doing it. But before we can ask why this should be so, we had better see what the evidence is.

The twentieth century has gone about its chores with a clear conception of where value lies. Value lies in the extraction of use or profit from the available world, whether it is the world of farm produce or familiar faces, of interlocking directorates or plays to be seen. The century has given all of its time and all of its energy to this work, the constant and apparently limitless accretion of value. Now, in the 1960s, as it studies its own image in whatever mirrors it can lay hand upon, it sees no values at all.

. . .

All games in which the mind is required to do work of a specifically mathematical nature belong not to the realm of pure pleasure—which may be taken for the moment as that intoxicating state in which the whole man finds himself centered on, and in, a sensation of having just been born and having just been set free and having been born for the freedom he is feeling —but to the realm of diversions. Pleasure is well-being itself; diversion is a temporary turning-away from a lack of well-being. Pleasure is time ransomed; diversion is time passed. Pleasure changes a man; diversion changes what he is looking at, though not the quality of his looking. Whereas pleasure actively recharges, diversion keeps the battery running at an even purr.

When we try to conceive of genuine pleasure, what we grope for is something more deeply felt and more expansively filling than the rather neutral and matter-of-fact satisfaction we take from games of skill which are really "changes of task." Finishing an evening at cards, we may feel that the tensions of our lives have been briefly reduced, or at least held at arm's length, by preoccupation with an interesting pastime; what we have done, in effect, is soothed ourselves with a harmless "hair of the dog."

But if we were to envision pleasure proper, pleasure in all the fullness of its eternally beckoning promise, we should ask that it achieve something more for us than this: we should expect it in some way to make us over.

Surely somewhere in this tantalizing universe an experience awaits us that is richer than canasta or George Harmon Coxe. Would men keep promising themselves some ultimate "pleasure" when all the work is done, would anyone have bothered to equate the pursuit of happiness with such important treasures as life and liberty, if "pleasure" began and ended with the barely tolerable aridities with which we occupy our free evenings? An instinct tells us that we were born to something better, a breeze that touches us unexpectedly as we are locking the doors at night fills us with a brief, vague distress over the joys of maturity we once thought were coming to us and never have come.

The question to be asked at this point in our inquiry is not: where are such wells of pleasure as these, wells at which we might drink as deeply as we like? It is this: sensing that such wells exist, why don't we look for them? Feeling the breeze, and knowing that there is something we have neglected to seize for ourselves, why do we suppress the sudden upsurge that should logically end in a quest, shut the door resolutely, and resign ourselves to the thinnesses of our time killers once more tomorrow night?

We are prisoners of our convictions, hostages of an inertia that permits us to hold two quite contradictory views in balance. We are inclined, on the one hand, to suppose that there must be profoundly pleasing experiences, more exhilarating than those in which we habitually indulge ourselves, which might make us feel bigger with life than we now do; and we feel obliged, on the other hand, to dismiss such possible experiences as unnecessary and even as unreal.

Of *course* there may be sensations of overwhelming delight—if one were to take the trouble to look for them—and the delight might very well prove restorative. But we dare not permit ourselves to grow sentimental about the matter. Sentimentality consists in lavishing more emotion on an object or experience than the object or experience is worth, and our precise scale of values tells us that idle play, sheer delight, and such pleasures as are held in the mind merely are—no matter how satisfying—without essential substance, devoid of worth. *Ergo,* the superior joy we are half imagining might indeed refresh; but, given our creed, we must logically and stoically conclude that the refreshment itself would be valueless. Fun, no doubt. Stimulating, no doubt. But unimportant, unworthy of a man.

The word "recreation" remains in our vocabulary, but we do not think highly of the activity it defines. Children need recreation. Give them a bat and a ball, take them out to the park, send them off on a hike from time to time: growing bodies and immature minds can stand a certain innocent flexing now and then. Deteriorating bodies and weary minds do not require it so much. Of course, *some* men should force themselves into the open air for a few minutes each week: they have not stopped smoking, and their lungs need clearing. Some men may be a bit better off for acquiring an untaxing hobby: the pressures at the office are often very fierce.

There is a "recreation" room in the basement, though it is not used as much as the family thought it would be when the work of paneling it was undertaken. Its principal fixture, and the one that has most nearly justified its cost, is a bar; there is probably a phonograph that has been used for dancing several times; there may well be a ping-pong table which can be moved to the center of the room if no one is going to dance and which has been standing in the center of the room for many months now (it will be used again if someone can find the balls).

"Recreation" is light exercise, taken therapeutically and most often under duress. It is a stamp album, a determined walk with the dog, an amorphous spectral necessity that confronts us whenever we are about to take another life-insurance examination. It is a term used to describe what adolescents are going to be doing in that room downstairs; it is an adult male's minimum gesture, the most he can afford, toward warding off incapacity; it is nothing at all, really, to the woman of the house, not a word she can apply to any activity that concerns her. When we speak of "recreation" we are referring to a brief and casual commitment that is usually physical, that is most often performed both unwillingly and perfunctorily, and that produces, at best, superficial benefits. We are not confused about the meaning of the term.

We are confused only when we read of the absurd claims some thinkers —luckily, most of these are seriously out of date—have made for it. Aristotle has been quoted earlier in these pages as stating, without qualm or qualification, that the men who create for us the necessities of life are less wise, less knowing, less worthy of being held in esteem than the men who create our pleasures. "Recreation" is the term Aristotle uses to identify, and gather together, these pleasures. It would seem to follow that in this philosopher's view recreation is more admirable than work, though why he should have thought so is beyond us. Yet Aristotle is not even concerned to argue the case. The arts of recreation were "naturally" always regarded as superior to the achievements of our labor, he tells us.

We do not pay much attention to ancient saints, even when they were thinkers. "No man can exist without pleasure," remarked St. Thomas Aquinas, who ought—if our understanding of the dour medieval mind is correct—to have been urging us to put away our playthings in favor of prayer. "Life would not be tolerable without poetry," announced St. Teresa of Avila, making it perfectly clear, in a parenthetical remark, that she meant it would not be tolerable even in a convent for contemplatives. St. Augustine thought that whenever a conflict arose between the enjoyable and the useful, the useful had to give way as being, in the ultimate sense, inferior. Many of the soberer thinkers of the past, including those who had by vow denied themselves most earthly pleasures, did not scruple to elevate what they called recreation to a dizzying position in the hierarchy of the worth-while. Indeed, "worth-while" is an inadequate word to describe the value they placed upon pleasure. No man could exist, life would not be tolerable, without such patently superior experiences.

The experiences we, in the twentieth century, tend to lump together as recreational forms—our distracted dalliance with *kitsch,* our bridge games, our dyspeptic Christmases, our sullen visits to the squash courts—do not honestly seem to merit the enthusiasm some minds have bestowed upon the act of play; nor do they afford us anything like the satisfaction we might rightly demand of activities held to be superior to our work. Someone is using a word in a sense that eludes us. However, since we do find our lives increasingly empty these days, it may be worth taking a few minutes to ask whose use of the term is faulty.

Begin with the dictionary—ours, not Aristotle's. Recreation signifies: " *1.* Refreshment in body or mind, as after work, by some form of play, amusement, or relaxation. *2.* Any form of play, amusement, or relaxation used for this purpose, as games, sports, hobbies, reading, walking, etc." Yes, there is the noun as we know it, and there is nothing in it to justify Aristotle. What of the verb, the act that presumably produces the noun? To recreate is "to restore, refresh, create anew; to put fresh life into. . . ."

There is an overtone here. "To create anew" and "to put fresh life into" begin to suggest what a profound pleasure may do and a hobby may not. Is this an echo of an ancient, and now mislaid, hope? If there were actually in the universe a regenerative power that could fill us with fresh life, that could add to our very being still more being, shouldn't we be willing to prize it more highly than the labors that seem to drain our being away? There is a hint, though only a hint, that our foolish diversions and ephemeral amusements belong to an instinctive strain in the human personality that, given its head and nursed to its highest, might place us in the unexpected and exhilarating position of being reborn. Some sort of rebirth is what we are asking for. The word beckons, faintly.

But how can so trivial an activity make good so vast a promise?

. . .

. . . [T]here is no solving the problem at the extremities, neither in the flight to the bedroom nor in the flight to the barroom, certainly not high in the branches of the old apple tree: the wasteland is already there, waiting. Until the mind can be convinced that pleasure is meaningful, until it can feel that pleasure is just, until it can quite simply and plainly be pleased with itself, there will be cakes and ale for nobody.

It is no doubt a mistake for me to mention cakes and ale at this point, for that is just what we conceive our pleasures to be: desserts, things we can and should do without. (Are we trying to convince ourselves that we should do with less sex in all those novels and plays, that we should care less for the flesh in all those paintings?) Pleasure itself is something more than that. Being pleased in our minds with our minds and with our bodies and with all that our minds think and our bodies do is something more than that. It is an interior experience of the rectitude of things, a seen certainty of the consonance of things. When I become aware that I am in harmony with my own being, I am pleased. When I become aware that I am in harmony with all other, or any other, being, I am pleased. One often thinks of pleasure as the satisfaction of an appetite, which it is. But what is the appetite, traced to its ultimate source, and what does "satisfaction" mean? The appetite is for fulfillment, completion. To "satisfy" means "to fulfill the needs, expectations, wishes, or desires of . . . to suffice, fulfill, or answer the requirements or conditions of." Insofar as I am, I have requirements that must be met if I am to continue to be. When they are met— when they are satisfied, as a true measurement in architecture is said to satisfy or as a just judgment in a court is said to give satisfaction—I am made fully myself, and it is this rightness, this perfect conformity of requirement and response, that I call my pleasure. Tracing the origins of the word "pleasure," one comes upon a curious early equivalent: agreement, mutual understanding. When I am in the right place, and all the world fits me, I am pleased.

In this ultimate sense of the word, pleasure becomes one of the mainsprings of the will. Being made certain that I am not a displaced person in a universe indifferent to me, I am able to move about in it. But if I have no direct, deep experience of how much the universe and I agree, I shall doubt the likelihood of our ever coming to a mutual understanding and so become either immobilized or very angry. The immobility is linked, fore and aft, to apathy; and there is a surprising apathy in some sections of the world today. The anger, conscious that movement is still possible but convinced that it is essentially random and therefore incapable of being satisfied, explodes into activity that is, and in the circumstances cannot help but be, irrational; we read of the irrational act, whether it is a private act or a vast public one, more and more often these mornings. Being pleased is not a mere matter of our being titillated; it is a condition of our being willing to go on. "No man can exist without pleasure," said Aquinas, and we may soon bump head-on into the appalling discovery that we cannot or—if the hour has grown late—that we could not.

I do see that these remarks attach what seems an excessive importance to an experience we think of as trivial. Therein lies our greatest stumbling block just now: a profound requirement of our natures is fixed in our minds as superficial.

Just as we equate "recreation" with the recreation room and not with rebirth—which is what the structure of the word truly signifies—so we habitually speak of pleasure as though all its implications were idle. "Well, one has to get some pleasure out of life" is not a proudly-held creed; it is an excuse, uttered by way of apology for an evasion of responsibility one is contemplating but of which one is transparently ashamed. Here is life on one side, over here. It is something to be got through, and the assumption is that getting through it will in no way be pleasing. But by the time one dies, one ought to have slipped in a few odd hours of dereliction of duty. A man is entitled to cheat a little along the way.

The roots of the word "pleasure," wriggling this way and that over the centuries, have taken a variety of turns, and some of these have headed in our direction. The medical term "placebo," for instance, is an offshoot of the Latin for "to afford satisfaction or happiness," and it suits our present understanding well. A placebo is "a medicine given merely to humor the patient; especially, a preparation containing no medicine but given for its psychological effect." That indeed is how we look upon the whole matter of delight: partly as coddling, partly as fraud, altogether as something from which true substance is missing.

But now we must face up to the implications of our attitudes; it is time to be entirely honest with ourselves. We hold two attitudes, and they are deadlocked. One is that, because we have been unable to provide pleasure with a value, pleasure is insubstantial, illusory. The other—and this is where our inquiry began—is that the value we do acknowledge, the abstract value we give to the thoughtful ratios of our labor, has also, and in spite of us, come to seem insubstantial, illusory. Between two negations, between two pathways felt to be slippery, is there no firm earth we can ever get beneath our feet?

Or is it possible that firmness, security, confidence, and joy—in this most mysterious universe—depend upon our willingness always to walk both paths at once, always to advance one foot on the right side and the other on the left so that we shall keep from toppling either way, always to accept the fact that the only way we can have one world is to admit and to honor the existence of two? There is a famous Chaplin image, at the end of a film called *The Pilgrim.* Chaplin has been ordered out of one country, literally kicked over the border. But across the border he is caught in the murderous cross fire of bandits engaged in guerrilla warfare. Where to turn? Swiftly shrugging his shoulders, he decides. The last we see of him, he is deftly and philosophically shuffling away from us, straight down the border line, one oversize shoe safely planted in this country, the other safely planted in that.

I say "safely." But, of course, there is something very tentative, eternally unresolved, in his teeter-totter journey to the horizon. And there is something about tentativeness, about teeter-tottering, that we do not like to allow in our own lives. We prefer to get things straight, to get things settled, to discover a single efficient way of hitching all we must deal with into single harness. We like to be single-minded, to have one rule of thumb, to define all that is diverse in the same simple set of terms—if we can possibly do it. The world is easier to manage that way, we feel.

But what if there is no single way to manage the world, no simple way of holding onto anything quite so supple—as though we were trying to lift a cobra with one hand when it really takes two? What if the world is as solid as rock and as yielding as water at one and the same time and man is a creature who needs the rock to sit on the the water to get under? What if man himself is essentially unresolved—partly granite and partly mercury, immaterial as his thought and material as his toenails, an unfinished sum and an unfinished symphony, an eternal spectacle in the mismatched socks he is wearing—and what if it is precisely in his failure, or his refusal, to define himself absolutely and to commit himself forever that his flexibility, his power of inventiveness, and his exuberance lie?

We are now being given hints that if this were the case, it would be an excellent thing. I quoted Teilhard a few chapters ago on the flexibility and playfulness of the kitten. I did not mention then that the very advance the kitten, along with its cousin mammals, represented in the evolutionary development of life stemmed from its superb sloppiness, its comparative inefficiency, its frisky escape from the drive toward automated perfection. It had left behind it, and well beneath it, a much better organized species, the single-minded insect. With the mammal, Teilhard remarks, "instinct is no longer narrowly canalised, as in the spider or the bee, paralysed to a single function. . . . We are dealing with an entirely different form of instinct in fact, and one not subject to *the limitations imposed upon the tool by the precision it has attained."*

The insect had been strict with itself, honed each of its parts to a specific function, tolerated no nonsense in the process of its self-organization. Having sorted out all things safely, and having co-ordinated them toward a single end, the busy bee and the admirable spider completed themselves —and thereby froze themselves. Out of perfection of a kind came a kind of death: the insect had formed itself absolutely and was now able to sustain itself indefinitely—but it could make no further contribution to anything outside itself or better than itself. The mammal, "no longer completely the slave" of its methodology, kept a response or two open— undetermined, uncommitted, untamable, elusive—and it was the open responses that enabled it to participate in further adventures. A loose character, the kitten.

If we are to believe the paleontologists, then, the looseness we notice in the strange ambiguity of our lives is one of the luckiest things we possess: something to be cherished, *as looseness,* rather than to be regretted as awkward. If we are, at our present stage of development, forced to do some things with one tool and some things with another, forced to labor on the boss's time and make love on our own, forced to advance upon the universe with both arms open and each hand prepared to make a rather different gesture, our advance in nature and in grace is not over. Something ahead of us invites us to test it this way and that, to strike it and to stroke it, to assault it and to steal up on it. If it is complex, we are still flexible and apt to surprise it in the unexpectedness of our approach. With a roller skate on one foot and a hiking boot on the other, we can switch tactics; it is by being free to switch tactics that most engagements are won.

But if we are ambidextrous wrestlers in a multiform world, doing some things intuitively and some things doggedly, now dancing about the arena and now showing what a straight line we can walk, where in all of this uninterrupted sparring can substance lie waiting for us? Must we posit that, given our odd natures and their apparent suitability to an equally odd universe, substance exists for us in the dimension that leaps into being when the two faces of the world are seen in a shimmering superimposition, one relieving the other with shade and the other lifting its companion into light? This is admittedly an unstable image for an unstable condition: the two do not absolutely merge; we cannot have the universe whole in one fell swoop. The two meet, and shield one another, and illuminate and shadow one another, in a meeting that is not quite a fusion: it is as evanescent as an eclipse, though it may be as thrilling. Are we vouchsafed the certainty of a sun and moon only while they are brushing contours, exchanging darkness and glow, fleetingly and ungraspingly making two faces one? Perhaps it is intolerable that substance, and value, and all promise should be as impermanently and dizzyingly known as this. But perhaps it is also the guarantee of our continued mobility, our malleability, our throbbing sensitivity to impressions that are themselves throbbing with life, a guarantee of our active partnership with an active, growing, changing, hallooing universe. Here nothing is frozen, not in our heads, not in the skies. We buzz, and bend, and beam together as we play hide-and-seek until dawn.

And see where we are, if any of this is so. Suppose that an eternal, hide-and-seek, mysteriously creative duality *is* so—a duality of thinking and seeing, of abstract and concrete, of action and contemplation, of cerebration and intuition, of work and play, of profit and pleasure, of assertion and surrender—and that our confidence and our exhilaration depend upon an alternating exercise of dual tools upon a double face—an exercise so regular and so rhythmic in its alternation that we come to have a lively sense of the sustained presence of both, finding substance in their iridescent interplay.

In that case, we are, at this precise moment in time, ready to declare ourselves a bonus. We have achieved a high degree of skill in one kind of groping, the hard kind, the theoretical kind. Our futures now depend upon a most attractive activity: upon our developing a matching skill in the easy kind, the loving kind, the arm-in-arm kind. Praiseworthy as we are in the work we have been doing, and certain as it is that more work will have to be done, our freedom to grow in stature rests unconditionally upon our ability to play. To keep our minds supple and the universe in focus, we are requested, most cordially, to exercise just those intellectual instincts which tend—in their contemplative listening and their intuitive rejoicing —to produce pleasure.

Can pleasure, then, be said to have a value, a value at least half as big as the total capital available to us, a value big enough to give us permission to pursue it? Intellectually speaking, I think so. It is, in essence, the value of The Other.

How much we have neglected The Other, and how strainingly we yearn for it, is not always clear to us. It is not clear to us because we have not fully realized how much of a burden, and how unnecessary a burden, we have conscientiously placed upon The Self.

One last, short recapitulation. When we decided that all value was extrinsic, and that no value was intrinsic or actually *in* things, we accepted a private responsibility that might well be called intolerable. We said that all that was touchable and all that was visible—from the grass outside the window to the face looking up at us from a chair across the room—was neutral and that worth was something we constructed for it in the adding machines of our heads. But this meant—though we barely noticed the implication—that all that was real, all that was worth-while, all that was valuable, was in *us*—in the equations we manufactured in the busy switchboard of our brains. Whatever vitality or continuity the universe possessed came from *us*. We were its guarantor, its prop, its collateral, its claim to being. We carried it on our shoulders like a willing, though perspiring, Atlas: the moment we ceased our cerebration, the moment we stopped supplying it with fresh charges in the shape of formulas, it would drop. The world about us, the womb in which we grow, had no other source of energy, no power of its own. Each of us, in the individuality of his thinking mind, had perforce to accept the responsibility not simply of knowing the universe but of creating it—abstractly—and of perpetually maintaining it in the sustained tension of his thought.

Without being in the least egocentric, we had got ourselves in the position of the man who does not trust airplanes and who therefore does one wholly unnecessary thing: he gets a grip under the armrests attached to his seat and helps hold the plane up.

To acknowledge the presence, the independence, the energy, and in some way the reality of The Other is to begin to put down the burden that makes us most lonely, most isolated, most exhausted—and to begin to take pleasure in the comfort, the mutual support, the "oh, *there* you are!" of friends.

The Other is that warmth in a field that would make the ground thaw and the wheat grow if I never happened by; when I do happen by, it is waiting not for the support of my thought but for the impress of my foot. It is that moment in a conversation when, toward the end of the evening, the few who are present sit back and realize, with a quiet leap of the heart, that each has touched something in the other and not merely imposed a rattle of entertainment upon him. It is a living face noticed across the aisle in a theater in which slightly parted lips and intent eyes and head held poised all, together, speak of a completeness I could not add to; or a face carved in marble, or in oil, that lifts the marble from the earth and the oil from dead cloth. Even when he is painting a self-portrait the artist must be stunned by the otherness he has trapped: this is he, but it is different from what he had thought. The Other is in this curious book we are reading in which an adolescent we have never known and could not have imagined does very strange things, and confesses to very strange thoughts, that bring him closer in his strangeness than our own children are in their familiarity. It is in the unfathomable chase Bach leads us, so urgent that there is almost not time to space the notes, after something that will escape him with a cry if he does not hurry; but he hurries, and it is still just there. It is in the movement that is not made in a dance, because the dancer is patiently permitting the invisible to pass him. What did you think the clown was crying about? He saw perfection, and it was not in him, it was somewhere else. And did you think he was unhappy crying? No. That kind of crying is a kind of happiness.

I am pleased in that instant when I discover that I am not alone. My joy, like the discovery, is profound.

chapter seven

Work and Leisure

What kind of social structure can give all people opportunities for fulfillment in work and leisure? Can various individual needs be reconciled with the needs of society itself? The quality of the work and leisure lives of the mass of people in American society has become a "problem," because the two spheres are generally seen as irreconcilable.

The four- and three-day workweeks are management innovations which open up new leisure opportunities for the harried industrial-age worker in a postindustrial era of less lifetime toil. The shortened workweek offers more choices to the modern worker who has relatively few personal options. While Americans are fairly free to spend the money they earn, the modern industrial regime typically denies the worker similar freedom in choosing the work routine by which he earns his money. Increased recognition that people's needs and rhythm of life differ has led to the belief that individuals should be permitted to pursue work and leisure according to their individual life style regimens.

In the discretionary-time conceptualization of leisure, the fundamental values around which behavior is organized are contained within work—not leisure. The valuation of the person is structured in terms of his work performance. No important judgment of the person occurs within the context of leisure per se. This conceptualization relegates aspects of life contained within the sphere of work and leisure to the status of spare time activity. Work and leisure involve definitions which are *not* conceptually equivalent. A fallacy—defining work implicitly in terms of behavior and leisure in terms of time—usually occurs when the significant variables of each concept are interpreted by professionals and laymen. This opposition of conceptual inequivalents created no particular problem so long as there was a relative scarcity of leisure and little reason to be concerned about what it might mean if explained in terms of behavior, as work has been defined. The difficulty of interpreting work and leisure has arisen in part from the singular and rather narrow discretionary-time reference given to leisure, a byproduct of the antiquated Protestant work ethic which still dominates postindustrial society.

WORK—THE DOMINANT RHYTHM OF LIFE

The discretionary-time conception of leisure, generated during the Industrial Revolution, is rooted within traditional American culture. Leisure is viewed as unobligated time to be earned and re-earned by the worker. Work (according to the blue model; see Figure 1, Chapter 1) is the dominant rhythm of society and leisure is valued as reward for people who are gainfully employed. One cannot claim *virtuous* leisure if he has not earned it; therefore, the central focus is a steady pattern of productive work. All other aspects of social life, including family relationships, existence requirements, engagement in community and civic activity, and political, educational, and religious participation, *gain significance in their relation to the work requirements of the culture.*

The traditional work rhythm of a scarce economy required people to work long hours and to be frugal with time and money, merely to survive. As the American economy has grown from scarctiy to abundance (green model), the resulting increases in nonwork time, longer vacation, rising income, earlier retirement, less physically arduous toil, and longer life are causing a shift of the individual's central life interest to the leisure domain. The definition of leisure as recuperation, relaxation, and reward for hard work is changing with decreased emphasis on the old rhythm in which one enjoyed work and was permitted limited relaxed nonwork activity. Margaret Mead[1] states that we need to revise the discretionary concept of leisure.

> This must be a revision which will make the members of a society—where delight in high proficiency should now replace dogged willingness to work long hours for very limited rewards—able to integrate the shorter hours of work and

[1]Margaret Mead, "The Pattern of Leisure in Contemporary American Culture," *The Annals,* 313 (September 1957), p. 15.

Figure 1.   Contemporary linear-sequential life patterning.

the new engrossing home rituals into some kind of a whole in which these outmoded sequences, heritage of an age of scarcity, can be overcome.

The sequential-linear pattern of living in traditional American culture is illustrated in Figure 1. It is oriented around the mechanistic work rhythm, which forces the postponement of exhilarating moments, events, and experiences until after work, next season, or retirement; this concept is being eroded by a "freer," more permissive psychological time reference. A more natural, rhythmical, cyclical pattern of human development, involving play, education, work, and disengagement (formerly known as retirement), would conceivably allow contemporary technological man to synthesize his experiences (as suggested by the turquoise model). Instead of suffering the sequential and inevitable terminal states of human development, man would hopefully be able to allow instincts to determine when he played, worked, or relaxed.

According to Figure 2, all aspects of human endeavor, including leisure, work, and study, are recognized as blending harmoniously into a common rhythm of life, not dictated by or based solely on the organization of work.

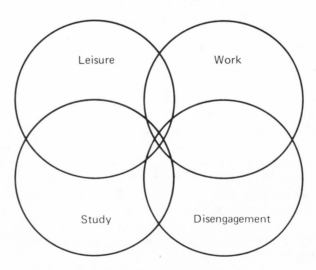

Figure 2.   Ecology of human life patterning.

Kenneth Roberts[2] notes that leisure activities are organized around the dominant work rhythm of life, and that various forms of entertainment, including theatre, television, park and community recreation programs, and spectator sports programming, are arranged to occur when the majority of the working population will be free. The nonworking population, including housewives, must gear their free time to fit the industrial work rhythm.

The way in which [free time] is distributed over time in a common rhythmic manner is one of the distinctive features of leisure in industrial societies. Specific periods occurring regularly and predictably are available for leisure and these periods occur in accordance with the dominant rhythm throughout the entire society.[3]

Outsiders. Roberts also notes that not everyone fits society's work rhythm. Leisure is not equally distributed among all members of society; although it has historically been dependent on positions and social class, the dispersion of leisure opportunities has made leisure potentially available to the mass of the working and nonworking population. However, outsiders who are cut off from the normal rhythm of life, including the unemployed, retired, ill, disabled, and those whose jobs necessitate working unusual hours, find it "difficult . . . to enjoy a normal style of leisure, thus emphasizing the extent to which the leisure of the vast majority of people is geared to a common rhythm of life."[4]

Roberts notes that enjoying leisure in contemporary society depends on having a job because, without employment, "a person's normal rhythm of life and his approach to the daily routine is undermined, and participation in normal forms of recreation and social relationships becomes impossible."[5] Howard S. Becker's study of jazz musicians[6] revealed that normal amusement and recreation were not available to them, and they had to develop a deviant style of life. Roberts suggests that people's pursuit of leisure interests differs between the working force, those people whose style of life is governed by the dominant work rhythm, and outsiders, who are for various reasons cut off from this normal rhythm.

It is becoming increasingly important to integrate outsiders into the mainstream. It is likely that the size of the group of outsiders will increase

[2]Kenneth Roberts, *Leisure* (London: Longmans Green and Co., Limited, 1970), p. 12.
[3]Ibid.
[4]Ibid.
[5]Ibid., p. 13.
[6]Howard S. Becker, *Outsiders: Studies in the Sociology of Deviance* (New York: The Free Press, 1963).

in the future, because (1) the proportion of older people in society is expected to increase (2) shift work and reduced work weeks are expected to become increasingly common, (3) acceptance of divergent subcultural groups will become more prevalent, and (4) growing alienation will frustrate people no longer gaining moral strength from the repetivitive tasks of assembly-line work.

The attitudes and values generated during leisure are carried into other social situations and influence patterns of social life. It is therefore important for social institutions to accommodate their values and structures to the leisure-based orientations of the public. The youth subculture or black subculture, for example, are the sources of values, attitudes, norms, and the basis of behavior and ideas of young people, white and black. It is increasingly important, therefore, that various social service agencies, including recreation and leisure service organizations, adjust to their life-style patterns and rhythms.

TOWARD THE WORK SOCIETY

According to Aristotle, work had a purpose outside itself (work was a means) while leisure was viewed as an end in itself. In ancient Greece and Rome work was explicitly connected with a slave class and leisure with the free classes (the elite aristocracy). In a primitive social order, work and leisure are fused, as are all institutions. In the preindustrial, feudal social order, the beginning of a work–leisure differentiation appeared—while the masses worked, elites, free from labor, engaged in intellectual pursuits. With the movement toward an industrial order the work–leisure distinction became fairly complete, with separate work–leisure roles, clothes, settings, expenditures, and the like. As American society becomes increasingly a postindustrial social order, a refusion process appears to be emerging: the work–leisure dichotomy is decreasing, and a neoprimitive synthesis of daily routine is breaking down the strict separation of work–leisure behavior. See Table 1 for a historical summary of the evolution of community life, work, and free time.

In primitive and preindustrial societies man was defined chiefly as a creature of leisure, *Homo ludens,* but with the appearance of bourgeois society in the industrialized culture, man became defined as a working being, *Homo faber,* a tool-making animal. Johan Huizinga[7] explores the play element in culture and concludes that the need to play is instinctive and that play engaged in simply for fun; it reaches beyond all moral, biological, and aesthetic considerations. *Homo faber,* in contrast was con-

---

[7]Johan Huizinga, *Homo Ludens: A Study of the Play Element in Culture* (Boston: Beacon Press, 1955).

Table 1. Transformation of culture: toward a society of leisure.

	Folk Society	Feudal Society	Industrial Society	Post-Industrial Society
Community Life	Small, isolated, non-literate, homogeneous communities with a strong sense of group solidarity. No distinction of class. Social structure is rigid. Mobility is slow and infrequent. Organic, human relationships.	Relatively large peasant population and small elite. More stratified and more heterogeneous. Small core of literate persons, priestly class. Some government apparatus. Integration of all phases of daily life for aristocracy.	Large community size and relatively dense population. Heterogeneity of people and cultures. Anonymity, transitory and impersonal relationships. Social mobility. Fluid class system, mass literacy. Predominance of secondary contracts.	Shared community decision-making based on pluralistic, cooperative relationships.
Work Life	Energies wholly oriented toward the quest for food. Little or no specialization of labor. No food surplus. People produce their own artifacts.	More occupationally differentiated than folk communities. Trade, commerce, and craft specializations well developed.	Occupational specialization, division of labor. Economy of scarcity dominated by manual labor, assembly-line work.	Economy of abundance, economic independence. Still large work force dominated by science and technology. Growing number of craftsmen and artisans characterized by individualistic, nonmachine and stylistic qualities.
Free Time	Behavior is traditional, spontaneous, spiritual, personal. Sacred prevails over secular. Leisure is part of living, condition interwoven into the main fabric of life.	Leisure available to an elite upper class, integrated into the rituals, celebrations, weddings, and day-to-day routines of the masses.	Mass leisure. Leisure a specific block of time, earned from work. Socially acceptable leisure behavior predominates.	Individualized and liberated leisure based on inherent right and specified by particular individual needs. Many personal options, diverse styles of life. Fusion of work–leisure relationships.

cerned with the Protestant work ethic, "the ethic of serving God by extreme restraint, by giving up pleasure, by constant work and the accumulation of means for spreading the material basis for work."[8] However, both conceptualizations, of man explicitly as a fun-seeking creature or a tool-maker, diminish man's characterization as *Homo sapiens*, a multidimensional being.

THE PROBLEM OF WORK AND LEISURE

The problem of leisure and the problem of work are seen as a dual dilemma. On the one hand, the quantity of leisure is increasing. On the other, continued routinization of work, application of automation in industry, reduction of physically arduous work requirements, and job compartmentalization have led to increased boredom among workers. Worker dissatisfaction is increasing; given more time off the job, workers tend to choose more income, a second job, and overtime instead of leisure. The continued development of automation and technological progress will ultimately mean that more people will choose leisure because the choice will not be dictated by economic necessity.[9] Contemporary society almost cringes at the notion of joy or pleasure, because, according to the Protestant work ethic, one should endure pain and suffering through labor. The future relationship of work and leisure, Stanley Parker suggests, should be complementary rather than one sphere of life having more value than another.

> ... experts in the various social sciences agree that both work and leisure are necessary to a healthy life and a healthy society. ... Maximum human development in both work and leisure spheres requires that they be complementary rather than that one be regarded as "good" and the other "bad."[10]

Parker cites some evidence that people who are minimally involved in their work are similarly uninvolved in their leisure, and that frustration in one area accompanies frustration in another. The antiquated work ethic has been rejected by youth and other "outsiders" who do not find the ideals and proposed means of a capitalist nation as free, self-fulfilling, and satisfying as promised. Fulfillment in both work and leisure seemingly will require a coordinated program to realize human potentialities.

[8]Jonce Josifovski, "Work and Leisure," *Society and Leisure*, 2 (1970), 11.
[9]Stanley Parker, *The Future of Work and Leisure* (New York: Praeger Publishers, Inc., 1971), p. 11.
[10]Ibid., p. 12.

The task of the worker is absurd when viewed out of context. A task has meaning only when it is related to the production of an object. Separating the task of the industrial worker from the point of completion or fulfillment has meant that much of the craftsmanship and meaning has been eliminated from work. Mass leisure pursuits, particularly various forms of mass entertainment and spectator events, also have weaned individual skill requirements, achievement, and spontaneity from experiences. In both instances, participation in modern technological society has become not a part of life, but a *means* to life, in which both working and playing are seen as things of merely extrinsic value, useful only if they permit the individual to escape the frustration and alienation of other spheres of life.

According to Leo Perlis,[11] we are faced not only with more leisure time off the job, but with a duller time on the job, and both problems require our attention.

> Assembly-line or push-button work in modern times is no great joy in itself. There is no diversity. There is no craftsmanship. There is no opportunity for achievement. There is no chance for excellence. There is only the time clock every day and the paycheck every week.
>
> There was a time when a man fulfilled himself in large part by the job he did. There are many men who still derive a sense of fulfillment from their occupation, although the complete man concept has rapidly been gaining ground so that the job no longer means as much as it once did.

ALTERNATIVE WORK–LEISURE PATTERNS

The movement from the customary five-day, forty-hour work week to a four-day, thirty-two- to thirty-six-hour work week has gained momentum during the last decade. According to J. D. Hodgson, former Secretary of Labor, the American worker during the last decade alone has gained some fifty hours a year in free time. Through a rescheduling of holidays, Hodgson claims, most of America's business and industry is already on a four-day week for 10 percent of the year.

Hodgson sees gains in leisure as a result of a reformation of our working life, attributable to (1) the five Monday holidays which provide new opportunities for the American worker to indulge in leisure-time pursuits; (2) earlier retirement, creating additional blocks of leisure for the American worker; (3) the sabbatical, which has become more extensive; and (4) shifts

---

[11]Leo Perlis, "Implications for Labor Unionism," in *Technology, Human Values and Leisure,* ed. Max Kaplan and Phillip Bosserman (Nashville, Tenn.: Abingdon Press, 1971), pp. 99–100.

in work life since the turn of the century, resulting in time free of the necessity of earning a living.[12]   Additionally, Hodgson reveals that the shift in the ratio of working hours to leisure hours has had the following effects on the average American worker: (1) it has made him more conscious of the opportunities of his leisure hours; (2) with more money in his pocket, he has become culture conscious; and (3) it has also increased the demand for professional recreation workers.[13]

The future arrangement of work and leisure may be very different from today's pattern. Phillip Bosserman[14] characterizes industrial society as one of uniformity, standaradization, and homogeneity, and the leisure (postindustrial) society as one of diversity, life styles, income, and discretionary time. Because individuals seek to be identified by their life style and cultural taste rather than by their occupations, an important shift in values and central life interests emerges in a post-scarce economy. With a renaissance of interest in the inner or affective side of life, the work order will have to promote human fulfillment as its primary conscious goal and foster an environment in which flexibility and options are available to the worker. Bosserman suggests several options which might be available to the worker, whose length of stay in any one job will decrease.[15]

Daily

½ days, 5 days a week
½ nights, 5 nights a week
2 days, 2 nights each week
3 days a week at 12 hours each day
4 days a week at 10 hours each day
Or any other combination, depending on the job and the employee.

Weekly

3 weeks each month
6 weeks on and 3 weeks off at 40 hours each week
Or any other combination, again depending on the nature of the work and the personal needs of the employee. Actualization is the goal.

Monthly

6 months on and 6 months off
3 months on and 3 months off
2 months on and 2 months off
8 months on and 8 months off
Any combination would be feasible, again considering the job.

[12]J. D. Hodgson, "Leisure and the American Worker," *Leisure Today*, 1 (1972).
[13]Ibid.
[14]Phillip Bosserman, "Implications for Youth," in *Technology, Human Values and Leisure*, ed. Kaplan and Bosserman, pp. 117–63.
[15]Ibid., pp. 162–63.

Yearly

2 years on and ½ year off
5 years on and one year off
Again, any combination is conceivable.

It is the task of society . . . not to impose a pattern of social relationships on the individual but to offer him a set of alternatives.[16]

MEANING OF THE FOUR-DAY WORK WEEK

Riva Poor and James L. Steele report the findings of twenty-seven business firms which converted to the four-day work week.[17] The social innovation of the four-day work week is considered an important step toward greater leisure and less lifetime toil.

Many manufacturers who have adopted the shorter work week cite recruitment as a factor; the theory is that a company which offers a three-day weekend should be a better place to be employed. Increase in efficiency has accompanied the adoption of the four-day week. Tardiness and absenteeism have been reduced, and increased productivity has generally also been achieved.

The four-day work pattern seems to offer new choices to the modern worker, who has relatively few personal options.

Poor and Steele reveal that the shortened work week allows "bunching" of leisure, opening up new leisure opportunities over the extended weekend. Spending, recuperation, and yard work have increased with the longer weekend.

The long-range benefits of automation and the four-day work week appear to be more creative and service-oriented outlets for workers' energies, because of the lower proportion of their free time needed to recuperate from work. More free time will theoretically mean that workers can acquire the skills necessary for engaging in participant activities, resulting in a decrease of time spent in spectator activities.

Increased free time is an important commodity for nonskilled workers who find it difficult to realize achievement and recognition at their work. Leisure outlets provide an opportunity for them to justify their existence and give meaning to their lives.

[16]Parker, *The Future of Work and Leisure,* p. 117.

[17]Riva Poor and James L. Steele, "Work and Leisure: The Reactions of People at 4-Day Firms," *4 Days, 40 Hours: Reporting a Revolution in Work and Leisure* (New York: New American Library, 1973), pp. 105–22.

THE INTEGRATION OF WORK AND LEISURE

As work becomes a less central life interest for many industrial workers, leisure and related family activities are emerging as the prime life interest. Parker has articulated this trend in an integrated, holistic (turquoise) philosophical premise of work–leisure relationships (see Table 2).

An individual, the parts of whose life are integrated, in that each aspect of his life affects and is affected by the others, has a work–leisure relationship characterized by an *ecological-holistic* configuration. "Extension of work into leisure (and vice versa) in the life of the person is paralleled by fusion of work and leisure spheres in the society as a whole."[18] On the other hand, a person who views the parts of his life as distinct segments relatively unaffected by each other is characterized by one of two types of segmentalist work–leisure relationships. A *contrasting* or *oppositional* leisure pattern of activity is deliberately unlike work, with a sharp distinction between what is work and what is leisure—a *polarized* work–leisure relationship. A *neutrality* pattern of work and leisure recognizes that each is generally different from the other and is fairly self-contained.

According to Parker's model,[19] work–leisure relationships may be interpreted at the individual level. Successful businessmen, doctors, teachers, and craft workers are characterized as embracing the holistic-extension work–leisure relationship. Minor professionals other than social workers embrace the separate-neutrality work–leisure relationship. Finally, unskilled manual workers, assembly-line workers, and so on are characterized by a contrast-opposition work–leisure relationship.

The holistic-integrated conceptualization of work and leisure is an attempt to maximize leisure but to fuse it with a uniquely satisfying form of work. According to Parker:

Table 2. The connection between philosophies and work-leisure relationships.

Philosophy	Work-Leisure Relationship
Holism	Identity
Segmentalism	{ Contrast { Separateness

From Stanley R. Parker, *The Future of Work and Leisure* (New York: Praeger Publishers, Inc., and London: MacGibbon and Kee, Ltd., 1970, p. 109).

[18]Parker, *The Future of Work and Leisure,* p. 102.
[19]Ibid., p. 109.

In this fusion, work may lose its present characteristic feature of constraint and gain creativity now associated mainly with leisure, while leisure may lose its present characteristic feature of opposition to work and gain the status—now associated mainly with the *product* of work—of a resource worthy of planning to provide the greatest possible human satisfaction.[20]

Essentially, segmentalists view work and leisure as separate, contrasting, and conceivably oppositional compartments of life, while holists see an interrelationship between work and leisure. The chief barrier to a closer integration of work and leisure is society's preoccupation with production at the expense of other values, and the traditional individual preference for more income at the expense of more leisure. "The central problem, then, is not one of maximizing some values (i.e. those associated with leisure) and minimizing others (associated with work) but of achieving an integration of both sets of values."[21]

While work is losing its significance for a growing number of alienated people, its absence would be severely felt by most people who are presently employed. Society has not provided the worker with a moral sanction which will embrace nonwork activity. Since goods in a surplus economy are generated primarily to stimulate increased material purchasing, standards of work, craftsmanship, morale, inventiveness, and purpose have been eliminated from the contemporary work scene. In an advanced technological society it becomes increasingly important for the *affective* or emotional aspects of life to be built into everyday life to overcome the rational, objective, efficiently productive work cycle, which provides little emotional gratification. The movement toward the four-day work week is seen by some economists and leisure-policy planners as a rare opportunity for the American worker to free himself from his humdrum existence and discover new forms of experience which he is free to choose.

[20]Ibid., p. 122.
[21]Ibid., p. 138.

the influence of leisure upon work

KENNETH ROBERTS

In nearly all the studies that have investigated the connections between work and leisure it has been implicitly assumed that if these two areas of life are related it is because work exercises an influence upon the way in which people spend their free time. This implicit assumption needs to be made explicit and openly questioned because today there are strong grounds for arguing that leisure exercises a reciprocal influence upon the nature of people's working lives.

In the nineteenth century, when extremely long hours of work in industry for six days per week throughout the year were normal, it may have been reasonable to treat work as the major determinant of an individual's total style of life. Marx viewed time spent off the job in a capitalist economy purely as a means whereby the supply of human fodder that fed the capitalist system could be maintained in working order, and such a concept of the relationship between work and leisure may have been justifiable in the nineteenth century. But today it is worth questioning whether work is still the dominant element that determines the style of people's lives. As the working population has won freedom from long hours of work for itself, and as rising standards of living have made it possible for people to use their free time in a variety of ways in accordance with their own personal interests, it may well be that the influence of work over how people use their leisure has declined, and it is even possible that styles of life, attitudes and interests that are based upon leisure may be exercising an influence upon industry itself.

Take the issue of the general rhythm of life in our society into which leisure is slotted. This rhythm of life has to be based around the needs of an industrial economy for people to be available for work at specific and predictable times, and it might therefore be inferred that it is the economic

From Kenneth Roberts, *Leisure,* by permission of Humanities Press, Inc., New York, and Longman Group Limited.

system that determines the rhythm of life and therefore the distribution of the leisure time that people enjoy. In the nineteenth century, when hours of work left the working population with few opportunities to develop leisure interests and pursuits, it would have been reasonable to regard the developing industrial system as the main factor that dictated the rhythm of life. But as the time available for leisure has progressively increased, society has been able to choose how to apportion out this newly-created leisure. There are many alternative ways in which additional spare time can be distributed. It could be used to give people longer annual vacations, or to make earlier retirement possible, or to provide more days off in a normal working week, or to reduce the number of hours in the normal working day. The actual form in which the leisure that has become available during this century has been taken has been determined to a large extent by the way in which the working population has preferred to have its spare time distributed. In negotiations with employers at both national and local levels the labour force is able to decide for itself how its hours of work should be reduced in order to structure its leisure time in the manner considered most desirable. The rhythm of life in a society such as ours has to be consistent with the needs of industry, but there are various ways in which this consistency could be achieved, and as the working population has progressively won more and more free time for itself the rhythm of the working life has become increasingly determined by the style of leisure that people have wished to cultivate. The rhythm of life and leisure is no longer determined solely by the demands of the economy, and to explain the rhythm of life that has developed during the twentieth century it is really necessary to pose questions about the way in which the population's leisure interests have influenced the type of working life that has become normal.

This is just one way in which, from originally being determined by work, leisure has gained considerable autonomy from the influence of employment and has itself begun to influence industrial behaviour. In recent years several industrial sociologists have come to the conclusion that it is necessary to refer to the styles of life and attitudes that employees have developed outside the workplace in order to explain the ways in which they behave and react at work. That such conclusions should have been drawn from investigations whose main concern was to explain work behaviour and attitudes is an indication of the recognition that is now being extended to the possibility of leisure influencing the structure and functioning of industry. One example of an investigation conducted in industry which led to such a conclusion is the study of the job attitudes of workers in an Australian factory from which Lafitte[1] concluded that

---

[1] Lafitte, *Social Structure and Personality in the Factory*, Routledge, 1958.

whether or not employees were satisfied with their jobs and conditions of work could only be explained in terms of expectations learned in the outside community. The different ways in which the employees studied reacted to work were quite inexplicable in terms of the characteristics of the jobs themselves. Miller and Form[2] come to similar conclusions about the extent to which work behaviour and attitudes are influenced by factors outside the work situation. In examining the available data on the career patterns of the members of the labour force in America, they noted that as individuals matured into adulthood their careers tended to become increasingly stable; job-changing declined and in particular, people became less likely to make switches in the direction of their careers into completely new types of occupations. Many of the reasons Miller and Form gave to explain why this settling-down should take place as people progress into adulthood concerned the roles that people play in society outside the workplace. As people grow into adulthood they normally assume family responsibilities. They also often sink social roots in the communities where they are living, forming personal friendships and becoming involved in clubs and associations. In order to maintain the responsibilities and the styles of life that they have developed during their free time people will seek security and stability in employment. In Miller and Form's view the manner in which careers become increasingly stable as people grow older is only fully explicable in terms of the way in which the patterns of life that they develop outside the workplace lead to new demands being made upon employment.

Perhaps the piece of industrial research that has placed the greatest emphasis upon the extent to which industrial behaviour and attitudes are influenced by the sort of lives people wish to lead in their free time is Goldthorpe's[3] study of *The Affluent Worker*. This British study was intended to present a picture of the type of employee who might become typical in the future as the labour force as a whole becomes more affluent, for the workers selected for study all earned incomes in excess of the national average at the time of the investigation. Goldthorpe and his colleagues found that their sample of workers possessed a predominantly instrumental approach to their jobs. They worked in order to be able to realize a particular style of life that they considered desirable. Many of them had chosen their jobs principally because of the high rates of pay and considerations such as the nature of the work itself were not felt to be important. How satisfied the workers were with their jobs was virtually unrelated to how interesting they found the work itself. The sort of work

[2]D. C. Miller and W. H. Form, *Industrial Sociology: The Sociology of Work Organisations*, New York, Harper and Row, 1964.

[3]J. H. Goldthorpe *et al.*, *The Affluent Worker: Industrial Attitudes and Behaviour*, Cambridge University Press, 1968.

they had chosen to do, and the way in which they reacted to it, were only comprehensible in terms of aspirations acquired outside the workplace, based upon a desire to be able to spend free time and money in particular ways.

These conclusions about the influence of leisure upon work are interesting because they have been drawn by industrial sociologists whose major concern has been to explain the attitudes and behaviour of people in employment. Industrial sociology has traditionally been based upon the study of industrial organizations and work-groups, and factors outside the work environment have only been resorted to in attempts to explain industrial behaviour because variables within the work situation itself have proved inadequate for such purposes. Some sociologists who have been primarily concerned with understanding the role of leisure in contemporary society have been even more definitive in their conclusions about the extent to which leisure influences work. Nels Anderson[4] has argued that, from being an unintended by-product of industrialism, created by the unforeseen productive power and prosperity that industrialism eventually unleashed, leisure has emerged to become the focal element in people's lives. The expansion of leisure, creating new opportunities for people to develop interests according to their own inclinations, combined with the meaningless nature of many industrial occupations, has led people to centre their lives upon their leisure. Historically leisure was created by industry, but today, Anderson argues, it is leisure that imparts a meaning to work for the bulk of the industrial population. People work in order to be able to do desirable things in their leisure time, and it is this instrumental role which has come to give work a meaning in people's leisure-based lives.

Dumazedier[5] has developed this line of argument still further. Upon the basis of investigations undertaken in France he alleges today, rather than their leisure being determined by the types of jobs that they do, people choose a job that will enable them to enjoy the type of leisure that they want. Dumazedier argues that decisions such as where to work will be taken with an eye on the scope of the leisure facilities available in a particular district. He asserts that leisure is so central in the life of modern man that industry is being obliged to adapt its own structure to accommodate leisure values. People wish to work in a pleasant environment; they will be attracted to firms that offer recreational facilities among the fringe benefits of employment; they insist that relationships within a firm should be agreeable and friendly; and they will demand a leisurely atmosphere to be provided by innovations such as 'music while you work'. It has traditionally been the practice to note the extent to which leisure is permeated

[4]N. Anderson, *Work and Leisure,* Routledge, 1967.
[5]Dumazedier, *Towards a Society of Leisure,* Collier-Macmillan, 1967.

by the values of industrialism. Commentators upon leisure in industrial societies have often observed the extent to which values such as competitiveness and orderliness have affected patterns of recreation. Today the accent is changing to stress the extent to which industry is being permeated by leisure values. Aspirations concerned with leisure activities and attitudes generated during leisure are carried by individuals into industrial life, and business organizations are obliged to modify their structures and methods of operation in order to accommodate the leisure-centredness of their employees' lives.

The evidence offered to substantiate claims such as these about the pervasive influence of leisure is far from totally conclusive and the views expressed by sociologists such as Dumazedier should be treated as hypotheses requiring further investigation rather than as definite conclusions. Nevertheless, they are hypotheses, the validity of which deserves to be explored for the implications of these views, not only for the sociology of leisure, but for all sociologists who are concerned with the inter-relationships between the institutions within modern industrial society, are considerable.

The inter-relationships between work and leisure in modern society are extremely complex and defining them can no longer be interpreted as a problem of simply determining the effects of occupational status upon the uses to which people put their free time. Whether it is the status accorded to a job or some other characteristic that an occupation possesses which has the most significant influence upon the leisure activities that people adopt is still uncertain; the extent to which leisure is compartmentalized off from the influence of work has still to be accurately determined; and the ways in which leisure may be influencing the working lives of the members of society have yet to be explored. The complexity of this problem of the relationship between work and leisure is matched only by its importance, for it is this relationship that sets the rhythm and style of contemporary life.

work and leisure:
the reactions of people
at 4-day firms

RIVA POOR and
JAMES L. STEELE

In 1899 Thorstein Veblen published his classic work, *The Theory of the Leisure Class,* in which he examined the life style of the upper class. At that time only the wealthy could afford leisure, but this is no longer so! The shorter workweek that has developed over the past 100 years has had the important social and economic consequence of transforming the working class into a new leisure class. The 4-day workweek further enhances the leisure available to the new leisure class by regrouping many of the hours into a 3-day weekend.

One objective of this study was to find out how employees react to this new leisure and to the companies that provide it. Other purposes included an examination of the effects of the 4-day workweek upon managers, upon employee spending patterns, and upon patterns of use of leisure. In short, what difference does the 4-day week make to people's lives, and how do they feel about it?

This study of people at thirteen 4-day firms was conducted in July and August, 1970, through the use of personal interviews (tape recorded, in some cases) and a survey questionnaire (included at the end of this article). The findings confirm and add detail to many of the observations made in previous chapters. Also, the fact that it was an intensive study lends increased credibility to the general proposition reported throughout this book that the 4-day workweek is working well at most places.

The responses of 168 people (including 20 managers) show that the 4-day week has been well received by both labor and management. As

"Work and Leisure: The Reactions of People at 4-Day Firms," by Riva Poor and James L. Steele. From *4 Days, 40 Hours: Reporting a Revolution in Work and Leisure* (New York: The New American Library, Inc., 1973).

noted in several of the previous chapters, managers report that it aids recruitment, cuts down absenteeism and tardiness, practically eliminates turnover, and, in general, results in improved company morale. Workers are delighted with the long weekends and the increased time available for family, travel, and many new activities.

While some report disadvantages, the employees of 4-day firms clearly feel that the advantages far outweigh the disadvantages. One hundred and thirty-six of 148 workers report they feel either pleased or very pleased about the 4-day week. Only 12 report feeling very displeased (2), displeased (5), or indifferent (5).

This high positive proportion (over 92%), like many of the other results reported in this study, is well above the 67% that we can normally expect from the introduction of almost any attempted improvement, regardless of type (The Hawthorne Effect).

Every manager interviewed in this study was pleased (2) or very pleased (18) with the way the 4-day week is working out for him and for his company. When one looks at what the 4-day week is producing for the companies, it is not amazing that so many managers are so pleased. . . .

THE SAMPLE

Managers constitute 12% of the sample. All are males, almost all are 30 years old or over (9 are 40 or over), and 4 are new at their firms. Because the managers' responses are different from the workers' responses in most cases—more positive and more company-oriented—we report their attitudes separately to avoid obscuring the workers' responses.

Workers constitute 88% of the sample (148 people). Fifty-seven per cent are males (84 males and 64 females). Twenty-eight per cent are under 30 years old (41 people)—one third of the males (27) and one fourth of the females (14). About 30% of the workers joined their firms after 4-day began (44 workers). Sixteen are females (11 under 30 years old) and 28 are males (9 under 30).

The 6 supervisors and foremen (2 females) are counted among the workers, because their responses to the questionnaire are more typical of the workers' responses than of the managers'. Almost all of the workers are factory personnel, but there are several each of office, sales, and professional personnel (e.g., quality control).

The firms include manufacturing, service, and retail businesses—3 of them unionized. Most are located in the greater Boston area, but a few are outside the area, in California, Florida, and Oklahoma.

Whether the responses of this sample are typical of those of the rest of the 4-day workers, we cannot discern. They probably are, though, because they match the responses reported by the managers, in other chapters, and by the other authors who interviewed workers for their chapters. The proportions of male and female workers, types of jobs, and so on, are similar. The 13 firms were selected because they were the ones we knew existed at the beginning of the study. (We discovered the other 4-day firms too late to add them to the study.) Almost 700 workers were given a written questionnaire, and received post-paid envelopes so their responses could be sent directly to us. A little over 100 sent their responses in time to be used in the study.

ADVANTAGES AND DISADVANTAGES
FOR COMPANIES

Greater commitment to the company.   One of the greatest benefits for the 4-day firms is an improvement in employees' attitudes towards the firm. Table 1 shows that only 5 of the workers like their company "less" after beginning 4-day, out of 100 workers answering the question. But 46 state they like their company "more." This positive change in attitude may be enough to make any manager ponder the feasibility of the 4-day week.

Both younger and older employees like their company more, although liking the company more is slightly more prevalent among younger workers. Fifty per cent of workers under 30 say they like their company more, and none likes it less, compared with workers over 30—45% like their firms more, but 5% like them less now. Older workers, or workers who have been with a company for a number of years, tend to report liking the company the same. It was a common thing to hear them say in an interview: "I like the company the same—I've been working here for 15 years.

Table 1.   Many workers report liking their company more on the 4-day week.

	Number of Respondents		
Attitudes	*Male*	*Female*	*Total*
"I like the company *more* now than I did when we were on 5 days."	25	21	46
"I like the company *the same* now as I did when we were on 5 days."	26	23	49
"I like the company *less* now than I did when we were on 5 days."	1	4[*]	5
Totals	52	48	100

[*]All factory workers over 40 years old, employed by one firm on a 10-hour-a-day schedule.

I like the 4-day week, but I like the company the same—it's a good company."

The responses of male and female workers are different only in that 4 of the 5 workers who like the firm less now are females. (It should be noted that they all work at the same firm.)

Do the managers recognize accurately how their employees feel about the 4-day week? The managers happily report that the attitude of workers towards their work is better than before 4-day, and that the general morale of the firm is excellent. In a company where there is no basis for comparison (because the firm *began* operations on 4-day) and in 2 companies where managers state that employee attitudes and morale are the same (always excellent), the survey shows that the attitudes and morale of workers is, in fact, very good. In only one firm did the manager's report of employee attitudes overestimate the satisfaction of his workers; this manager reported that the workers were 100% in favor of 4-day, but the actual responses in a sample of 33 out of a few hundred workers and managers show that 25 are pleased, 4 are indifferent, and 4 are displeased. In every other company, the managers either were correct or slightly underestimated the satisfaction of their workers with the 4-day week.

One should recognize that the positive attitude of workers towards the company may reflect a stronger commitment to their 4-day *job*, rather than their 4-day *company*. Our statistics do not make this distinction for us. One worker who says she likes her company more now also states that she probably would quit "if they ever go back to 5 days." The comment may mean she is committed to the job itself, as opposed to the firm. If 4-day jobs were plentiful, and she could choose among 4-day companies, her commitment to the company might diminish or be based on something other than the 4-day workweek. As one manager said: "If all companies did it, we wouldn't have an advantage."

Aids worker recruitment.   Certainly, until the 4-day workweek is a common phenomenon in American industry, the company that operates on a 4-day schedule has an important advantage in the competition for workers. Table 2 shows that increased leisure as a form of payment is very attractive to workers. This point is demonstrated by the fact that a little more than 3 out of 4 new workers joining firms already on 4-day indicate: "The 4-day week was a very important reason for my joining this firm." Fewer than 1 out of 4 says that it had little to do with their joining, and not even one worker says that the 4-day week is a disadvantage.

Of the 44 new employees who responded to this question, 16 are females and 20 are under 30 years of age. Of the females, 13 out of 16 state the 4-day week was an important reason for joining the firm (81% compared to 67% of the males). Several women say they returned to work because the 4-day week gives them more time at home for family and housework. Of the group under 30 years old, 16 out of 20 say 4-day was

Table 2. Most new workers state that 4-day was a very important reason for their joining the firm, and none says 4-day was a disadvantage.

	Number of Respondents		
Attitudes	Male	Female	Total
"The 4-day week was a *very important* reason for my joining this firm."	21	13	34
"The 4-day week had *little* to do with my joining this firm."	7	3	10
"The 4-day week was a *disadvantage* in joining this firm."	0	0	0
Totals	28	16	44

important to their decision (80%, compared to 75% for the over-30 group). The long weekend is the most attractive feature of the 4-day week for this group.

Three of the 4 new managers say 4-day was important to their joining. Seven of 16 continuing managers say they like the firm more now, and none of the managers like it less than before although in some cases they have some inconveniences on the new schedule. Ten managers indicate that recruitment is now easier, 2 find it to be the same as on 5-day, and the other has no basis for comparison because they always had 4-day. Together, these facts illustrate that the 4-day week is a boon to companies that find it difficult to compete in the labor market.

Disadvantages for the company. The disadvantages of the 4-day week are hard to find. Ten of the 20 managers mention no disadvantages for themselves nor for their company. A few managers mention problems with work scheduling, particularly when 4-day is first implemented, or recount difficulties they had educating customers to the fact that they simply would not be open on Fridays, for instance.

Some managers report having to pay for more overtime work now, but they say it with a smile. As one manager put it: "Anybody knows that if you've got the orders and you need to work your people overtime, you can afford to pay them." And an important advantage of the 4-day schedule is that it provides an *extra* day for overtime when it is needed.

MOONLIGHTING AND OVERTIME

Moonlighting interests many managers. To some companies it is an advantage, and to some a disadvantage. One manager remarked: "If they are caught, they are fired. It takes too much out of them." At other companies moonlighting is positively encouraged. For example, men who work the night shift at one company are permitted to work a day shift as well if they desire—at a guaranteed salary of $200 per week per shift. Despite the differences in managements' attitudes, we found no significant difference in the incidence of moonlighting at firms that oppose it and those that encourage it.

Second-job holders in American industry usually number about 5% of the labor force. A comparable percentage of the 4-day workers (4%) state they held a second job during the 5-day workweek. But the figure more than quadrupled when workers began the 4-day week. Twenty-five out of 141 of the respondents (17%) indicate that they now hold more than one job. There is reason to suspect that even this high figure does not accurately report the prevalence of moonlighting among 4-day workers. One manager states he would be surprised if fewer than 25% of his workers have second jobs. And when workers were asked in interviews about the moonlighting of fellow workers, their responses always suggested a higher number of second-job holders than indicated in the questionnaire survey.

Moonlighting is more prevalent among male workers (20% of the males moonlight on 4-day), but it increased among the females too. While only 2 females report moonlighting on the 5-day week, 6 of 64 report moonlighting on 4-day, a jump from 3 to 10%—5 times higher than the national average for women on 5-day (2%).

The form that moonlighting takes among 4-day workers is varied. In addition to extra shift work, some companies provide their employees with the opportunity for extensive overtime, ranging as high as 20 hours a week. Many workers consider this an important advantage of 4-day. Some have similar jobs at other firms, a few have their own businesses (especially, farms), and others serve as part-time policemen or firemen.

What is the relationship between the 4-day workweek and moonlighting? Although there are problems of defining moonlighting, gathering accurate data, and isolating the many variables at work, it is evident that the 4-day week contributes significantly to moonlighting. But Professor Paul Mott points out that while the shorter workweek is a major factor in contributing to the prevalence of moonlighting in our society, other factors are important too, such as, the presence of shift work in the community, high economic aspirations of the workers, and inadequate opportunities in the community to exercise free time. Especially important, we think, is his statement "the worker must have adequate physical energy and the appropriate psychological traits if he is to be a successful moonlighter."[1] Since

---

[1]Paul E. Mott, "Hours of Work and Moonlighting," in Clyde E. Dankert, *et. al.* (eds.), *Hours of Work* (New York: Harper and Row, 1965), p. 76–94.

no pay cuts are involved and no other factor emerges to correlate with moonlighting, it appears that 4-day itself makes these attributes *operative* in an additional set of people, amounting to over 13% of our sample. The implication, too, is that the longer days of the 4-day schedule are not unduly fatiguing for many workers, including females—in fact, quite the reverse.

The long-range effect of 4-day on moonlighting is difficult to predict. The increased spending reported below could lead to increased moonlighting. At any rate, at present, about 80% of 4-day workers use their new time for leisure, rather than to gain additional income!

ADVANTAGES AND DISADVANTAGES
FOR EMPLOYEES

Bunching of leisure. The workers are overwhelmingly pleased with the 4-day workweek although there is a slight, but definite difference between male and female reactions. Although most men and women have positive responses to 4-day, more men report a greater degree of satisfaction from 4-day. Of the 96% men pleased or very pleased about 4-day, 82% are *very* pleased; of the 92% of women pleased or very pleased, only 75% are *very* pleased.

Worker satisfaction with 4-day stems primarily from the leisure advantages it offers, rather than from the longer hours of labor on the job each day. Most workers are delighted with the bunching of their free time, inasmuch as it makes the leisure hours more useful for old and new activities. The most frequent response to the open-ended question, "Please name one or more advantages . . . to the 4-day week," is simply "the long weekend!" Others state that they like the extra time it gives them with their families, and some say that it provides a weekday for conducting personal business, such as keeping appointments with doctor or dentist, or going to the bank. A number of women say they like 4-day because it gives them an extra day for housework while still leaving them a 2-day weekend. (This may explain why the women are somewhat less enthusiastic than the men—most of them work second jobs at home.) Table 3 shows the frequency with which advantages and disadvantages are cited by the 4-day workers.

Little negative reaction. Eighty-seven of the 141 labor respondents cite no disadvantages, reporting advantages only. Forty-six cite both advantages and disadvantages, and only 8 report no advantages. Although it is the older workers who have all but one of the negative reactions to 4-day (one worker under 30 says he is indifferent to it), oddly enough it is the

Table 3. The workers cite many more advantages of the 4-day week than disadvantages.

Advantages and Disadvantages	Number of Citations[*]
Advantages	
Long weekend or more leisure	65
More time for family	
(excludes travel to relatives)	25
More time for personal business and errands	14
More time for housework	11
More overtime	11
More time to putter around house or garden	9
More time for travel	
(includes visits to relatives)	8
More time for shopping	4
Miscellaneous reasons	13
Total	160
Disadvantages	
Longer day is fatiguing	23
Loss of former job or pay benefits[**]	
(includes loss of overtime)	11
Longer day disaccommodates meals, car	
pools, or other schedules	5
Work load is high on the day after the weekend	3
Miscellaneous reasons	9
Total	51

[*]87 of the 141 respondents (59%) cite advantages only, while 8 respondents (5%) cite disadvantages only.
[**]The bonus system imposes a large penalty on those who are late or absent from work without a bona fide excuse.

older workers who report the fewest disadvantages. Almost 65% cite no disadvantages at all, compared to 54% of the younger group.

The disadvantages mentioned most frequently are "longer hours per day" and "too little rest time during the day." Managers and foremen also mention having to work harder the first day after the weekend. One manager interviewed on a Monday morning pointed to a large stack of mail and remarked: "This is what Monday is like on the 4-day week!"

One significant factor bears mentioning again. Most of the negative attitudes towards the 4-day week are reported by workers of a single company. The reasons for this negative feeling are varied. It reflects discontent with the bonus system which has the effect of a rate cut for those who are late or absent without an important excuse. It also reflects some disapproval of the shift system employed by the company and the manner in which overtime is arranged. It is only fair to point out, however, that 75% of the respondents from this company state they are pleased with 4-day, and also our sample from the company is small.

Some writers have suggested that with increased free time the average worker would be troubled by boredom. This study indicates otherwise. Only 6 out of 168 people report being bored with free time. (Four are males, one is a manager, and none is under 30 years old.) In contrast, 2 report they were bored on 5-day. With the arrival of 4-day, one got a second job and is no longer bored. The discussion (below) of workers' activities during their new free time indicates that most workers do not experience a problem in finding new outlets for their time and energies on 4-day. Whether they would be bored on an even shorter week is a different issue.

Adjustment problems. In an attempt to learn if the *transition* from a 5-day workweek to a 4-day workweek presents problems for the workers and managers, they were asked if there were problems in adjusting to the 4-day week and, if there were, to give an example. Of 142 labor respondents, only 37 state they experienced adjustment problems. The problem mentioned by nearly half of these workers is "longer hours," but several add that this was just "in the beginning." Some mention that they had to adjust to standing on their feet extra time, but one worker volunteers "O.K. now!"

Female workers report more adjustment problems than male workers; 23 of 61 female workers answering the question (38%) say there were problems in adjusting to 4-day, and 14 of 81 male workers (17%) indicate adjustment problems. But these are the females over 30 years old. Of the workers under 30, 73% report to adjustment problems (the same for females as males). Only 15% of the older males report adjustment problems, while 40% of the older females report problems, and 35% of the managers (7 out of 20) do so as well. It seems that the problems are more related to a person's functions and responsibilities than to age or sex alone.

The thing that stands out is that most adjustment problems are experienced early in the transition and tend to disappear with time while, most importantly, most workers report no adjustment problems at all (74%). Adjustment problems occur primarily with the more strenuous jobs and at the firms that schedule the longest workdays (10 hours, rather than 9½ or 9 hours).

Fatigue. Fourteen per cent of the employees (about ½ male, ½ female) cite fatigue as a disadvantage of the 4-day workweek—which generally has a longer workday. But despite citing fatigue as a drawback, almost every one of the 23 employees is pleased or very pleased with 4-day. Also, as mentioned above, 19 additional employees obtained second jobs after 4-day started, an increase of moonlighters from 4 to 17% of the work force.

It appears that fatigue from the longer workday—which might be expected to be a big problem—is not a big problem for almost all of the workers. Why? For one thing, the new workday is not much longer than before, while the total hours in the workweek is now somewhat reduced.

Secondly, morale is now higher. But perhaps most important, the weekend is now 50% longer.

The difference that a longer weekend makes may be explained by a look at the problems found with the shorter weekend of the 5-day week. The following is from an article headed "Five-day Workweek Too Long, Study Claims" (*Boston Sunday Globe,* August 23, 1970):

Associated Press

> OSLO, Norway—A Norwegian medical study says the 5-day week fails to provide a relaxing weekend, and people need longer vacations. . . .
>
> The study [by a medical association committee] quotes an expert on leisure as saying: "Medically viewed, the five-day week is meaningless, even absurd. It is injurious to health."
>
> The committee chairman, Odd Bjerke, observed: "In a [two-day] weekend people don't get the relaxation they need. The rush to use the leisure hours produces a stress situation like the rest of the week."

It appears that the 4-day workweek's longer weekend more than makes up for whatever additional fatigue, if any, that may result from its usually longer workday.

Employee evaluation.   With all its advantages and disadvantages, its problems in adjusting, and the changes it causes in the everyday lives of the workers, the 4-day workweek is appreciated more *after* experience with it than before. This is seen in the change in the workers' opinions between the time they first heard about 4-day and after they have had experience with it.

Eighty-nine per cent of the workers (125 out of 141) say they favored the 4-day week initially. Ninety-seven per cent of this group (121 out of 125) indicate they are pleased or very pleased *after* working the 4-day week. Only 1 person reports being indifferent and only 3 say they are displeased. (One complains: "Now I get home too late at night to have supper with my family after 9½ hours a day.")

Of the 16 people who report that they did *not* favor the 4-day week initially, 8 say they are pleased or very pleased now, and 2 report they are indifferent. Five continue to be displeased and 1 gives no opinion. In short, acceptance of 4-day is a little higher after experience with it than before it has been tried—92% favor 4-day afterwards, compared with 89% beforehand. (Managers' attitudes are omitted here since they are all in favor of 4-day both before and after experience with it.)

While these statistics indicate a very favorable attitude towards 4-day, they certainly do not convey the enthusiasm that 4-day workers express in conversation. An example of this enthusiasm is expressed by one excited young worker who said in an interview: "The 4-day week has been the turning point in the life of my family. Why, it almost made a Christian out of me! I used to go to the tavern every Friday after work, but now I've stopped drinking and smoking—and I spend the weekends with my family. I take care of the kids on Fridays now, and give the wife a chance to go shopping. Then on Saturdays, we go camping. I was a Green Beret in the Army, and I like to teach the kids woodlore and that kind of stuff. . . . The 4-day week is great, man!"

That the 4-day week *is* very important to most 4-day workers is clearly seen by the positive responses of both males and females, regardless of age. As one manager put it: "You probably couldn't get this high a percentage of our workers to agree on anything else. But they like the 4-day week!"

CHANGES IN PEOPLES' LIVES

New spending patterns. During the pilot interviews with workers it was discovered that many were spending more money since beginning the 4-day week. In an effort to discover how widespread was the increase in spending, employees were asked: "Do you find that you are spending more money for free-time activities since you began the 4-day week?" One third of the workers (44 of 137) replied "yes." One worker says that the problem became so severe for his family that he and his wife "had to sit down and talk it over." They began to plan their activities in order to keep their spending within limits.

In his case the increased spending resulted from too many weekend trips, but other items are mentioned by other workers. Increased spending for recreation in general is the item mentioned most frequently. Traveling is cited often, as are such things as eating out, going to the beach, boating, dating, and shopping. Nine people purchased vacation homes. This figure appears very high considering that most have experienced 4-day for less than a year.

Although two thirds of the workers do not report increased spending, it seems likely that the *patterns* of spending for almost all employees are now changed somewhat, because most report spending their *time* differently (reported in the next section).

Increased spending seems to be some function of age. None of the 6 respondents over 60 years of age reports increased spending, but one fourth of those 30 to 50 years old report increased spending, 40% of those under 30 report increased spending, and 60% of those 50 to 60 years old spend more (mostly, the men). Spending is also a function of income level: 65% of the managers say they spend more money now.

Changes in leisure activities.   One way in which the 4-day workweek is effecting changes in the lives and the spending habits of workers is seen in the ways workers use their increased free time. The workers were asked to indicate on a checklist both those activities in which they regularly participated when they worked a 5-day week and also the activities in which they participate regularly during the 4-day week. All free-time activities increase with the increase in usable leisure time that comes with its regrouping. The results are shown in Table 4.

One important leisure activity for workers is recuperation. Nearly 70% of the workers say they spend some of their new free time resting, relaxing,

Table 4.   All leisure activities increase when the same employees go from 5-day to 4-day workweeks.

Activities	Numbers			
				Per Cent
	Cited on 5-Day	Cited on 4-Day	Increase on 4-Day	Increase on 4-Day
1. Work around the house	94	116	22	23
2. Spend time with family	76	102	26	34
3. Travel	29	73	44	152
4. Go to ballgames, fights, hockey games, etc.	19	38	19	100
5. Fishing and hunting	22	43	21	95
6. Other hobbies	22	49	27	123
7. Engage in some form of athletics (bowling, golf, baseball, etc.)	26	43	17	65
8. Read more	16	41	25	156
9. Go back to school or learned a trade	7	8	1	14
10. Active in school boards, P.T.A., Boy Scouts, etc.	9	14	5	56
11. Got another part time job	5	24	19	283
12. Joined social club	6	11	5	83
13. Engaged in political action work	2	6	4	200
14. Rest, relax, loaf, etc.	26	96	70	269
15. Swimming, boating	16	67	51	319
16. Work on car	17	39	22	129
17. Church activities	9	14	5	56
18. Bought or buying vacation home	2	6	4	200
19. Bored with free time	2	5	3	150
20. Visit relatives	28	62	34	121
21. Watch television a lot	27	44	17	63
22. Attend movies, theater, concerts, etc.	22	44	22	100
Respondents citing at least one regular activity	118	138	20	17

and loafing. The figure is far greater than the 22% reporting this as a regular activity on 5-day. Whether this recuperative activity derives from the pressure of the 4-day workweek or is simply an activity that workers enjoy and can afford to increase with extra time, one is unable to say. It is probably a bit of both.

Workers increase their "creative" activities (hobbies, reading, and returning to school), and 85% report that 4-day gives them more time to work around the house.

Seventy-five per cent report spending more time with their families. It is very likely that the 4-day week will contribute to the strengthening of family ties in many homes. Thirteen women say that they like the 4-day week because it gives them more time with their families, and 10 males report this advantage. (Several women report that they would not have returned to work but for the 4-day week, because they want more time at home with their children than the 5-day week permits.) The extra day at home will enable many fathers to play a more important role in the family and the lives of their children.

Another example of 4-day's strengthening family ties is that one of the largest per cent increases in activities is visiting relatives (121%). A foreman told how his wife had arranged to get her own job at another firm onto a 4-day schedule. Now they visit their son and his family every other weekend, a trip of over 300 miles. Before the 4-day week they were able to visit them only once every 2 or 3 months.

The most striking increase is reported in the category of participant activites (travel, fishing and hunting, other hobbies, athletics, swimming and boating). More than half of the workers state that they travel regularly now, compared to one fourth beforehand. The vast changes that would result from increased travel if the 4-day week were to become widely accepted are difficult to imagine. One can only speculate that the demand for recreational facilities and travel services would mushroom beyond our wildest current imaginings.

The large per cent increase in workers reporting regular participation in swimming and boating (319%) is one of several items indicating that the new leisure class wants recreative action. Regular participation in athletics showed a 65% increase, fishing and hunting increased by 95%, and participation in hobbies was up by 123%. An avid camper exclaimed: "The 4-day week is the greatest! Thursday afternoon when I get home, the wife and kids are packed and ready to go. Thursday night we are in Maine or Vermont or the Adirondacks. When everybody else is fighting the commuter traffic Friday morning, I'm lounging around the camp, or fishing in the lake. And we don't have to fight the Friday crowd for a campsite!"

Although 4-day workers seem action-oriented as individuals, they also indicate that they can be spectators. Compared to 20% on the 5-day week,

30% state that they regularly attend each of the following: ballgames, fights, hockey games, etc. (a 100% increase); movies, theater, concerts, etc. (also a 100% increase); and watch television a lot (a 63% increase).

The thing which does not seem to "turn on" the 4-day workers is participation in voluntary associations. There is only a small increase in the number who report joining social clubs, working in service organizations, and engaging in political and church activities. (But these are in some cases large per cent increases.)

When one attempts to correlate free-time activities with variables such as particular type of 4-day schedule, job category, firm, or shift, one finds no significant relationships. Whatever the type of worker, and whatever his circumstances, he finds plenty to do with the increased usable leisure time provided by the 4-day week.

Actual vs. anticipated use of leisure time. In an article in which he discussed the effects of automation upon leisure time,[2] William Faunce suggested that with increased leisure time workers would probably seek more creative and service-oriented outlets for their energies, inasmuch as there would be a decrease in the proportion of their free time needed to recuperate from work. He further hypothesized that more free time would enable workers to acquire the skills necessary for engaging in participant activities, resulting in a decrease of participation in spectator activities. In an attempt to test his hypotheses, Faunce conducted a study of automobile production-line workers in which the workers were asked how they might use increased free time if it were to become available through longer vacations or a shorter workweek.

The present study of 4-day provided an opportunity to compare Faunce's hypothetical results with those collected from actual experience. There are difficulties in comparing the 2 groups, however. Faunce's study was of workers in automated automobile manufacturing plants, considered by some social psychologists the most alienated workers in American industry. To the extent that the samples were drawn from different populations, the comparison is weak. To the extent that the comparison may provide insight into actual vs. anticipated use of increased leisure, it is of value. The responses of all 4-day workers are included in Table 5, inasmuch as there was no significant difference in free-time activities reported by those on continuous process and other types of jobs.

The table shows that 4-day workers somewhat exceed in action the increase in creative activities the workers in the Faunce study anticipated. Whereas 26% of the auto workers said they would spend time with hobbies, 36% of the 4-day workers state hobbies are a regular activity. As to

[2]William A. Faunce, "Automation and Leisure," in Erwin O. Smigel (ed.), *Work and Leisure* (New Haven: College and University Press, 1963), p. 85–96.

Table 5. Proposed use of increased leisure time differs from actual use. People spend more time on unorganized or relaxed activities and less time on organized or disciplined ones.

	Per Cents	
Activities	Faunce Study (N=125)	4-Day Study (N=138)
1. Work around the house	96.8	84.1
2. Spend time with family	76.8	73.9
3. Travel	53.6	52.9
4. Go to ballgames, fights, hockey games, etc.	48.8	27.5
5. Fishing and hunting	42.4	31.2
6. Other hobbies	25.6	35.6
7. Engage in some form of athletics (bowling, golf, baseball, etc.)	24.8	31.2
8. Read more	24.8	29.7
9. Go back to school or learned a trade	19.2	5.8
10. Active in school boards, P.T.A., Boy Scouts, etc.	17.6	10.1
11. Got another part time job	16.8	16.7
12. Joined social club	15.2	8.0
13. Engaged in political action work	12.8	4.3
14. Rest, relax, loaf, etc.	11.2	69.6
15. Swimming, boating	4.8	48.6
16. Work on car	2.4	28.3
17. Church activities	1.6	10.1

Note: Items 18 through 22 included in Table 4 are omitted here, because they were not studied by Faunce.

reading more, the results are nearly identical: nearly 25% of the respondents in the Faunce study indicated they would read more, and nearly 30% of the 4-day workers report readying more.

The creative category "go back to school or learn a trade" provides a negative difference between anticipated and real experience. Almost 20% of the auto workers said they might go back to school or learn a trade, but only about 6% of the 4-day employees indicate that they attempt this. Furthermore, most of these respondents are managers, or are students working their way through school. One can only conclude that the "best laid plans of mice and men" too often go astray.

Excluding church activities, the 4-day workers fall short of fulfilling the expected participation in organizations that might be considered service-oriented. Ten per cent of the 4-day workers report they participate in school boards, P.T.A., Boy Scouts, etc., compared to nearly 18% of the workers in the Faunce study who anticipated participation in such organizations. Whereas 13% of the Faunce workers predicted they would engage in political activity, only about 4% of the 4-day workers report this as a regular activity. Although the 4-day workers did increase their participation in organizations, they did not attain the high levels anticipated by the workers in the Faunce study. Although the 2 groups are different, one suspects that the actual use of increase leisure by workers in the Faunce study would also fail to measure up to their anticipated use.

Faunce was correct in predicting that workers with more free time would engage in participant activities to a greater extent than in spectator activities. (This increase may have nothing to do with the job's degree of automation, though.) The most striking difference between the 2 groups was in the number reporting interest in swimming and boating. Only about 5% of the workers in Faunce's study indicated that they would engage in swimming and boating, but 49% of the 4-day workers state that this is one of their free-time activities. (Perhaps geographical differences account for some of this variation.)

While participant activity does increase among workers with increased leisure, spectator activity also shows a marked increase over the 5-day level, while education and service-oriented endeavors do not match expectations. Again, it must be stressed that the groups are different, that the time is different, and that the use of leisure may change as employees experience it over longer periods. But the theme seems to be that the workers choose unorganized, relaxing activities over organized or disciplined ones, and that the use of leisure may not be a function of type of job.

Managers' use of leisure time.   Contrary to what some might expect, most managers also report having increased free time as a result of the 4-day workweek. In some companies there is no increased leisure for top management, while in others the 4-day week applies to everyone, or the managers shift their times so that each gets a long weekend once a month.

Also contrary to what one might expect, there is little difference in the overall pattern of use of leisure by managers and labor. Managers do engage more in "creative" activities (hobbies and reading). The number of managers reporting that they read more compared to the number of workers who do so is significantly different at the .01 confidence level. (Another statistically significant difference at the .01 level is in the greater number of managers who report buying vacation homes. Three out of 12 managers [25%] report buying vacation homes, compared to only 6 of 141 workers [4%].) In participant and spectator activities, management and labor are very similar although labor indicates a higher interest in television and movies. What differences there are are probably more a function of educational level than of type of job.

Informal group ties. An interesting speculation about the 4-day week is the potential change it may create in the informal relationships of workers on the job. In some 4-day companies the official coffee break was eliminated, and furthermore, most employees work only 36 to 38 hours now (but are paid for 40 hours). When one considers these factors, together with management's desire to increase or maintain the previous level of output, it seems that one result of the 4-day workweek could be a lessening of informal group ties due to a reduction of free time at work.

The fact that most 4-day companies report increased output for fewer hours indicates what every manager already knows: that very few companies operate at optimum capacity. Although many variables are at work, it is obvious that the old production norms established by informal consensus among the workers may have been broken by the 4-day workweek in some companies. As one worker put it: "When you've got that carrot [the 3-day weekend] hanging out there, you just work harder!"

This is not to imply that 4-day is some insidious plot by management to get more out of labor. On the contrary, 4-day is mutually desirable for both management and labor. If labor *can* maintain or increase production, and is *willing* to do so for the extra day off, then it is in the best interests of both management and labor for management to provide the opportunity. But it is still too early to say what the long-range effects upon the informal structure of 4-day companies will be. The increased morale reported may mean the interactions are more intensive as well as more positive, instead of reduced and negative.

Alienation and the 4-day workweek. A subject of concern to some American sociologists during the past 15 years has been the so-called "alienated worker." The problem was first brought into prominence by Karl Marx, although his purposes in dealing with alienation were different from those which motivate today's industrial sociologists.

> What then do we mean by the alienation of labor? First, that the work he performs is extraneous to the worker, that is, it is not personal to him, is not part of his nature; therefore he does not fulfill himself in work, but actually denies himself; feels miserable rather than content, cannot freely develop his physical and mental powers, but instead becomes physically exhausted and mentally debased. Only while not working can the worker be himself; for while at work he experiences himself as a stranger. Therefore only during leisure hours does he feel at home. While at work he feels homeless. His labor . . . satisfies no spontaneous creative urge, but is only a means for the satisfaction of wants which have nothing to do with work.[3]

[3]Karl Marx, "Alienated Labor," in Eric and Mary Josephson (eds.), *Man Alone: Alienation in Modern Society* (New York: Dell, 1962), p. 97.

Although we did not set out to study alienation among 4-day workers, the results of our study suggest that workers on the 4-day workweek may be less alienated from their jobs than 5-day workers. We make a distinction here between *job* alienation and *work* alienation. It is possible for a worker to be alienated from work, to view it as a necessary evil in life, to find no sense of achievement or satisfaction through it, and yet to be strongly commited to his job. This is exactly the impression we gained about many workers on the 4-day workweek. It seemed clear that some feel a sense of alienation about work generally. But trade their 4-day job for a 5-day job? Not on your life! Alienated from work they may be; but alienated from their 4-day job or 4-day company, they certainly are not!

Leisure—a new salvation.   For many workers the increased free time permitted by the 4-day workweek may be a kind of salvation.[4]   The salvation of which we speak is the need every person has to justify his existence, his reason for being, both to himself and to the significant others in his life. (Essentially, the significant others for us are those persons whose opinions and judgements we value highly.)

It isn't difficult for a manager or a skilled craftsman to justify his existence in terms of his work. He is an important member of the management team, or he is an artistic, highly skilled laborer, and respected for it. With the increase in automation and the spread of bureaucracy it is increasingly difficult for some workers to realize their needs for recognition and achievement in their work (Theory Y management notwithstanding).

Many workers may have turned to leisure activities to justify their existence to their significant others. At the lake cottage or mountain retreat they are somebody! In their boat, camping trailer, motor home, or the motel pool they are for real! In his free-time activities the workingman is accepted as he is, something he seldom experiences on his job. No longer is he a cog; he has become a wheel. He is important to himself and to the others to whom he desires to be important. In short, it is in his leisure that he may find salvation.

It is through increasing this leisure that capitalism may have created the answer to the problem cited by Marx. Our society is wealthy enough to permit an emerging Leisure Ethic to replace the declining Protestant Work Ethic for the so-called workingman, member of the new leisure class.

IS IT WORTH IT?

In conclusion, what are we to say about the 4-day workweek? The effects upon the company are very positive. It results in a more positive

[4]Our thinking at this point has been encouraged by Dr. Raymond L. Gold of the University of Montana.

attitude among employees, and aids recruitment. Most companies increase production and improve their service to customers. Absenteeism and worker turnover decline or are eliminated, and the attitude and general morale of the workers are excellent. The disadvantages are few and seem to appear mainly in the period of transition.

Employees are delighted with the new leisure, because the bunching of free time provides opportunity for activities that otherwise would not be possible—including just resting, relaxing, and loafing more. While many workers report spending more money for free-time activities, most do not see this as a disadvantage. They report that more time is now spent with their families, working around the house, and engaging in participant and creative leisure activities. They are enjoying life more. That the change was

Figure 1. Work and leisure questionnaire.

worth it for them is undeniable. They could not be more pleased, and many jokingly ask: "When are we going to 3 days?"

The fact that every manager reports being satisfied with the 4-day week, that they do not anticipate any erosion of the gains they have made, and that they would recommend it to other companies is "proof in the eating" that the 4-day workweek has been worth the change for the companies that have tried it. The most threatening disadvantage to most managers is the fact that the 4-day workweek is being adopted by more and more companies. This is a prospect they do not relish!

chapter eight

The Future
of Leisure:
Toward a Holistic
Framework

Any inquiry into the future of work and leisure is at best highly speculative. However, because change has become a permanent fixture in our lives, it is important for social planners, educators, and leisure-policy makers to make judgments about the future. Don Fabun states:

> We have, in our society at the present have, almost no concept of training people for a life of leisure, we do not know even whether people can accept leisure as a way of life.
>
> We are on the threshold of a time when leisure is at last possible for most people in our society, and we are doing almost nothing to prepare them for this new dimension of human life.[1]

The challenge of the future in our postindustrial society seems to be for our economic system to recognize and then implement the consequences of the changed energy flow of production and with it the demand for new ways of perceiving work and leisure. Maryjane Dunstan and Patricia W.

[1]Don Fabun, *The Dynamics of Change* (Englewood Cliffs, N.J.: Prentice-Hall, Inc., 1967), p. 21.

Garlan state that as we move from an industrial to a postindustrial society, where computers and machines increasingly take over our work, we will face four crises:

> The first is an *economic crisis*. If a human being has no role as productive worker, how does he feed his family, clothe his children, and provide for the other necessities and the luxuries of a full life?
> The second is a *crisis of identity*. If a human being in our society can no longer identify himself by his job ("I am a teacher," "I am a printer," etc.), who is he? How does he define himself?
> The third is a *moral crisis*. Of what worth is a man, if he cannot earn his place in society by working?
> The fourth is a *crisis of meaning*. If a man can no longer work, what can he strive for? What makes his life itself worthwhile? What can he do instead of working?[2]

It seems prudent to add a fifth crisis, the *energy and natural resource crisis*, which may result in limited use of petrochemicals and electricity and the depletion of natural resources. Postindustrialism calls on man to develop inner strengths and to rely less on conveniences of the material culture. Neighborhood and home-centered leisure behavior patterns may increase as a result of the exhaustion of nonrenewable natural resources.

As we move into an economy of abundance, our needs will change from lower- to higher-level ones. When everyone's needs for food, clothing, and shelter can easily be met, we will concentrate our energies more on the goal of *self-actualization* through cultural activities, conceived as play on a high level. Economic principles have given man a one-sided attitude which deprives morality and nonutilitarian striving of their rational basis. According to Walter Weisskopf:

> The "economic man" is the prototype of alienated man. He is confined to conscious, deliberate action. All spontaneous, emotional, nonutilitarian behavior is suppressed. Economic theory has, in spite of its lip-service to economic freedom, eliminated real freedom from its image of man by maintaining that perfect consciousness and knowledge permits only one, unequivocally determined kind of action, that is, action which leads to the maximization of material gain measured in terms of money. . . . This has led to a disintegration of those aspects of life where this measurement is inapplicable. Friendship, love, charity,

[2]Maryjane Dunstan and Patricia W. Garlan, *Worlds in the Making: Probes for Students of the Future* (Englewood Cliffs, N.J.: Prentice-Hall, Inc., 1970), p. 196.

creative activity, aesthetic, and religious experiences cannot be calculated according to the economic principle.

In order to balance the economy we have to integrate work with leisure, material need satisfaction with spiritual and intellectual pursuits. . . . A person will have to be rewarded rather on the basis of what he is than of what he does in the market place.[3]

Work is no longer the central life interest for most people in postindustrial society. Historically, life styles have been defined by economic class and occupational status. Rationality, efficiency, and the notion of time as money were pervasive concepts and attitudes in a nation oriented to a scarce economy.

By and large, modern life styles have lost this mandatory component and inflexibility. Work and occupational role no longer determine so directly the life styling of individuals in a nonwork-oriented culture. The detachment of the way of life from the way of earning life, or living, does not replace work with leisure, but alters the meaning of both terms; it is not nonwork or leisure, but the decline of exclusively economic measures for human activities.[4]

John McHale predicts that in the future the factors which have traditionally determined role and life style will no longer be relevant—ways of earning a living, occupational status, economic and geographic location will not be important constraints. Man and his social and physical milieu will be seen increasingly as interdependent and coexistent. Therefore, it will no longer be meaningful to conceive of various societal components as separate, compartmentalized sequences. "The overlapping of work/vacation/weekend living is also accompanied by the flexible adoption of appropriate styling for the many different social roles that the individual now occupies."[5]

LEISURE AND THE ELECTRIC AGE

The evolving postindustrial society is a somewhat eclectic model of social behavior and attitudes, characterized by the disappearance of the distinctions between work time and leisure time. According to Marshall

[3]Walter Weisskopf, "Existence and Values," in *New Knowledge in Human Values,* ed. Abraham H. Maslow (Chicago: Henry Regnery Company, 1959), pp. 116–17.
[4]John McHale, *The Future of the Future* (New York: Ballantine Books, Inc., 1969), p. 320.
[5]Ibid.

McLuhan, man will not be freed from work to indulge in play. Rather, man should be freed to develop his innate potential through a new kind of work known as self-development. McLuhan's concept is inherently in tune with the biological striving of the human organism toward maximum self-development.

To be relevant in the future, the provision of leisure service must merge with other human service offerings to serve the central goal of human development. The use of the full environment represents the merging of sensory and intellectual experiences which is the hallmark of the new electric age, and therefore of the *new* leisure. Bertram M. Beck[6] states that "as man is freer to integrate experience and ideas, he is more able to develop his total being." The evolving postindustrial man perhaps will be ready for and seek integration rather than segmentation of experience.

According to McLuhan, man is presently experiencing a tear between the world of ideas and the world of senses which is essentially disruptive and neurosis-producing.

> The medium, or the process, of our time—electric technology—is reshaping and restructuring patterns of social interdependence and every aspect of our personal life. It is forcing us to reconsider and reevaluate practically every thought, every action, and every institution formerly taken for granted.
>
> Innumerable confusions and a profound feeling of despair invariably emerge in periods of great technological and cultural transitions. Our 'Age of Anxiety' is, in great part, the result of trying to do today's job with yesterday's tools—with today's concepts.[7]

Sequential-linear allocations of time in an industrial social order have ceased; space has vanished in the electric age. The development of automation in an age of electric technology has resulted in a vastly altered sociopolitical environment.

> It ends the old dichotomies between culture and technology, between art and commerce, and between work and leisure. Whereas in the mechanical age of fragmentation leisure had been the absence of work or mere idleness, the reverse is true in the electric age. As the age of information demands the simultaneous use of all our faculties, we discover that we are most at leisure when we are intensely involved, very much as with the artists in all ages.[8]

[6]Bertram M. Beck, "Recreation and Delinquency," in *Recreation and Leisure Service for the Disadvantaged,* ed. John A. Nesbitt, Paul D. Brown, and James F. Murphy (Philadelphia: Lea & Febiger, 1970), p. 67.

[7]Marshall McLuhan and Quentin Fiore, *The Medium is the Message* (New York: Bantam Books, Inc., 1967), pp. 8–9.

[8]Marshall McLuhan, "Automation: Learning a Living," *Understanding Media* (New York: McGraw-Hill Book Company, 1964), p. 300.

McLuhan also notes that we now live in a *global* village—a simultaneous happening. In a postindustrial society, people desire total involvement and reject fragmented, specialized goals or jobs. Societies have been shaped more by the nature of the media by which men communicate than by the content of their messages. The alphabet and print technology fostered and encouraged a fragmented process of specialization and detachment. Electric technology fosters and encourages unification and involvement. The "new" environment compels commitment and participation. We have become irrevocably involved with and responsible for each other. The establishment of a global network has resulted in a change in our conception of the human central nervous system. While it is recognized as an electric network, translating impulses and initiating action, the central nervous system also represents a "single unified field of experience." Each encounter of an individual in society is no longer interpreted as an isolated, fragmented happening.

The synchronization of experiences as a result of cybernation means that the organism can react to the world as a whole, in much the same manner that the brain serves as an interacting place where impressions and experiences can be exchanged and translated. This process constitutes an "organic unity", which terminates the mechanical-industrial age of specialization and linear-sequential life patterning. The electric age ushers in a new concept of societal involvement and participation and releases man from the mechanical and specialist servitude of the preceding machine age. McLuhan states:

> We are suddenly threatened with a liberation that taxes our inner resources of self-employment and imaginative participation in society. This would seem to be a fate that calls men to the role of artist in society. It has the effect of making most people realize how much they had to come to depend on the fragmentalized and repetitive routines of the mechanical era. Thousands of years ago man, the nomadic food-gatherers had taken up positional, or relatively sedentary tasks. He began to specialize. The development of writing and printing were major stages of that process. They were supremely specialist in separating the roles of knowledge from the roles of action. . . . But with electricity and automation, the technology of fragmented processes suddenly fused with the human dialogue and the need for over-all consideration of human unity. Men are suddenly nomadic gatherers of knowledge, nomadic as never before, informed as never before, free from fragmentary specialism as never before—but also involved in the total social process as never before; since with electricity we extend our central nervous system globally, instantly relating every human experience.[9]

[9]McLuhan, *Understanding Media,* pp. 310–11.

CHANGING DIMENSIONS OF LEISURE

We are accustomed to life in a fragmented world. Now we suddenly find ourselves considering a world that is all one piece, because any part of it can be experienced by us instantaneously. We have reached the beginning of an economy of abundance, and electronic advances have created the basis for a participative society for everyone.

THE NEW LEISURE ENVIRONMENT

The electronic environment, a cool medium, creates an *implosion*, according to McLuhan, which unifies the nervous systems of all men into a single contemporaneous whole, bringing everyone back to the tribal village, this time on a world scale. The introduction of print, a hot medium, created an *explosion* which resulted in the separation and isolation of various societal components. This resulted in a movement from intimate to complex relationships, *Gemeinschaft* (refers to a society based on close personal ties of friendship and kinship) into *Gesellschaft* (refers to a society in which social relationships are formal, contractual, impersonal, and specialized), tribalism into nationhood, feudalism into capitalism, craftsmanship into mass production, and lore into science.

The aural requirements of speech keep people together and develop dialogue, response, feedback, complex and intricate patterns of personal relationships, family-centered societies, and the like. The electronics medium accelerates hearing and touch and carries emotion as well as meaning. The traditional approach to recreation and leisure service delivery, concerned primarily with the provision of separate classes in painting, art, drama, music, and so on, are seen as obsolete in the new electronic environment. The electric-age participant seeks involvement in all recreation classes simultaneously. Fabun[10] offers such an idea:

RIDERS OF THE ELECTRONIC SURF

A journey—any journey—is a lonesome thing. However long or short the way, it inevitably involves the traveler in experiences that are not shared by those he left behind. Whatever he may have been when he left, the traveler returns—to some extent—a stranger. The tribal cohesion of the early hunters, whose individual weakness led them to roam in packs, and of the early farmers, who for mutual protection tilled their plots within shouting distance of each

[10]Fabun, *The Dynamics of Change,* pp. 19–20.

other, was fractured when the first traveler turned his back on them all and set off on his lonely journey.

The vehicle itself is a capsule of loneliness, its passenger-carrying ability limited by the capacity of its power train. The people who take a trip together are never quite the same as those who did not take it, and their number is always limited by the size of the vehicle. When man began to travel in vehicles—whether on horseback, raft, or dugout canoe—he began a process of separation which, amplified over the centuries by advances in vehicular technology, broke society into little pieces, and made strangers of us all.

In recent years, this fragmentation has been attributed to the invention of printing, with its formalized breaking down of human experience into standardized bits and pieces that can be arranged into linear sequences. This, it is said, was later translated by advancing technology into the standardization of parts (pieces of type), the assembly line for mass production (sentences on a printed page), and the specialized and repetitive actions of workers, which was reflected in the separation of our arts and science; in the compartmentalization of our formal education, and the over-specialization of our economic lives. The result was the breaking down of what had once been the continuous, flowing interaction between organisms, each other, and their environment, into static, standardized bits and pieces. Our intellectual, emotional, social and economic lives had been reduced to a series of "still" pictures which, if sequenced properly and run through the machine at the "right" speed, gave us the illusion of life, but not the feeling of it.

We thus have finally begun to reap the harvest of our affair with the vehicle —a sometimes bitter harvest. But is it possible that we are coming to the end of this long and lonely journey and that we may embark upon a quite different one. Our new electronic technology offers us, at least in theory, the possibility that all of us can share in the same experience simultaneously. The hard glow of the television tube may weld our fractured world together, and offers us the opportunity to restore identity, process and continuity to our inner lives. It may be that *this* is the road we will take—together. Someone has referred to this as "an insurmountable opportunity." Perhaps it is—but if we keep in mind the long way we have come, and the way we may go, it may not be so insurmountable, after all."

CULTURAL CHASM: CHANGE AT THE INTERFACE

We are presently experiencing "future shock"—the relationships of things no longer make sense. The rate of social and cultural change is so swift that our nervous systems have not had enough time to establish identifiable patterns or relationships, and this has disrupted our equilibrium. The experience is painful, and we therefore seek to resist change. Since we cannot control it ourselves, we seek to control the rate at which it affects our lives through institutions (including leisure service). We create institutions to preserve change which we feel is good and to slow down the rest.

Fabun suggests that accelerated change is more likely to take place along *interfaces* where culture meets culture or neighborhoods rub shoulders along a common street. In urban environments, social and cultural change are likely to occur along the boundary layers—those discontinuities where different races, economic classes, religions, or ideologies confront each other. With the advent of the McLuhanistic concept of the global village communications network, the interface has leaped neighborhood lines and national borders. Electric circuitry has overthrown the regime of time and space and deluges us instantly and continuously with the concerns of all other people. Electronic information means that no minority or subculture can be ignored.

There are two basic types of interfaces—*locale* and *location.* A locale is a site for many differing activities carried out by members of varied social groups, such as a downtown street of theatres, restaurants, and shops. Physical segregation is at a minimum. A location is an area occupied largely by a single social grouping, such as a completely ethnic residential block. Physical segregation is at a maximum. People indulge openly in ceremonial and ritual gestures, and the outsider knows he is out of place. Most people's social orbits (the range of locations and locales used by individuals living according to particular life styles) of work and leisure take them beyond their immediate residential neighborhoods; most people do not identify with or feel comfortable with other people who frequent these areas. The widening network of communication and shared symbolism has resulted in social orbits becoming increasingly more diverse and oriented toward nonwork concerns. This has meant that leisure, not work, is responsible for the most important changes and conflicts in our society.

Future shock, a result of greatly accelerated rates of change, is characterized by a society of impermanence among structures, values, and relationships. This occurs even in the recreation setting.

> In New York City, the Department of Parks has decided to build twelve "portable playgrounds"—small. temporary playgrounds to be installed on vacant city lots until other uses are found for the land, at which time the playgrounds can be dismounted and moved elsewhere. There was time when a playground was a reasonably permanent fixture in a neighborhood, when one's children and even, perhaps, one's children's children might, each in their turn, experience it in roughly the same way. Super-industrial playgrounds, however, refuse to stay put. They are temporary by design.[11]

[11]Alvin Toffler, "Things: The Throw-away Society," *Future Shock* (New York: Bantam Books, Inc., 1971), p. 59.

Future shock is psychologically distruptive to people who rely on static structures, values, and relationships for personal meaning and purpose. Large amounts of free time pose a sociopsychological dilemma for those who have traditionally gained purpose and identity from work and other obligatory functions. That self-fulfillment and meaning can occur during nonwork time means that the basic values and beliefs underlying many people's patterns of everyday life have been undermined.

Although the new freedom, product of advanced science and technology, is creating uneasiness, anguish, and even guilt for some, it is posing new, enriching challenges for those who are no longer constrainted by the demands of scarcity and labor. The Puritan Work Ethic is being replaced by a new Fun Ethic; people who fail to find satisfying rewards in work are beginning to search for deeper meaning in leisure. Because the work role and even the opportunity to work have lost prestige, many people attempt to search for identity through play: "The number of play identities will increase, work (boring anyway) will take more and more a back seat to hobbies."[12]

Orrin E. Klapp speaks of a "new romanticism," pervading America's youth and working class, which involves a search for new sensations in many types of amusements. "The new romanticism asserts the right to a self; fun is legitimatized as a way of fulfilling oneself, not just because it is part of one's right to happiness."[13]

The attitudes derived from such experiences will generate feelings of ultimate validity and legitimatize the play experience as part of self-identity. This opens the way to the exploration of offbeat experience for even higher identity, as the individual tries to understand psychological "triggers" and to discover those efficient methods of self-realization. Klapp sees the new romanticism escalating because people no longer seek amusement or relaxation as a respite from work, but as part of a search for identity. People deviate more in the recreation setting because they are bored and need meaning. Various kinds of leisure experiences can seem to be the highest and best possible. Conventional experiencing is being replaced by reality with a fun orientation. According to Klapp,[14] the new romanticism, or the pursuit of "kicks," gives us an understanding of why people pursue deviant leisure expressions.

Once "fun" stops being what people do for amusement or relaxation from work and becomes part of a search for identity, it provides a basis for a theory

[12]Orrin E. Klapp, *Collective Search for Identity* (New York: Holt, Rinehart and Winston, Inc., 1969), p. 184.
[13]Ibid., p. 185.
[14]Ibid., p. 200.

of why people deviate. The stress is not so much the failure of social control (anomie) or rebellion at the frustrating opportunity structure, but, rather, just what people do who are bored, want to have more meaning in their lives, and make certain choices in their leisure. This search for meaningful fun, for "kicks," leads from banal forms of amusement to realizing ones, it takes the seeker to offbeat experiences, cults, poses, and bizzare drama. The movement is essentially an esthetic and a moral one; it is one of alienation, of moving toward what may be real.

The trend toward cultic play has become more urgent, according to Klapp, because of certain tensions of self-defeat within the modern leisure age. "Leisure invites a man to find himself, and the new romanticism proclaims that he has a right to do so."[15] There are increasing expectations of self-fulfillment in an age of computer technology, particularly among those who find it impossible to realize themselves within the alienating forces of a mass society. Those who feel cheated or insufficiently rewarded by conventional games in society rationalize the new romanticism by seeking contact with ultimate values and a rebirth of self through activities and symbols with which to restore or find new identity. Klapp hypothesizes that

> ... squares have firm identity and are satisfied with the opportunities of the status quo; therefore they do not need, do not understand, and are likely to condemn the offbeat adventures in identity which one sees in cultism, style rebellion, avante-garde drama, "sick" humor, and the entire philosophy of kicks. Those with identity problems, on the other hand, feel cheated by the status quo, disdainful of its opportunities, and search for new identity along the "trail of kicks." Nonsquares do not feel these directions are wrong because they have a small stake in the conventional order, an urgent need for identity, and the support of the new romanticism.[16]

According to Klapp's interpretation, individuals who are seeking identity and deeper meaning through play should be viewed positively rather than as engaging in negative escape or rebellion against a dehumanizing technological, social, and political environment. In contrast, Victor Ferkiss sees the emergence of a new philosophy from the postindustrial technological age, in which "the totality of the universe is a dynamic process, a constant moving and becoming."[17] Ferkiss has a clearer, less fearful under-

[15]Ibid., p. 210.
[16]Ibid., p. 201.
[17]Victor Ferkiss, *Technological Man: The Myth and the Reality* (New York: New American Library, 1970), p. 206.

standing of technological man. Ferkiss identifies three principles of the technological age—the new naturalism, the new holism, and the new immanentism—which give society an ecological basis and recognition of the interrelationships of men with each other and the total environment.

The *new naturalism* asserts that man is part of nature, not apart from it. The *new holism* recognizes interrelationships among all things and implies that no part is meaningful outside the whole, that no part can be identified or understood except in relation to the whole. The *new immanentism* states that the social order cannot be determined from outside, but must be viewed from within. All three principles recognize that to make any decision, any change, one must see everything within the total system as a part of the whole.

TOWARD A HOLISTIC-INTEGRATIVE LEISURE BASE

According to Max Kaplan, leisure is best understood in terms of its dynamic nature, particularly when viewed from a holistic perspective, as a total way of life. Almost anything can be identified as leisure, as elements of leisure may be found in work, family, religion, and education.

> Leisure, then, can be said to consist of relatively self-determined activities and experiences that are seen as leisure by participants, that are psychologically pleasant in anticipation and recollection, that potentially cover the whole range of commitment and intensity, that contain characteristic norms and constraints, and provide opportunities for recreation, personal growth and service to others.[18]

According to Kaplan's construct, the following conditions are of highest importance: (1) Leisure must be seen as *continuous* or *bulk time,* not chopped up, as in work life. There is instantaneous access to people and places through travel and study, and to the world through the mass media. Thus, a major new element in leisure is experiences that require relatively continuous periods of attention. (2) The loss of the full-time production role among many groups, particularly the elderly, disaffected youth, workers on three- and four-day work cycles, and the like, requires that men seek alternative sources of moral strength and value from an eroding work ethic.

[18]Max Kaplan, "Implications for Gerontology from a General Theory of Leisure" (paper presented at the Third International Course, "Leisure and the Third Age," Dubrovnik, Yugoslavia, 15–19 May 1972).

This condition of the new leisure raises important questions about the usefulness of values from the work life.

Additionally, the evolution of a new concept of leisure is characterized by a convergence of elements, a neoprimitive fusion. "Elements of leisure, . . . pleasant expectation or self-growth—become ideals in the work situation; meantime, elements of work—such as the fulfillment of oneself, discipline and craft—find their way into leisure."[19]

Kaplan has articulated a model or concept of leisure which provides a dynamic description of various ideal sociohistorical orders and shows a futuristic cultivated society, in which all aspects of life, including work and leisure, are integrated, representing a neoprimitive social order. Figure 1 depicts this sociohistorical process.

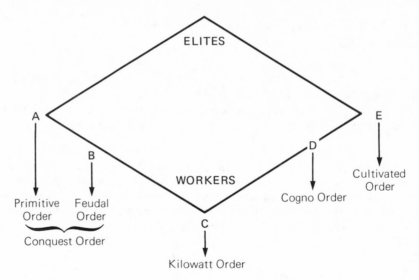

Figure 1. Constructs of social orders and leisure.[20]

According to Kaplan,

The [Conquest order] . . . subsumes primitive and feudal patterns, largely agricultural, pre-scientific, manual, simple, organic human relationships. Workers and rulers become divided in the feudal principle, and by the time of Kilowatt, or industrial structure, class and power lines are well delineated. But by now the middle-class emerges, together with machine power, urbanization, complex social institutions, science democratic movement, and relative abun-

[19]Ibid.

[20]From Max Kaplan, "Leisure and Design" (paper read at the American Iron and Steel Institute, Chicago, Illinois, 23 March 1972).

dance for the common man. At its end, the industrial order moves toward cybernation, and inevitably to man's search for values. . . . Hence the Cogno order seeks to know itself, to find new identity in the new Heaven of material splendor. This transitional stage, in which American currently finds itself, is one of reexamination in which the worker faces the problem of radical transformations in his economic, political and philosophical systems. Finally, as we seek to establish the post-industrial—hopefully, the "Cultivated" society, a major direction has apparently become discernible—a general return to the fusions of work and nonwork which characterized the first part of the social model. . . ."[21]

Primitive or Conquest societies evidence maximum fusion between the various institutions. In the feudal or preindustrial society, elements of culture and various social roles become more delineated. In the industrial or Kilowatt social order, work and leisure are finely distinguished to the extent of separate clothes, hours, companions, status positions, places, and even languages for each. During the Cogno social order, in which Kaplan claims we presently live, a general fusion among institutions and concepts occurs. The emergence of a Cultivated or postindustrial society results in a fusion of social institutions and roles, a form of neoprimitivism.

Time in the Conquest-primitive societies is cyclical and oriented to the seasons; in Conquest-feudal orders time is fundamentally geared to occasions and rituals; in Kilowatt societies time is mechanized and oriented to work specifications; finally, in the emerging Cultivated-postindustrial society, the precision of the clock is less important for service and knowledge industries and the notion of time may conceivably revert to primitive, natural temporal orientations. Kaplan states that societies move from the dictates of the stars to the priesthood, the clock, and finally to neoprimitive poetic integrative temporal orientations.

A. W. Bacon[22] suggests that leisure is a multidimensional concept composed of many elements which interact to generate particular styles of life. The present behavioral and value orientation of leisure demonstrates the fusion of institutions and social relationships of a postindustrial society in which "work is becoming more like play and play like work,"[23] and provides evidence of the interaction between work and leisure relationships, meshed in earlier, preindustrial societies. Bacon suggests that the *unitary* essence of leisure appears to be an important research consideration; we can no longer view leisure as an isolated residual sphere of unobligated behavior, as we did in industrial society.

[21]Max Kaplan, "Leisure and Design" (paper read at the American Iron and Steel Institute, Chicago, Illinois, 23 March 1972).

[22]A. W. Bacon, "Leisure and Research: A Critical Review of the Main Concepts Employed in Contemporary Research," *Society and Leisure,* 4 (1972), 83–92.

[23]Ibid., p. 89.

Indeed it is probable that a different conception of leisure will be needed to investigate the nature of social cohesion in sections of society where poverty has largely been eliminated, where prosperity is endemic and where work is declining in importance in favour of non-working or leisure oriented life style.[24]

According to Stanley Parker, the relationship between work and leisure in the individual's life is paralleled by the relationship between these two spheres at the societal level. Parker sees two basic interpretations of the work-leisure spheres in an urban-industrial society. *Segmentalists* see the parts of their lives as separate segments, comparatively unaffected by each other. Segmentalism is likely to have either (1) an opposition (polarized) pattern of work and leisure, or (2) a neutrality pattern of work and leisure, in which work and leisure are fairly self-contained. A person who views the parts of his life as integrated is likely to have an extension pattern of work and leisure (paralleled by fusion of work and leisure spheres in the society as a whole, or at least in his social circle).[25] Integrating the work and leisure spheres of society, a leisure policy maker would attempt to tackle the problems together, while a segmentalist would tackle the problems separately.

IMPLICATIONS OF SEGMENTALISM

Preindustrial societies knew no confrontation between work and leisure, because work included leisure-like attributes. However, during our present phase of industrialization, with reduced work week, greater affluency, and earlier retirement, leisure has emerged as a significant aspect of life. Each phase of living should be designed to promote maximum fulfillment.

Those who advocate the differentiation of work and leisure as the solution to at least some of the problems in either sphere do so on the assumption that the segmentation sphere is characteristic and desirable in modern industrial society.[26]

Society should not impose a pattern of social relationship on the individual, but provide him a series of alternatives. Accordingly, the differentiation approach to the problems of work and leisure could be ameliorated in the following manner:

[24]Ibid., p. 90.
[25]Ibid., p. 99.
[26]Ibid., p. 116.

First, there must be a revaluation of work, which, to be complete, must be carried out simultaneously on three different planes, intellectual, social and moral. Secondly, there must be opportunities for self-realization and self-development for the individual in non-work activities.[27]

IMPLICATIONS OF HOLISM

Research carried out by Robert Dubin and others has shown that work is not a central life interest for most manual workers and business-type nonmanual employees. The division of life into spheres which can be ordered in varying degrees of individual satisfaction is seen as somewhat artificial. This finding agrees with a study of Japanese industrial workers, who favored an integrated (work and leisure) pattern of living combining business with community activities, recreation, and personal activities. "It is difficult to distinguish working time from leisure time, and the businessman often entertains his clients with a trip to the golf course or a party with entertainment by geisha girls."[28]

The aim of integration is to maximize leisure, but also to fuse it with a uniquely satisfying form of work. Parker notes the implications of the integration of work and leisure.

> In this fusion, work may lose its present characteristic feature of constraint and gain the creativity now associated mainly with leisure, whily leisure may lose its present characteristic feature of opposition to work and gain the status —now associated mainly with the *product* of work—of a resource worthy of planning to provide the greatest possible human satisfaction.[29]

The goal of leisure service agencies in the future must be the advancement and provision of enriching and satisfying free-time opportunities, particularly because of the increased emphasis in industry on more flexible, shorter working schedules, earlier retirement, the prospect of some form of guaranteed annual income, and like developments. The central focus on the part of leisure service advocates should not be to maximize leisure values and minimize those associated with work. Holists recognize a relationship between work and leisure. Therefore, the central focus of leisure service should be *encouraging individual initiative and choice.*

Parker suggests a laissez-faire doctrine of leisure as a self-determined, natural, spontaneous experience which cannot be engineered or unneces-

[27]Ibid., p. 118.
[28]Ibid., p. 65.
[29]Ibid., p. 122.

sarily influenced by various agencies. The individual nature of the leisure experience is diminished if leisure service agencies attempt to direct people's energies into specified channels in advance of participation. "We should aim instead to nourish the individual's potentialities so that each, according to his capacity, could find his own solution."[30]

Parker notes that our traditional planning approach has considered leisure as a luxury for a few; for the masses, work considerations were of high priority and whatever time remained was to be passed as "wholesomely" and as cheaply to the community as possible. This outmoded leisure policy, which survives widely today,

> . . . concentrates on the requirement of the work environment, giving high priority to efficient physical relationships among factories, offices, schools, shops, houses and transport routes. The residual "open space" that remains is regarded as adequate to meet leisure requirements. Very little attention is paid by planners to a positive approach to leisure by understanding and forecasting leisure-time behaviour, and by developing resources in line with estimating demand.[31]

Whatever leisure policy, segmentalist or holistic, is ultimately used by leisure service agencies, it will have broad social planning implications. A segmentalist approach would provide leisure facilities for a certain type of people who need them; a holistic approach would stimulate an awareness of the possibilities of leisure behavior in a variety of situations.

While future work–leisure patterns are uncertain, there is some feeling that work will not be totally enveloped by free time. Whatever pattern emerges, the fundamental concern of leisure planners should be on providing opportunities for individuals to determine leisure choices from a variety of options in a variety of situations and to realize personal fulfillment in leisure that either complements or takes the place of work. "The extent to which the advantage is taken of such opportunities must, of course, remain the choice of the individual."[32]

[30]Ibid., p. 139.
[31]Ibid., p. 140.
[32]Ibid., p. 143.

new concepts
of leisure today

MAX KAPLAN

How does one interpret the impressions of recent travels far into eastern Europe; the visual scenes—endless sheep being led up to the mountains of Yugoslavia, the picturesque dorfs of Romania, the Kesckemet market near Budapest or the teeming bazaars of Sarajevo, Skopje and Istanbul; the aural contrasts on the car radio of modern symphonic sounds a tiny millimeter away from endless folksongs, the intellectual exchanges of unguarded home conversations, and the more formal interviews with cautious academic and political figures?

In Bucharest, the head of research for Romanian television, discussing political controls over mass media, insisted that TV has a life of its own, but that in contrast to McCluhan's "world village," his listeners are joining the "world metropolis." Television is only 11 years old and already one of every 20—half a million people—have sets; their favorite program is on science, followed by melodrama shows. He used this contrast to say that social change is therefore inevitable, not only in industrial and institutional life, but in values as well.

This duality in change came out of all the conversations, and with it, a hunger for scientific studies from the USA, where the change in lifestyles through industrialization has been longer under way. Hungary is just now becoming a consumer-oriented society; Yugoslavia, longer experienced in the determination of its economic policies, is now anxious for our studies on aging. But throughout western Europe as well, in studies of leisure which go to the heart of national directions, we find this pairing of issues: (1) a growing accessibility to more goods, services, and knowledge; (2) an implicit question of changing values, traditions and attitudes, not only among the young but of all ages. East and west, there is a concern with the future, not only in a general sense, but in systematic study, with leisure

Max Kaplan, "New Concepts of Leisure Today," *Leisure Today,* I (1972).

as one overall clue to what people will need and want beyond maintenance. They see in leisure a summation and indicator of aspirations as well
as an adaptation of the new and the old, one affecting the other.

This research goes on everywhere, in universities, academies of science,
or, as in Bucharest, in the research unit on social aspects of medicine which
is now seeking to conceptualize the relationships of emotional, mental, and
biological health. The University of Zagreb has a large department for
studies of leisure within their Institute for Social Research; it has completed studies on retirement (especially of those formerly active in sports),
community studies of Zagreb and 74 small towns, the nature of youth
clubs, family life, and leisure patterns at the university itself. The Government Survey Service of England has published a national study of outdoor
recreation. Major studies of sample populations across the USSR have been
aimed at reducing commuting time and household work. The group in
Paris, headed by Joffre Dumazedier, the foremost authority in our field, not
only heads the seven-nation team of which our Florida Center is a part but
has carried out intensive inventories in the town of Annecy and elsewhere,
as well as theoretical tasks. Similar work is being done in Holland, Den-
mark, Italy, and elsewhere, but the question is not to catalog but to interpret this growing body of independent and comparative study. The
tendencies which I see are toward a new view of leisure as (1) holistic in
conception and function, (2) dynamic and developmental in its methods,
and (3) futuristic and policy-oriented in its intent.

HOLISTIC CONCEPTION AND FUNCTION

A holistic, rather than a segmentalist approach, embraces the two formerly opposed conceptions of leisure, as ends or as means. The first was
derived from Greek aristocrats who, living off slavery, could afford to meet
in their academies to speak eloquently of grand themes such as justice or
beauty, to participate—as "volunteers," we would say—in the political
process, or to enjoy the great plays and sports events. This is the use of
nonwork time in developing the mind, the conscience, the good life. Sebastian deGrazia in his volume *On Time, Work and Leisure* brings this notion
up to date in brilliant fashion—the notion of *paidaia:* leisure as an end, as
contemplation, joy, scholarship, something beyond the material base or
value. The catholic philosopher, Joseph Pieper, sought in *Leisure, the Basis
of Civilization,* to revive this pro-Protestant ethic and to stress leisure as
celebration of life.

The second view, grounded in the ethic of work and post-Hellenic
Christianity, is to look upon leisure as therapy, rest, relaxation, social
control, re-creation for subsequent productive effort—and generally,

therefore, as instrumental in character. Identified with the needs of the workers of history, the last century has also seen this approach broadened into the dimension of leisure as a symbol of the rich, most notably in Veblen's work; as a tool for status by all; and most specifically, as part of the personality configuration in David Riesman's work.

We seem to have attributed the so-called Puritan ethic to the laboring classes, not the rich. We have forgotten how difficult it was in the early decades of the English industrial revolution to get people adapted to factory schedules, and we have seen how quickly the common man gets used to such comparative luxuries as the two-day weekend. I was told in Czechoslovakia that their Russian "guardians" have been unable to get the workers back to a six-day week after the Czechs had been enjoying it for only the one year before 1968.

The whole subject, therefore, was approached almost to the middle of this century on the one hand in either a general, philosophical, moralistic tone, or on the other hand with a suspicion of mass culture by the intellectuals. It was not surprising, therefore, that when social scientists took up the subject of nonwork, an inescapable inquiry in observing social change, they reacted by detailed studies of consumer expenditures, time uses, class distinctions, and the like. These were often correlations, such as Havighurst's studies of activities with factor analysis, Wilensky's work on the leisure of various types of "organization men," or the work of the Lazarsfeld group on uses of mass media.

The current holistic tendency, when one looks at the balance of European as well as American research, seems to blend these two traditions —leisure as an end and as a means of relaxation and revitalization. An attempt at this synthesis comes, interestingly, from the Russians, who do not speak openly now of leisure as time for potential service to the socialist society, but of personality growth. However, they hang on to the "parks for culture" tradition by their own interpretation of personality, as in this statement from three members in the Siberian Department of the USSR Academy of Science. "In the capitalist society," they say, "rest and entertainment are held as most valuable; they are connected, first of all, with consumption of goods and services and take people away from the sphere where a highly developed personality can express itself (politics, arts, technological activity)."

In the western countries, too, we seem to be looking for a conception broad enough to include both views, not because a scientific theory would be easier, but because we are interested now in leisure as a social phenomenon. Objective data, correlations, hypotheses, experiments, and other tools of hard science remain useful to this larger conceptualization, but the newer task demands more. As Dumazedier notes, the subject is now too large for merely a quantitative elaboration of such categories as play, sports, arts, social life, etc. "Seen in the complex of its multiple relations to other aspects of our mechanized and democratic civilization, leisure is no longer a minor item, postscript to the major ones, to be studied or not, depending on whether there is time or money left. . . . Leisure is, on the contrary, the very central element in the life-culture of millions upon millions of workers. It has a deep-going, intricate relatedness to the largest questions of work, family, and politics, and these, therefore, must now be reexamined and reformulated."

In this light my own conceptualization is that leisure is not an activity, but a construct of elements which are emphasized with roles that are pertinent to it rather than to economic, political, educative, religious, or marital life. These elements may, in modified form, be found in other institutions as well. Leisure, then, can be said to consist of relatively self-determined activities and experiences that fall into one's economically free-time roles, that are seen as leisure by participants, that are psychologically pleasant in anticipation and recollection, that potentially cover the whole range of commitment and intensity, that contain characteristic norms and restraints, and provide opportunities for recreation, personal growth, and service to others.

This conception, it seems to me as I work out the implications of every phrase, permits both traditions to be observed in union and separately— leisure as manifestation of man's desire to be man (his "essence") and man's desire to develop symbols and tools in the mastery of himself and his environment (man as "history").

DYNAMIC AND DEVELOPMENTAL

I have talked at some length of the holistic approach to leisure. More briefly, I turn to its new dynamic and developmental approach. Riesman's *Lonely Crowd* illustrates one such example. Thrasher's old gang studies, Becker's work on marijuana, Lynd's observations in Muncie, deJager's research of symphony audiences in Utrecht, chapters by Margaret Mead and others in volume 22 among reports of the Outdoor Recreation Resources Review Commission—all these and others are not snapshot or static views of leisure; they seek to examine processes, dynamics, developments. Every form of data is useful. For example, there now exists an enormous collection of time-budget studies, covering 13 nations (including the USA), engineered by a genius at such cross-cultural endeavors, Alexander Szalai of Budapest, presently deputy chief of research training for UNITAR. This is the most successful cross-cultural study that has ever been done; two volumes on the uses of time summarize and interpret the data of 130,000 cards and 50,000 interviews. They tell us much about how people in Jackson, Michigan, Gyor, Hungary, and other communities spent a specific 1440 minutes of their lives in the middle 1960s. Such data *per se* is useful as a beginning. We now know, for example, that in the socialist countries, men spend 7% of their leisure in study and self-education, only 2.3% in capitalist countries; that, except for the use of mass media, a remarkably comparable period emerges in both for such items as social activity, sports, entertainment, rest, reading, and talking.

However, a dynamic view would have to place such data against each milieu in a complex of explanatory factors. The Szalai group does some of this, of course, but within the material it has uncovered. Many questions can be raised, combining humanistic with scientific inquiry. Subject A reports, truthfully, that he attended an opera yesterday; what is unreported, and crucial to his life meaning, is why he went, how often he has gone before, what it has meant for his aesthetic sensitivity, whether he intends to go again, whom he met, what he eliminated from his normal routine, and so on. Thus longitudinal studies are one corrective, despite the difficulty of eliminating the intervening variables.

Recently, some of my college students carried out family interviews on leisure. They began with the resources of the community and neighborhood, observed the outside of the home, inventoried relevant objects inside, obtained basic data about the family, asked about individual, subgroup and joint activity, then turned from a tentative conclusion about the dynamics of *this* family to a hypothesis about families with similar characteristics. Or, starting from an activity as such, listening to a lecture or drinking beer, we interrelate four components-objective conditions, selection, use, and meaning—as the first level of explanation; this is placed within a level of related pairs (person-family, group-subculture, community region, nation-world); all this falls within the cultural pattern (systems of energy, social organization, values and symbols); finally a classification of social orders completes the whole, proceeding not by historical periods, but by types of structures which I privately call conquest, kilowatt, cogno, and cultivated social orders. Thus we have moved, in an accumulation of complexity, from the fact that someone who does not have to is at this moment listening to a dull lecture, all the way to the type of utopia he conceives or at least implies in his symbolic leisure selection.

This study of large configurations is interdisciplinary. It draws from history, economics, psychology, sociology, linguistics, anthropology, philosophy, and common sense. I see this dynamic approach developing in the gerontologists' use of the term "aging" rather than "aged." Criminology has long ago left a static explanation or treatment—at least in the books —as has family work, services to the handicapped children, and other fields.

Students of leisure can contribute by interpreting nonwork as diagnostic or explanatory clues for lifestyle. The social sciences can contribute to the leisure student by noting characteristic behavior in various social situations that help us to understand the milieu behind leisure uses. Urban planners, for example, are coming to the position that cities are more than storehouses for goods and services, but also scenes of drama, human aspirations and relationships, and living tradition.

FUTURISM AND POLICY

Thus, leisure is now seen as both holistic and dynamic. A third new conception is its relation to futurism and policy.

The futurology movement—we think of such men as Buckminster Fuller in Illinois, Bertrand deJouvenal in Paris, Herman Kahn on the Hudson, Robert Jungk in Vienna—has had to look at time as a new basic resource. Omar Ozbekan of the Rand Corporation has spelled out to this new discipline the sticky problem of assessing or projecting changing values.

For the traditional social scientist, futurology is a new discipline which succeeds or fails on its careful projections. However, the scientific heretic seeks not to eschew his tradition but to synthesize his knowledge with the pragmatic policy-making segment of society; the future is in some part a matter of our making. As U Thant has said, yesterday we used to assess our resources and set our goals; today we can establish priorities and create the necessary resources. Look, for example, at only a few striking elements that enter the future in relation to leisure.

1. American business and industry seem to awaken to the worker's right to distribute his time in accord with his rhythm of life. Thus there arises a significant difference between his use of what I call his "bulk" time in contrast to his "fragmentary" time. So-called practical men who rule business are naively surprised that many workers prefer to work 40 hours per week, but within four days. Yet how long should it take personnel men and managers to discover that the person will be more productive, loyal, and happy if he has some choice and flexibility in his distribution of work and nonwork hours? A concentrated 13-week paid sabbatical among steel workers is far different from a distribution of 58 off-days over a longer period of time.

2. Without analysis, I submit the increasing uselessness of all comparative data based on hours or on income and more than a quarter century old because an hour is not an astronomical unit of time but, socially, an interval which provides opportunities, and these possibilities (as in travel and communications) keep going up as the value of the dollar keeps going down.

3. There is a new fusion—I call it the "neoprimitive" aspect of the post-industrial society—between day and night, far and near, young and old, male and female, domestic and international, inside and outside, urban and rural, work and retirement, labor and leisure. Even our familiar indexes of poverty are to me increasingly useless if we go beyond hunger itself and deal with access, not only to food and shelter, but to literacy, distance, friendships, and to the world itself.

4. There emerges a new flexibility in lifestyles: the prospect of the four-hour day for the many, of retirement at 38 by 2000 A.D., or of normal and healthy life to the ages of 90 and 95 projected by Alex Comfort and other gerontologists. This suggests that the old sequential pattern of social roles may be radically shaken. The worker may prefer to work one week all day and not at all next week, or—as Juanita Kreps of Duke University suggests—half a year, or half a lifetime.

Our field might, if these broad propositions hold up under careful analysis, contribute enormously in conceptualizing some bold outlines for this flexibility-time life. Can scenarios—in Herman Kahn's language—be created to envision family life where the father works half a year? Can adult educators conceive new roles to serve a potential ongoing clientele of many more millions? Can government units on all levels, together with private service agencies, invent new leisure occupations, as Dennis Gabor suggests in his important volume, *Inventing the Future?* Can the Nixon program to develop a unified national effort for volunteerism be given the help it needs from us all in vision, courage, and innovation?

These policies cannot, in our society, be as unified as in the socialist nations I recently visited. But even there, as I was told in each country, "we want to know what you are doing, but we must develop the Romanian way in our politics and our traditions." So, too, in the United States. Our post-industrial material base is available, in spite of sizeable poverty. But even poverty has different origins and meanings in every culture; so, I would add, does abundance. The question that looms before us all is not the distribution of our trillion-dollar gross national product. That we can do if we wish it. What we have not achieved in a mature fashion is a theoretical frame for the study of leisure of our time, or a philosophical position on values for its application in the emerging social order.

As to those values, the most important clue is what the youth are saying, not in a systematic way, but in the setting aside of material goals, even if not the artifacts themselves. The questions they ask are familiar ones, but they come from a generation raised, as far as they are concerned, already in the post-industrial society where physicists are moralists, old political processes do not respond to change rapidly enough, education prepares them to produce what can better be made by machines, adults became neurotic over such playful symbols as long hair, and their nation sends them to die in a costly war which they see as immoral, useless, and founded on an historical fraud. These are children of leisure who are by now experts at organization and at tweedling even the federal bureaucracy by gestures of opposition and affirmation, whether in Estes Park or Washington.

These, then, are several new undercurrents that I see in our field—holism, dynamism, futurism. As we collectively face the problem of constructing a thesaurus for computerizing the flood of data, we must realize our internal differences and theoretical gropings. But each of us needs to stand up, state his piece, and know when to sit.

This is our problem, to relate the older tradition and the newer tradition of man with the help of such miracles as electronics, computers, and Boeing 707s. But let us not confuse the trip itself with the substance of the old or the new. As Thoreau said it, let man in the technological society not become the tool of his tools. Leisure is both a tool and an end, what we do now with our time will be entered into the passport to the future. As Eric Hoffer reminds us, let us make sure we do not forge that passport. To enrich the leisure of today will be to arrive at our goals tomorrow, and deserve to travel into it.

living with timewealth

MILLARD FAUGHT

Would you realize what Revolution is, call it Progress; And would you realize what Progress is, call it Tomorrow.
VICTOR HUGO

Great debates over its *economic* impact, resounding with money statistics, will attend the advent of the Three Day Work Week. Yet many of its most profound and revolutionary forces for change will not be money measurable; rather, the Three Day Work Week will set in motion a human time-use revolution unprecedented in history. It will present an incredible challenge to us whose luck it will be to pioneer the transition adaptations to this new species of personal "Timewealth" in abundance.

TIMEWEALTH—A NEW TERM FOR A NEW PHENOMENON

Even less advisable than putting new wine in old bottles is it to try to squeeze the new and abundant time use potentials, which the Three Day Work Week will bring, into the already inadequate time value concepts and semantics which we have inherited from the personal-use-time-scarce past.

It is immediately relevant to the miracle we want to talk about here to note that history never provided us with an adequate word to describe the time that a person might have for his very own personal use. And it is the *reason* for this omission that is so illuminating: man has had precious little of such time and has been made to feel pretty guilty about what little he has had.

Traditionally man's time has been for working, interrupted only by still work-related essentials of eating, sleeping, maintenance chores and a Spartan-spent Sabbath. That "leisure" for the few was supported by the sweat of slaves or exploitation of the many gave that word a historically bad name; and "leisure" has since been abused into all manner of shapeless and usually invidious meanings. Nor are we overly accomplished at the "arts" of leisure. Many tackle the expenditure of leisure more strenuously than they work.

For some time now we moderns have theoretically had a lot of "new" leisure, from our shortening work days. That we have turned this into a new kind of "rat race" is due in no small part to the fact that our new non-work time comes to us *fragmented*—in bits and pieces strung through the week; most of these fragments of free time are too short to do much with uninterruptedly.

From the human point of view, this free time fragmentation is the prime self-defeating aspect of the five day week. Its total work time on the job is short, but the gross time it takes out of the day and week is long. Forty hours or less it may well be, but it is a *work week*. Except for some work-night televiewing, most functional "leisure" of today's typical job holder is crowded into the two end-of-week days.

It is in this now-frustrating time-use context that we should take due note: the Three Day Work Week not only adds two days to the job holder's personal-use time, it *consolidates* his non-work time into a 108-hour, four-day-five-night contiguous stretch of time, uninterrupted by a single trip to or from the job; and this *every* week, not even counting vacations. Some revolution!

What we have here, as the more-than-money-can-measure aspect of the Three Day Work Week, is a brand new thing in human experience— vast amounts of uniquely useful *personal Timewealth.* I have invented this word, "Timewealth," for it simply because there is no established word for such species of wealth, of a sort that man-in-numbers has never had before. No matter what we might call it—"time income," "personal-use time" or the like—we will truly be pioneers in its consumption.

A NEW "NOUVEAU RICHE"

This new kind of pioneering won't be easy, even though becoming the timewealthiest generation in history is a mighty nice challenge as challenges go. It may even take a generation or two before man really begins to adjust to the Timewealth potentials and consequences of the Three Day Work Week—and the Four Day Weekend.

Not to get the inventory of prospective results off on the wrong foot, among the early consequences of the Three Day Work Week may well be:

An increase in the divorce rate;
A rise in admissions to mental institutions; and
A mounting bankruptcy rate.

Yet, close on the heels of, and tending to reverse, such trends, we may reasonably expect:

A strong resurgence and strengthening of the traditional family unit in American life;
A lowering of the crime rate and of juvenile delinquency;
A general lessening of the slum-bred crisis pressure on megalopolis living; and
A massive expansion of new and new-type enterprises in the nation, especially of a service nature.

But, to go behind any such illustrative generalizations, let's start with some assured changes in the environment which Split-Week-Living will bring about; you can be your own judge of how human nature will likely react.

IMPACT ON THE FAMILY UNIT

Some of the strongest and earliest impacts for change, growing out of the Three Day Work Week, will center on the family; on the individual job holder, yes, but mainly in the context of the worker *and* his family.

It is no news that family life in the United States has had a rough time from analysts in recent years, even to the point of suggestions that marriage and the family pattern of life are passé.

If so, then such fears add reasons for hurrying along the advent of the Three Day Work Week; it has potentials for restoring a lot of fundamental support that the family unit may have lost—and for adding unprecedented new support. And the number one factor in these potentials is that the Three Day Work Week will "bring Dad home."

The degree to which the American family has become a "matriarchy" turns directly on the lop-sided division between Dad's job-time demands and the residual hours he has at home. The fragmented nature of the latter hours, as noted, allows for only transient attention to the complexities of modern family life, except on a resultantly crammed weekend.

One commentary on this patent pattern is the almost frenzied (and often fatal) zeal with which we exploit three day "holiday" weekends. And no wonder the recent bill (to add five more such three day "holiday weekends" to the calendar) sailed through Congress, irrespective of their historical logic. The pressures in labor contract negotiations for more paid holidays, more than for shorter hours, attest the same basic point; it is not just more time we covet, it is more *useful* time. What a quantum jump, then, to a Four Day Weekend *every* week.

I believe that it is a simple statement of fact that such a restructuring of the work week, considering the long-accumulating frustration pressures and latent yearnings it will release, will set off the most fundamental peaceful revolution in history. Though time-use centered, it will affect every facet of American life.

And having the father back in the family household for most of the week, every week, will be one of the prime factors in this all-pervasive revolution. The results won't all be conjugal or parental sweetness and light either.

A case can be made—and often has been made—that contemporary husbands and wives and/or parents and children are the most relative "strangers" in the whole history-tradition pattern of such relationships. Wives' respect for husbands is alleged to have declined because the wives have had to take over too many of absent father's duties—like disciplining and otherwise "raising" the kids. Much juvenile delinquency is attributed, similarly, to this same dilution of the father image and presence.

Well, Dad will sure be home a lot more in the Split-Week Era. And he'll have a *lot* of time to be a husband and father. A lot of volatile potentials hang thereon:

Will the divorce rate go up indeed? ... until husbands and wives learn to "stand" one another so much? Or will it go down because there is really time to live together more rewardingly?

Will the birth rate go up, because the mates are together more and/or because the parent-child environment has new potentials?

Will the "generation gap" between the parents and children narrow or widen as familiarity breeds either more contempt or more respect?

To trot out a lot of pat prognostications, in the face of such unprecedented potentials and no historical comparisons, would be an affront to the reader's intelligence. Families have never had so much time together since the "job-for-pay" way of life began, as they will have with the Three Day Work Week; and never that much non-work, personal-use time. But is there any questions at all that the yawning contrast in conjugal and familial "togetherness," as between the now situation and that of a four-day-five-night weekend would be pregnant with enormous "household" change?

ACCENT ON THE POSITIVE

Having pondered this whole ramified complex of potentials for a long time, I believe there is a fundamental reason why the gains for constructive human desires, and the social arrangements that serve them, will triumph enormously over the many adaptive problems of man finally having Time-wealth in great abundance. My strong ally in this conviction is good old stubborn, persistent Human Nature itself.

When we run through the inventory of problems that rate highest editorial lament contemporarily, there is small evidence that our *goals* have changed, whether of being a better parent, a better citizen or, what is basic to all other roles, a better person. What seems to impede our reaching the traditional imagery of such goals is the ever greater amount and complexity of *things to cope with* along the way. We lead the most complex lives in history.

We also have the greatest array of complex facilities, tools and gadgetry for living, too. And how many of these are called "time-saving" conveniences! But one thing we don't have—as conspicuous functionally as it is overlooked philosophically—we don't have any more time per day. This blunt truism merits some real thought.

TIME-SAVING IS A FALLACY

Sure, we live twice the average lives of our ancestors, and we work at our jobs half as long. But we've still got 60-minute hours and 24-hour days, And, cliches to the contrary notwithstanding, we can't *save* a second of time; we can only use it or waste it as it goes by.

It is out of this factor of the overlooked-obvious that the colossal pinch comes in the pattern of our contemporary lives. The passing time flow is unchanged and immutable; but within it we have more coping-with-life demands on our time than any generation ever had. And what gives the pinch its most painful twist: we have to *adapt to more change* and *faster* than any generation has ever been called upon to do.

Divide our same-old-rate time flow by the number and complexity of the demands on our time, and we are the time-SHORTEST people ever. And this is no hocus-pocus of semantic arithmetic; this is what produces that which we call the "rat race."

This circumstance is obviously part of that amorphous thing we call the "price of progress" but how long need we over-pay? As I have declared, and I repeat, our present ridiculous five day work week (ridiculous because it is now an obsolete nonnecessity for creating the means-of-living in our advanced technology) is a prime and central cause of our compounding time rat race. To recap the reasons:

It rips up the very "free time" which the heralded 40-hour week gives us, into a lot of relatively useless bits and pieces of alleged "leisure;"

And even while so doing, it creates a whole new and unnecessary bunch of demands on our same-old-rate-of-flow time, just to cope with the megalopian mess of a five day economy—in which job and home have to be not too many traffic jams apart

Now let's switch the focus back again from worker to father role. It takes *time* to be a father; more than a hasty growl or two at the kids over early morning breakfast, as Dad girds himself for that traffic rassle to work. And it takes more than fragments of a weekend, already full of deferred home and car repairs, shopping, and the put-off list of living roles that adults want to play, besides being parents. Small wonder that participative citizenship and beyond-the-household facets of our rat race lives get small shrift these days.

MORE THAN DOUBLE

Before we can realistically assess what the Three Day Work Week might do for the present defaults of parenthood, citizenship or other roles of the average person or family, we should correct (or avoid further acceptance of) a fallacious assumption: namely, that with the Three Day Work Week we would simply have "double size versions of our now typical weekends—or that we would just have lots more of the present types of limited "holiday weekends." These assumptions are wrong, both as to quantity and quality.

Almost from the beginning of their inception, the regularly-recurring Four Day Weekends would begin to modify drastically (and very salutarily) much of the pattern of either a present 48-hour standard weekend, or those now special holiday weekends. And the basic difference sums up in one word—"pressure."

Under present patterns, our five work days are relatively useless for other than job-related demands and functions. They allow for little more than some highly-routinized short-time-span investments in matters of personal living. Even a lot of the default investments of time in TV watching are due to a feeling of, "What the hell, there isn't time to start and finish something else."

And throughout the week, the pressure builds up a deferred list of things to do on the weekend—even including getting enough sleep. (Remember that researcher who has discovered that we have been sleeping less and less over the past decade because we keep stealing sleep time to compensate for the growing total demands on us during that ever-limited 24-hour cycle.)

We defer and accumulate still further those things for which "more than a weekend" is required to do. So, come a holiday weekend, we all get out on the highway; and the ones who don't come home dead come home exhausted. Whatever else they may be said to be, none of the "typical" patterns of an American weekend are exactly "restful" or "re-creational" phenomena. The not-enough-time pressure never really relaxes.

RELEASE FROM PRESSURE

Because we have been born and raised in this high-pressured time-scarce milieu, the advent of a "normal" Four-Day-Five-Night weekend is going to be a mighty *abnormal* environment for a while.

Some of the old pressures will be *off*. We won't have to drive to hell and gone out to Uncle Joe's *this* holiday weekend; *any* weekend will do. In fact, there will be lots of time for lots of trips and lots of projects formerly out of the *time* question.

But some new pressures will be *on* too. Now, in the Split-Week Era, there's plenty of time to fix the roof or add a playroom; the old "no time" excuse is gone. And there's time to be a scoutmaster or take a course in astronomy; even finish college or high school or get another degree. Basically, there is more time to start *and finish* an incredible number of things previously not practical when free time came in bits and pieces. Split-Week living will call a lot of bluffs.

One sad certainty: many persons, when initially confronted with regularly-recurring long weekends, are going to come down with acute cases of *boredom*. Ours is not a society—and hasn't been one for a long time—which breeds well-rounded individuals, resourceful at self-direction and self-fulfillment. We perforce have become occupational specialists whose jobs entail little creative satisfaction, and whose non-job lives have become highly vicarious. As the Newly Timewealthy, we will start out as The Great Unskilled.

A lot of things and circumstances have aided and abetted our acquired ineptitudes. We have one group of versatile gadgets which "save" time (and participation) for us; and another batch of equally if not more ingenious gadgets that help us use up all this saved-from-work time—mostly while we occupy a sedentary position. We have thereby become the greatest collection of spectators in history. It will take us a while to become re-involved participants in activities of our own choosing, creating and directing.

But we will cope with the challenge—and with the old traditional American gusto. The reason is simple: basic human nature is glacially slow to change, even though it may adapt to pressures in ways that become habits. We now have adaptive habits geared to the "rat race." Little risk attends predicting that these habits will soon and willingly re-adapt, in the face of some no mean transitional struggle and frictions, to the challenging exploitation of abundant, unpressured, personal-use Timewealth.

DO-IT-YOURSELF—AND THEN SOME

Some of the broader change patterns are quite readily foreseeable. And one of the most certain will be a coming out of dormancy of the personal skill and creative resourcefulness of Americans. The do-it-yourself "craze," as we have hailed it in the past, will be as a mere preview of life when there is *really* time to build things and *really* time to use them, once built.

When Split-Week Living (overviewed widely in the next chapter) begins to take hold, the whole "housing industry" as we know it may well become a sort of adjunct of the do-it-yourself movement; production by "amateurs" may well rival that of the "pro's" in many fields; and the translation of personal Timewealth into new wealth of personal possessions and services will certainly give those who now compute the "Gross National Product" a case of the fits.

There is now almost no limit to the new materials, tools, gadgets and techniques open to individual use, without much or any professional guidance required. Add great new quantities of *time* and we will have a market revolution panting to keep up with a manual dexterity of resurgence. Thorstein Veblen avowed that man's "instinct of workmanship" rates second only to his sex drive; this innate desire to be creative with head and hands has had about all the rat race frustration it can stand.

HOME, THE FAMILY FILLING STATION

Due note has been made that ours is a job-centered society. But historically man has also, and much more so, been a *home*-centered (family-oriented) animal. And many of our most-lamented contemporary problems stem for a weakening of the home environment by pressures (many job-related) which cut down on family-time-at-home. Rectifying this imbalance and thus restoring the home (family) to its traditional center of gravity position in individual life will, in my view, be the singly most "revolutionary" effect of the Three Day Work Week.

More than just a matter of restoration; the Timewealth use potentials of the Four Day Weekend will be permissive of a pattern of home-family-life more dominant and pervasive of human affairs than history has ever seen. No culture has *ever* had a formula where "time for living" exceeded "time for working for a living." And it is patent that if most of the Timewealth for the individual, evolved by this revolution, is taken (a) from job time and (b) from the fractionated and wasted time of the rat race, and is added mainly to *time in the home* or to *family time use* patterns, then home is where this revolution is going to center.

Clearly, as a first aspect of such change, home is going to lose some of the "family filling station" characteristics it has acquired in all too many households. And some frictions will ensue no doubt in those where the transient family members are now not much more than first name strangers. They will have the time and the onus to get acquainted.

But it would be selling the family way of life short, in the face of its durable and all-important-to-man history, to suggest that more time to *be* a family will be of detriment to the family *way* of life. If it is optimistic to believe that the Three Day Work Week will usher in the greatest chapter, in all respects, in the history of the family as a human institution, then I hasten to be the first such optimist in line.

NEW COMMAND POST FOR CHANGE

And the heart reason for my conviction (more than just optimism) centers on the new *command* which the new Timewealth of Split-Week Living will give the family unit for coping with the ever-changing challenges of modern living.

List the problems for yourself which now harass family life: the "generation gap" and all its attendant frictions between parents and siblings; the tedious conflicts of interest between what the various family members want to do *right now* (because there is so little time for alternatives); and the always so little time to communicate among family members. There is so little time for other than expedient conversation in most households today that anything approximating philosophical exchange is thought to have gone out with the Greeks who wore togas.

Yet this is also the era in which all-wise commentators prate forth from the TV screen about the "knowledge revolution." Indeed there is constantly more that needs knowing. But what numbs the poor viewer is realization that he always has more questions than answers, and tomorrow it will be worse. There is never enough time to find out—or to *think.*

Is it naive to expect that a lot of the new Timewealth from Split-Week Living will go into getting better command, by the individual, of the knowledge explosion? Into more knowledge acquisition and use? More formal education? More thinking for oneself ... and thus becoming a better person, parent, citizen?

I believe a very substantial portion of the new Timewealth will be consumed in such areas of "intellectual-do-it-yourself." And even where there is no particular increase in "intellectuality," I believe that from sheer mutual exposure over more time, as between parents and siblings in a more mutually participative home, the "generation gaps" will narrow. There will be fewer "drop-outs"—either from home, or school, or life.

And there are some other "gaps" that will equally benefit from more time for human exposure, one to another. The "friend gap" and the "neighbor gap" and the "citizen gap" will, I believe, have a salutary narrowing when people have the time to do much more than just hurry past each other in the rat race.

And why not? Breathe there many so reclusive as to think that man has really lost any of his instinctive gregariousness? On the contrary; he is mighty sick of being at one end only of the canned conversation that comes to him electronically. But where is the time *now* to seek out good conversation? This art was never in such low estate.

Given ample new personal Timewealth, one of the things we will do with it, virtually instinctively, will be to learn to *communicate* again, one with another. And the results will be exponential. There will be more and better *public* opinion because more people will have more time to develop their own *private* opinion about more questions.

And does it not follow that men and women who know more about what they think, and think more about what they know, make better: persons? spouses? parents? neighbors? friends? citizens?

Yes, indeed, a Timewealthier America is going to be a lot nicer place to live.

And work.

the future of work:
three possible alternatives

DENIS F. JOHNSTON

Current interpretations of the meaning of work in American society range from a reassertion of its traditional significance to the view that its fundamental *raison d'etre* is about to be removed by advances in automation—advances which have been heralded as the "cybernetic revolution."[1] A corresponding range of views is evident with respect to the meaning of work in the life of the individual—from the assertion that work will continue to provide a central focus for personal

Denis. F. Johnston, "The Future of Work: Three Possible Alternatives," *Monthly Labor Review*, LXXXV (May 1972), 3–11.

[1] See Seymour L. Wolfbein, *Work in American Society* (Glenview, Ill., Scott Foresman, Inc., 1971); Sebastian de Grazia, *Of Time, Work, and Leisure* (New York, Doubleday & Co., Inc., 1964); Walter S. Neff, *Work and Human Behavior* (New York, Atherton Press, 1968); Alan Fox, *A Sociology of Work in Industry* (London, Collier-Macmillan. Ltd., 1971), chapter 1; and C. Gilbert Wrenn, "Human Values and Work in American Life," in Henry Borow, editor, *Man in a World at Work* (Boston, Houghton Mifflin Co., 1964), pp. 24–44.

satisfaction and status achievement to the argument that our traditional work ethic is undergoing rapid erosion, to be displaced by new criteria of personal worth and achievement unrelated to work performance.[2]

The three "scenarios" which follow depict possible alternative directions of change which may emerge in our society with regard to the role and significance of work. The first is labeled the "green" scenario, in deference to the controversial work by Charles A. Reich.[3] The second is labeled the "blue" scenario; it is basically antithetical to the first, and implies a strong commitment to full employment and the preservation of the traditional role of work in our society. The third scenario, representing a synthesis, is labeled the "turquoise" scenario. These scenarios are deliberately simplified "ideal type" constructs; they are intended to be exploratory and should not be construed as forecasts of expected outcomes.

In the long run, the size and age distribution of the population are significant factors influencing both the felt needs of the society and the supply of workers to meet those needs. For this reason, the description of the three scenarios is followed by a summary of two alternative sets of population and labor force projections, designed to illustrate the cumulative effects of different fertility levels over a span of 70 years. Different fertility levels influence the likelihood that our society will evolve toward one or another of the scenarios, and are in turn influenced by the changing values and life styles expressed in the different scenarios. These relationships are considered briefly in the concluding section.

THE GREEN SCENARIO

In this scenario, the displacement of workers by increasingly sophisticated, self-regulating machinery is assumed to extend rapidly from basic activities of production and distribution into white-collar and service occupations as well.[4] An increasing proportion of the population of working

[2]Compare, for example, Garth L. Mangum, "Guaranteeing Employment Opportunities," in Robert Theobald, editor, *Social Policies for America in the Seventies: Nine Divergent Views* (New York, Doubleday & Co., Inc., 1968), pp. 25–55, and the statement of the Ad Hoc Committee on the Triple Revolution, W. H. Ferry, Chairman, reprinted in John A. Delehanty, editor, *Manpower Problems and Policies: Full Employment and Opportunity for All* (Scranton, International Textbook Co., 1969), pp. 140–149.

[3]Charles A. Reich, *The Greening of America* (New York, Random House, 1970); Philip Nobile, editor, *The Con III Controversy* (New York, Pocket Books, Inc., 1971); and Henry Fairlie, "The Practice of Puffers," *Encounter*, August 1971, pp. 3–13.

[4] Ad Hoc Committee on the Triple Revolution, statement, March 1964. The three "separate and mutually reinforcing revolutions" are the cybernation revolution, the weaponry revolution, and the human rights revolution. The document stresses the implications of the first of these.

age is unable to find a need for their services. Concern for economic security or for material goods is no longer a significant motivation for the expenditure of work effort, since the supply of these goods is ensured by increasingly automated processes, and their distribution among the members of society is ensured by a variety of social mechanisms. With the provision of material needs and related services assured, the desire for growing material affluence is gradually displaced by concern for psychic and social enrichment in nonwork settings.

An underlying assumption here is, of course, a nearly complete separation of work and rewards. Members of such a society would share in the consumption of goods and services in much the same way they presently share in the use of such "free" goods as air and water. Under these conditions, conventional definitions of labor force, work, and employment would lose much of their relevance. The society would evolve into a two-caste system, comprising a small elite of highly trained cybernetic engineers and a growing majority of persons whose primary relationship to the economy would be limited to consumption. The life styles of this majority would be oriented toward highly diversified forms of expressive behavior—a veritable greening of America.[5]

The notion that the importance of work in our society will continue to diminish can be supported by statistical indicators reflecting the decline in the length of the average working day, the increase in the length of paid vacations, and the reduced proportion of life spent in the labor force. The following tabulation,[6] showing the change in expectations of the average

[5] The "Elitist" implications of this scenario are but dimly perceived by Reich, but they are clearly delineated by Donald N. Michael, "Cybernation: The Silent Conquest," in *Automation: Implications for the Future,* Morris Philipson, editor (New York, Random House, 1962), pp. 78–128. See also the classic work of Jacques Ellul, *The Technological Society* (New York, Random House, 1964), translated from the French edition of 1954 by John Wilkinson.

[6] The estimates of life expectancy discussed above are from conventional life tables. Those relating to the average expected duration of working life reflect the proportions of the surviving population of males who were in the labor force at successive ages at the specified time. For a detailed explanation of the derivation of conventional tables of working life, see U.S. Department of Labor, Manpower Adminstration, *The Length of Working Life for Males, 1900–60,* Manpower Report Number 8, July 1963, and Howard N. Fullerton, "A table of working life for men, 1968," *Monthly Labor Review,* June 1971, pp. 49–55. If trends in average hours of work per week observed during the first six decades of the twentieth century are extrapolated, the average amount of time spent at work during the year would be about two-thirds its present level by the end of the century. On this subject see Stanley Lebergott, "Labor Force and Employment Trends," in Eleanor Bernert Sheldon and Wilbert E. Moore, editors, *Indicators of Social Change* (New York, Russell Sage Foundation, 1968), pp. 97–143, especially table 2, and Mary A. Holman, "A National Time-Budget for the Year 2000," *Sociology and Social Research,* October 1966, reprinted (in part) in Marion Clawson, "How Much Leisure Now and in the Future?" in *Leisure in America: Blessing or Curse?,* James C. Charlesworth, editor, Monograph 4 (Philadelphia, American Academy of Political and Social Science, April 1964), pp. 1–20. For recent analyses of trends in the direction of increased leisure and its utilization, see Geoffrey H. Moore and Janice N. Hedges, "Trends in labor and leisure," *Monthly Labor Review,* February 1971, pp. 3–11, and Janice N. Hedges, "A look at the 4-day workweek," *Monthly Labor Review,* October 1971, pp. 33–37.

20-year-old working man, reflects the declining proportion of life spent in the labor force:

	1900	1950	1968
Life expectancy	42.2	48.9	49.2
Work life expectancy	39.4	43.1	41.5
Retirement expectancy	2.8	5.8	7.7
Percent of life in retirement	6.6	11.9	15.6

Although comparable estimates and projections for women are not available, it is apparent that the increasing labor force participation of women compensates, at least in part, for the reduction in work effort among men. Nevertheless, both sexes are entering the labor force later and retiring earlier, so that a continued reduction in the total proportion of time spent at work is likely.

If work absorbs less of an individual's time, it does not necessarily follow that it has less meaning or importance for him. However, a few studies and a larger number of impressionistic accounts have pointed to the emergence of life styles in which work is no longer regarded as intrinsically or personally valuable, but is accepted primarily for the monetary rewards it brings.[7] In one such study, only about one-third of the jobs surveyed were found to be "ego-involving," with the bulk of these concentrated in the upper white-collar groups. The remainder, including the overwhelming majority of entry-level positions, were classified as "society-maintaining."[8] As the new entrants to the labor force acquire both the habits of industry and the requisite skills in their chosen fields, they may be expected to search for an adult "identity" in terms of their work role. To the extent that this search is frustrated by the paucity of challenging or "ego-involving" jobs, a further erosion of the traditional work ethic may be ahead.[9]

The intuitive appeal of our first scenario is undeniable. It envisions a society which enjoys the ultimate liberation—from both the fear of want and from the need to submit to the disciplines of work. But its implications

[7] Ben B. Seligman, *Most Notorious Victory: Man in an Age of Automation* (New York, The Free Press, 1966), p. 368, as quoted in Walter S. Neff, *Work and Human Behavior* p. 241. Also see Ben Seligman, "Automation and Labor," in Ellis L. Scott and Roger W. Bolz, *Automation Management: The Social Perspective* (Athens, Ga., The Center for the Study of Automation and Society, 1970), pp. 138–52, and Bruce Mazlish, "Obsolescence and 'Obsolescibles' in Planning for the Future," in Stanford Anderson, Editor, *Planning for Diversity and Choice* (Cambridge, Mass., M.I.T. Press, 1968), pp. 155–69.

[8] Robert J. Havighurst, "Youth in Exploration and Man Emergent," in *Man in a World at Work*, pp. 215–36.

[9] *Ibid.* Compare Walter S. Neff, *Work and Human Behavior,* chapter 15, pp. 236–51, and Harvey Swados, "Work as a Public Issue," *Saturday Review,* Dec. 12, 1959, pp. 13–55 and 45. Also see Paul Goodman, "Youth in the Organized Society," *Commentary,* 1960, pp. 95–107.

are profoundly disturbing, and its underlying assumptions can be challenged. Most disturbing is the likelihood that reliance upon an automated system, controlled and understood by a select minority, implies an elitist control of the majority.

But the conceptual leap from a vision of what is technologically feasible in theory to the conclusion that such a vision is about to be realized involves a non sequitur of classic proportions. Our experience with the impact of automation does not thus far indicate the disappearance of work to be done—especially when we consider the mounting social and ecological problems associated with increased production and consumption.[10] Undoubtedly, rapid technological advances will continue to produce major changes in the nature and content of work, but it does not necessarily follow that the need for, and importance of, work will be diminished.

Moreover, our green scenario may also be flawed by its misconception of the value orientations of the youthful dissidents and apostles of "deviant" life styles. Those who refuse to participate in a "corrupt" society, or who reject the notion of engaging in "meaningless" work or ritualistic and "irrelevant" education are not necessarily denying the values which underlie these pursuits; they may instead be advocating reforms designed to reassert them in purer form.[11] The emergence of an increasingly cybernated technology, accompanied by increasing levels of education and aspiration among persons of working age, may indeed produce dramatic changes in the relative emphasis given to the economic, social, and psychological components of job content and performance, but work is likely to retain its traditional position as a major factor in orienting the individual within the society.[12]

THE BLUE SCENARIO

The essential characteristic of this scenario is the realization and maintenance of a full employment economy, together with the progressive re-

[10] Victor C. Ferkiss, *Technological Man: The Myth and the Reality* (New York, The New American Library, 1970). Ferkiss argues that the emergence of "technological man" would ensure the employment of technology in the service of social and humanitarian goals. *The Technological Society*, is not so optimistic. On this issue, see Hasan Ozbekhan, "The Triumph of Technology: 'can' implies 'ought,' " in *Planning for Diversity and Choice*, pp. 204–33. Ozbekhan argues that technology should not be more than a means to ends prescribed by social values; "can" does not imply "ought."

[11] Nicholas Rescher, "Value-Considerations in Public Policy Issues of the Year 2000" (paper presented at the Technological Forecasting Conference, 1969, sponsored by the Industrial Management Center, Inc.). For a fuller exposition of methods assessing trends in values, see Kurt Baier and Nicholas Rescher, editors, *Values and the Future* (New York, The Free Press, 1969).

[12] Harold L. Wilensky, "Varieties of Work Experience," in *Man in a World at Work*, pp. 125–54.

moval of remaining barriers to the employment of those groups whose desire for employment has been frustrated by a variety of handicaps or by discrimination. Two basic assumptions differentiate this scenario from the one preceding. First, the pace and direction of technological change is modified and channeled by the introduction of measures which ensure a sustained high level of demand for workers. Second, this demand is matched by a supply of appropriately trained persons willing to work.

On a number of counts, this is a plausible outlook. First, our experience with the impact of automation thus far suggests a continued expansion in the number and variety of professional, technical, and service occupations geared to the operation of automated machinery. Second, our attempts to reduce the social costs of the externalities associated with our current patterns of production and consumption may require substantial inputs of labor-intensive work effort rather than increased automation. For example, a drastic reduction in the use of chemical pesticides and fertilizers might well entail a considerable expansion in the labor inputs required to maintain production of agricultural products in the future. Third, it is conceivable that the United States, in concert with other highly industrialized countries, might attempt to boost production and income in the less developed countries. The resulting expansion of effective demand for U.S. goods and services would generate increased demand for U.S. labor. Fourth, the demand for work and the income it brings is far more pervasive in our society than the demand for income unrelated to work. Evidence of the strength of this value is the Employment Act of 1946, which expressed the need to create and maintain conditions under which useful employment opportunities would be afforded to those who are "able, willing, and seeking to work." This act provides the necessary legislative underpinning for a "full employment" policy. Should attempts to achieve full employment conflict with efforts to attain other national objectives, there is ample leeway, under the carefully qualified wording of this act, for the development of policies and programs designed to ensure "reasonably full" employment. If such policies were to include measures which reduced other sources of income to those deemed able to work while at the same time effectively removing existing barriers to the employment of those who are willing to work, our blue scenario would be quite realistic.

Finally, efforts to achieve our national goals in a number of areas are likely to generate a high level of demand for labor, thus facilitating the achievement of full employment. Assuming national commitment to 16 major goals, Leonard A. Lecht of the National Planning Association first estimated the dollar cost of attaining each of these goals, and then translated these costs into estimates of associated manpower requirements. Lecht's major findings strongly contradict the view that millions of workers are about to become redundant because of the spread of automation; he found, instead, that full achievement of these goals by the mid-1970's would require the employment of about 10 percent more workers than are expected to be in the labor force by that time.[13]

Other experts foresee neither the displacement of workers nor the abandonment of work as a means of livelihood, but rather the emergence of government (particularly at the State and Local levels) as a dominant employer of *first* resort.[14] This argument is based on the conviction that solutions to our mounting social and environmental problems can be developed only through governmental initiative and coordination. They envision new forms of public-private collaboration in dealing with these problems, recognizing the key role of government in developing and monitoring the large-scale programs which may be called for. The significance of their findings lies in their agreement that continued increases in productivity do not necessarily imply a reduction in demand for labor, particularly if the society devotes more attention and resources to the difficult public problems emerging.

THE TURQUOISE SCENARIO

This setting assumes continued improvement and application of automated machinery and related technological advances in meeting the growing needs of the society. It differs from the first scenario, however, in regard to the life styles which are seen to accompany this advance. In the turquoise setting, the economic security and material wealth generated and maintained by an increasingly cybernated technology are accompanied by sustained demand for work in four major areas: (1) a core of highly trained technicians and engineers needed to maintain and improve the machinery of production and distribution, supplemented by a growing corps of ombudsmen to provide the feedback information needed to direct this machinery in accordance with public wishes and agreed-upon social values; (2) a growing number of workers in the fields of public and personal services; (3) a growing number of craftsmen and artisans whose handiwork continues to be valued because of its individualistic, nonmachine characteristics and stylistic qualities; and (4) a major expansion of employment in what Toffler has aptly termed the experience industries—a blending of

[13] Leonard A. Lecht, *Manpower Needs for National Goals in the 1970's* (New York, Frederick A. Praeger, 1969). Fifteen of these goals were initially described in the Report of the President's Commission on National Goals, *Goals for Americans* (The American Assembly, 1960). A 16th goal, relating to space exploration, was later added. The outcome of such an exercise is, of course, heavily dependent upon its assumptions. Imprecise specification of goals and of attainment of a given goal were critical problems here. Lecht provides details on his procedure in appendix C.

[14] Irving H. Siegel and A. Harvey Belitsky, "The Changing Form and Status of Labor," *Journal of Economic Issues,* March 1970, pp. 78–94.

recreational and educational opportunities packaged to appeal to the interests of an increasingly affluent and educated population enjoying greater amounts of leisure time.[15]

In this scenario, work retains much of its conventional significance, both in economic terms and in sociopsychological terms. However, unlike our blue scenario, it envisions a major transformation in the relative importance of economic and noneconomic work needs. As a shrinking proportion of workers is engaged in the basic tasks of production and distribution, more and more workers are involved in occupations whose productivity grows slowly, or in modes of work for which conventional measures of productivity are inappropriate. This shift links the economic sector more closely to noneconomic forces, such as changes in life styles, so that nonmaterial cultural values tend to become the primary determinants of what we produce and consume.[16]

The salient feature of this scenario is the gradual reunification of work and leisure into a holistic pattern as was characteristic of most preindustrial societies. Such a reunification may already be observed in the guise of coffee breaks, informal on-the-job socializing, and increasing concern for the amenities of the work setting. But these are only the surface manifestations of more profound changes. The proliferation of on-the-job training courses, for example, reflects an increasing concern with the need to elicit from workers a greater sense of commitment by increasing their opportunities for growth and fulfillment within the work setting. What is significant in these developments is not the claim or belief that such innovations are conducive to increased productivity, but rather the fact that they represent an attempt to humanize the work setting.

The basic pressure for continued modifications in these directions stems from the increasing educational attainment of workers, together with the progressive removal of barriers to the employment of individuals whose participation in the labor market was formerly restricted. The more highly educated individuals now entering the labor force in rapidly increasing numbers have acquired high aspiration levels and expectations concerning their work roles and careers. Their enormous potential cannot be tapped without opening up new channels of communication for mutual education and sharing of experience and outlooks.[17]

A corresponding set of accommodations may be expected if the goal of

---

[15] Alvin Toffler, *Future Shock* (New York, Random House, Bantam edition, 1970), chapter 10.

[16] Ibid., p. 453.

[17] Bertram M. Gross, editor, *A Great Society?* (New York, Basic Books, Inc., 1966), p. 338. Compare Margaret Mead, "The Changing Cultural Patterns of Work and Leisure," U.S. Department of Labor, Manpower Administration, Seminar on Manpower Policy and Programs, January 1967.

equal opportunity for meaningful work is to be achieved by the "disadvantaged." The possible measures to be adopted or expanded in this area range from a variety of training courses—remedial education, skill upgrading, and the like—to the provision of facilities such as day-care centers designed to permit the fuller participation of those persons in some way handicapped in seeking and holding jobs. A continuation of these trends under conditions of technologically induced productivity increases suggests that a considerable share of these increases might be absorbed in the form of measures which promote a more socially and psychologically satisfying work experience.[18]

An important consequence of this type of change would be a continued expansion of the labor force as conventionally defined. This expansion would be accompanied by a gradual reduction in average hours worked per year, together with a more subtle blending of work and leisure activities.

POPULATION AND LABOR FORCE PROJECTIONS

Through their effects on size and age distribution of the labor force, fertility patterns are likely to affect the future role of work in our society —and the range of alternatives available.

The population projections summarized in table 1 illustrate the cumulative effect of two alternative fertility levels. Series B represents the adoption of a three-child family norm; Series E represents the adoption of a two-child norm.[19] The accompanying labor force projections illustrate the effects of these alternative fertility levels at 20-year intervals upon the size and age distribution of the labor force.

By 1980, the lower (two-child) series yields a labor force 1.7 million larger than the higher (three-child) series, because under the postulated patterns of child-spacing, the two-child series implies a smaller proportion

---

[18]For a balanced treatment of the alternatives of a "segmentalist" versus a "holistic" approach to work and leisure, see Stanley Parker, *The Future of Work and Leisure* (London, MacGibbon & Kee, Ltd., 1971, and New York; Praeger, 1971), chapter 10. For a persuasive argument in favor of a holistic approach see Joffre Dumazedier, *Toward a Society of Leisure* (New York, The Free Press, 1967, translated from the French by Stewart E. McClure), chapter 4.

[19]An average annual per capita increase in total output per worker of 2.2 percent (in real terms) is consistent with an assumed rise in productivity per man-hour of 2.5 percent per year, and a decline in hours worked per worker of 0.3 percent per year. Both of these rates of change are approximately consistent with long-term trends in the United States. These simple calculations are, of course, purely illustrative, and do not take account of a host of factors which might affect both productivity and its measurements over the 70-year span of our projections.

of women with young children, which in turn implies a higher percentage of women in the labor force, other things being equal. By the year 2000, the effect of the higher labor force participation of women in the two-child series is overshadowed by the smaller number of young workers who have been born under this series. As a result, the labor force of 127 million is 9.8 million smaller than that which would occur under the three-child series. Beyond the year 2000, the cumulative effect of the difference between Series B and Series E fertility levels is dramatic. By 2020, the Series B labor force would be 45 million larger than the Series E projection; by 2040, 107 million larger.

The contrast between the two series is even more striking when the amount of the average annual net increase in the labor force is considered. In the higher series, the labor force rises from an annual average of 1.5 million during the 1960–80 period to 3.5 million a year during the 2020–40 period. The corresponding increase in the lower series is from 1.5 million a year in the 1960–80 period to only 300,000 a year in the 2020–40 period. In other words, both the population and the labor force of the lower series approach a constant level by around the middle of the next century, but the higher series implies exponential growth.

The age distribution of these alternative projections reveals a number of significant differences, particularly after the year 2000. During the 1960–80 period, the projected labor force increase in both series is roughly the same: 35 percent of the increase will be young adults (age 16 to 24 years), while about 12 percent will be older workers (55 years old and over). During the next 20-year period, 20 percent of the projected increase in the high series consists of young workers, while older workers contribute about 5 percent of the increase. In the lower series, the number of younger workers actually declines, so that nearly all of the increase is accounted for by workers in the central working ages, 25 to 54.

The contrast between the two series is even more striking during the following period (2000 to 2020). In the higher series, older workers account for only a slightly larger proportion of the labor force increase than younger workers, 17 and 21 percent respectively. But in the lower series, less than 2 percent of the projected rise occurs among younger workers, while 72 percent occurs among workers 55 and over. By 2040, about 21 percent of the labor force under the high series would be under age 25, and 14 percent would be 55 and over; the corresponding percentages for the lower series are 16 and 19 percent, respectively.

In summary, the salient feature of the higher series of the labor force projections is the continued rise in the number of workers, sustained by the ever-increasing supply of new young entrants to the labor force. The outstanding characteristic of the lower series of projections, on the other

Table 1. Illustrative projections of total population and total labor force, by age and sex, 1960 to 2040.

	1960	1970	Series B (3-Child Norm)				Series E (2-Child Norm)			
	Actual	Actual	1980	2000	2020	2040	1980	2000	2020	2040
POPULATION[1]										
Numbers in thousands:										
Total, all ages	180,525	205,397	236,797	320,780	440,253	598,179	225,510	266,281	299,177	317,382
Male	89,281	100,752	115,941	158,051	218,103	297,002	110,178	130,253	145,284	154,716
Female	91,244	104,645	120,856	162,729	222,150	301,177	115,332	136,028	152,893	162,666
Percent distribution:										
Total	100.0	100.0	100.0	100.0	100.0	100.0	100.0	100.0	100.0	100.0
Under 16 years	32.9	30.7	29.4	31.4	32.1	32.1	25.9	24.2	22.5	22.0
16 to 24 years	12.2	15.7	16.0	15.6	14.6	14.7	16.8	13.6	12.2	12.2
25 to 54 years	37.6	34.9	35.7	36.9	35.7	36.4	37.5	42.9	39.4	39.3
55 years and over	17.4	18.7	18.9	16.1	17.6	16.8	19.8	19.4	25.9	26.6
TOTAL LABOR FORCE[2]										
Number in thousands:										
Total, 16 and over	72,104	85,903	101,096	136,422	185,814	255,312	102,818	126,660	141,138	147,724
Male	48,933	54,343	63,574	84,249	114,183	156,367	63,574	77,388	85,576	89,182
Female	23,171	31,560	37,522	52,173	71,631	98,945	39,244	49,272	55,562	58,542
Percent distribution:										
Total	100.0	100.0	100.0	100.0	100.0	100.0	100.0	100.0	100.0	100.0
16 to 24 years	17.6	23.2	22.8	22.2	20.9	20.9	22.9	17.7	16.0	16.2
25 to 54 years	64.6	59.9	61.0	65.0	64.1	64.8	61.2	68.5	64.2	65.1
55 years and over	17.7	16.9	16.2	12.8	15.1	14.4	15.9	13.8	19.8	18.7

NOT IN LABOR FORCE

Numbers in thousands:										
Total, all ages	108,421	119,494	135,701	184,358	254,439	342,867	122,692	139,621	158,039	169,658
Male	40,348	46,409	52,367	73,802	103,920	140,635	46,604	52,865	60,708	65,534
Female	68,073	73,085	83,334	110,556	150,519	202,232	76,088	86,756	97,331	104,124
Percent distribution:										
Total	100.0	100.0	100.0	100.0	100.0	100.0	100.0	100.0	100.0	100.0
Under 5 years	18.5	14.8	19.2	18.3	18.6	19.0	15.6	14.1	13.3	12.9
5 to 15 years	36.3	37.9	32.1	36.4	37.0	37.0	32.0	32.0	29.3	28.1
16 to 64 years	33.9	33.4	33.8	31.5	30.5	30.6	36.0	35.6	34.9	33.4
65 years and over	11.4	13.9	14.9	13.9	13.9	13.4	16.4	18.3	22.5	25.5
Dependency ratio[3]	1.50	1.39	1.34	1.35	1.37	1.34	1.19	1.10	1.12	1.15

[1]Data relate to total population, including Armed Forces abroad, as of July 1 of the specified year. Estimates for 1960 and 1970 are current estimates as of those dates. Projected data were prepared by the Bureau of the Census for the Commission on Population Growth and the American Future, and are consistent with the projections published in Current Population Reports, Series P-25, No. 448.

[2]Data include Armed Forces, and are annual averages for the specified years. Data for 1960 and 1970 are estimates based on then current population estimates. Projected data were prepared by the author for the Commission on Population Growth and the American Future, and are not official Bureau of Labor Statistics projections.

[3]The "dependency ratio" is the number of persons of all ages who are not in the labor force divided by the total labor force.

NOTE: The Series B projections of population represent the growth patterns that would result if the future fertility of American women were to follow a trend such that women now entering the child-bearing ages and all subsequent cohorts of women would have 3,100 children ever born per 1,000 women. The Series E projections represent the growth patterns that would result if these succeeding cohorts of women were to have 2,110 children ever born per 1,000 women, which is just enough to barely replace each generation, given current mortality levels. Both series assume the same trend in mortality, and both assume the same annual net migration to the United States of 400,000 persons per year.

The corresponding series of labor force projections were developed to illustrate the effects of different levels of fertility on the size and age-sex distribution of the labor force. These fertility differentials were assumed to affect only the economic activity rates of women of child-bearing ages. The projected rates of labor force participation for both sexes are extrapolations of actual trends observed during the postwar period; they assume no sudden or drastic change in the propensity of different age-sex groups to enter or leave the labor force.

The labels "B" to "E" used here are two of the five arbitrary designations the Bureau of the Census has employed to identify different series of population projections they have prepared in recent years. The five series "A" to "E" may be defined in terms of the number of children born per 1,000 women throughout their childbearing period: Series A=3,350; Series B=3,100; Series C=2,775; Series D=2,450; and Series E=2,110. Series A, which represents a reasonable upper limit for the birth cohorts of women who entered childbearing ages at the start of the post-World War II "baby boom," has been dropped as being above the range of reasonable current expectations for future fertility of American women. Therefore, Series B now represents the highest series considered to be attainable in the future, Series E, at the lower extreme, represents the fertility needed to barely replace the current generation. Because Series B approximates an average fertility of three children per woman, it has been referred to as the "3-child norm." Similarly, Series E, approximating a fertility rate of two children per woman, is termed the "2-child norm."

hand, is the sharp fluctuation in the age distribution of the workers, tend-ing, in the long run, toward an older, more slowly growing labor force. Thus, each of these projected series would give rise to a different pattern of stresses in accommodating the potential supply of workers to the de-mands of the economy.

PROJECTIONS AND SCENARIOS

The relationships among our three scenarios and the two series of popu-lation and labor force projections can only be described in general terms; the tentative and conjectural nature of these generalizations must be stressed.

At first glance, a return to the higher growth pattern of Series B would appear to be consistent with our traditional self-image as an expanding society—a society which continues to equate growth with progress in all spheres of life. However, the longrun implications of such continuing growth portend the emergence of serious and historically unprecedented stresses which would tend to reduce the range of options open to the society and would adversely affect the climate in which choices must be made in the future. By the year 2000, a Series B population of about 320 million people, enjoying a national per capita productivity which has con-tinued to rise at the conservative rate of, say, 2.2 percent per year (in real terms) would be producing—and consuming—nearly three times the vol-ume of goods and services it presently utilizes. By the year 2040, such a population, then numbering close to 600 million, would on the same as-sumption, produce and consume over 13 times our current output.[20] Not only would such a growth pattern generate unprecedented pressures on the supply of natural resources and trigger vast environmental side effects, but it would also produce a host of social strains and psychological frustrations as the growing affluence of each individual inevitably impinges upon that of his fellows. In the long run, any society which is geared to an exponen-tial pattern of demographic and economic growth is bound to encounter a series of progressively severe "shocks" as its demands surpass the avail-able supply of all those elements—such as breatheable air, potable water, and usable space—which are not growing exponentially, and may in fact be rapidly diminishing.[21]

[20]Such enormous growth is roughly comparable with the growth we have experienced during the past 70 years. Compare Herman Kahn and Anthony J. Wiener, *The Year 2000* (New York, Macmillan, 1967), chapter 3, pp. 167–84, and E. J. Mishan, *The Costs of Economic Growth* (New York, Praeger, 1967). Also see Professor Mishan's article, "On Making the Future Safe for Mankind," *The Public Interest*, Summer 1971, pp. 33–61.

[21]See Barry Commoner, "Economic growth and ecology—a biologist's view," and Walter W. Heller, "Economic growth and ecology—an economist's view," *Monthly Labor Review*, November 1971, pp. 3–13 and 14–31, respectively.

One possible outcome of our attempts to overcome the challenges posed by such enormous growth would be a forced adoption of certain features of our "green" scenario. For example, the social and environmental costs associated with the increased production needed to sustain our growing population might induce such rapid adoption of new technologies that the normal growth in the labor force could no longer be fully absorbed. The resulting imbalance between the supply of potential workers and the demand for their services could then create a need for increased reliance upon mechanisms of support unrelated to work.

Alternatively, any failure to meet the demand of increased production and distribution by technological means, or an inability to solve the associated problems of pollution, waste disposal, and the like by such means might force increased reliance upon labor intensive efforts. Under these circumstances, our evolution towards the blue scenario would be associated with declining productivity and corresponding declines in the level of living of the population as a whole. In short, a return to the growthmanship of the higher series implies movement into an environment of heightened stress whose challenges are likely to impose drastic changes in our way of life, whether or not these challenges are successfully met by means of technological innovation.

The consequences of a continuation of our current trend toward reduced fertility are generally more hopeful, if only because the sheer volume of the population increases much less rapidly. If we again assume, for purposes of illustration, that real per capita productivity grows at 2.2 percent per year, we find, by the year 2000, a Series E (two-child norm) population of about 270 million producing and consuming about 2.4 times our current volume of goods and services. By the year 2040, this population, then approaching a constant number of about 320 million, would produce about seven times our current output.

Many of the same types of problems associated with the higher series would still emerge under the lower series, but the growth pattern of the lower series would afford the society considerably greater leeway in managing these problems before they assume crisis proportions. Moreover, the gradual aging of the population resulting from the Series E growth pattern is less likely to produce sudden crises; instead, the society is likely to experience a gradual shift from concern with the problems of youth toward concern with those services and facilities designed to meet the needs of the older population. Under these circumstances, the realization of our turquoise scenario would be greatly facilitated. The older age distribution of the Series E population and labor force would seem to imply a greater interest in the introduction of changes which preserve the traditional meaning of work while improving the conditions under which it is performed. The relatively greater concern of such a population with the adjustments of aging and retirement would encourage further experimentation with various conbinations of work and leisure, while the smaller number of new young entrants to the labor force could more readily be absorbed into meaningful and satisfying career patterns.[22]

The major conclusion which emerges from these brief speculations is that a return to the Series B growth patterns may be expected to generate an atmosphere of much greater social and economic stress than would occur if the Series E pattern was realized. Both series of future growth give rise to serious problems, but the lower growth pattern would afford the society a greater degree of freedom from the pressing demands of undiminished population growth and would thereby facilitate both the emergence of a wider range of alternatives for our future societal development, and a more rational choice among these alternatives.

[22]See David Riesman, "Leisure and Work in Post-Industrial Society," in Jack Douglas, editor, *The Technological Threat* (Englewood Cliffs, N.J., Prentice-Hall, Inc., 1971). pp. 71–91.

Selected
Bibliography

CHAPTER 1

Bacon, A. W., "Leisure and Research: A Critical Review of the Main Concepts Employed in Contemporary Research," *Society and Leisure*, 4 (1972), 83–92.

Burch, William B., Jr., Neil H. Cheek, Jr., and Lee Taylor, *Social Behavior, Natural Resources and the Environment*. New York: Harper & Row, Publishers, 1972.

Burdge, Rabel J., and Donald R. Field, "Methodological Perspectives for the Study of Outdoor Recreation," *Journal of Leisure Research*, 4 (Winter 1972), 63–72.

Charlesworth, James C., ed., *Leisure in America: Blessing or Curse?* Monograph #4. Washington, D.C.: American Academy of Political and Social Science, April 1964.

Fabun, Don, *The Dynamics of Change*. Englewood Cliffs, N.J.: Prentice-Hall, Inc., 1967.

Gray, David E., "This Alien Thing Called Leisure." Paper presented at Oregon State University, Corvallis, Oregon, 8 July 1971.

Green, Thomas F., *Work, Leisure and the American Schools*. New York: Random House, Inc., 1968.

Johannis, Theodore B., and Neil Bull, eds., "Sociology of Leisure," *Pacific Sociological Review*, 14 (July 1971), 243–367.

Kaplan, Max, *Leisure in America*. New York: John Wiley & Sons, Inc., 1960.

———— and Phillip Bosserman, eds., *Technology, Human Values and Leisure*. Nashville, Tenn.: Abingdon Press, 1971.

Kraus, Richard, *Recreation and Leisure in Modern Society*. New York: Appleton-Century-Crofts, 1971.

Larrabee, Eric, and Rolf Meyersohn, eds., *Mass Leisure*. New York: The Free Press, 1958.

"The Leisure Enigma," *Quest*, Monograph #5. The National Association for Physical Education of College Women and the National College Physical Education Association for Men, December 1965.

Matejko, Alexander, "Culture, Work and Leisure (Basic Concepts)," *Society and Leisure*, 3 (1971), 21–42.

Meyersohn, Rolf, "The Sociology of Leisure in the United States: Introduction and Bibliography, 1945–1965," *Journal of Leisure Research*, 1 (Winter 1969), 53–68.

Miller, Norman P., and Duane Robinson, *The Leisure Age*. Belmont, Calif.: Wadsworth Publishing Co., Inc., 1963.

Roberts, Kenneth, *Leisure*. London: Longman Green and Co., Ltd., 1971.

Staley, Edwin J., and Norman P. Miller, *Leisure and the Quality of Life*. Washington, D.C.: American Association for Health, Physical Education and Recreation, 1972.

CHAPTER 2

DE GRAZIA, SEBASTIAN, *Of Time, Work and Leisure*. New York: The Twentieth Century Fund, 1962.

GREEN, THOMAS F., "Time and Leisure," in *Work, Leisure and the American Schools*. New York: Random House, 1968, pp. 46–75.

LINDER, STAFFAN, *The Harried Leisure Class*. New York: Columbia University Press, 1969.

MURPHY, JAMES F., "A Rediscovery of the Spiritual Side of Leisure," *California Parks and Recreation*, 28 (December 1972/January 1973), 22–23.

PIEPER, JOSEF, *Leisure: The Basis of Culture*. New York: Pantheon Books, Inc., 1952.

CHAPTER 3

BRIGHTBILL, CHARLES K., *The Challenge of Leisure*. Englewood Cliffs N.J.: Prentice-Hall, Inc., 1963.

BUTLER, GEORGE D., *Introduction to Community Recreation*, 4th ed. New York: McGraw-Hill Book Company, 1967.

CARLSON, REYNOLD, THEODORE DEPPE, and JANET MACLEAN, *Recreation in American Life*, 2nd ed. Belmont, Calif.: Wadsworth Publishing Co., Inc., 1972.

CLAWSON, MARION, and JACK L. KNETSCH, *Economics of Outdoor Recreation*. Baltimore: The Johns Hopkins Press, 1966.

NASH, JAY B., *Philosophy of Recreation and Leisure*. Dubuque, Iowa: Wm. C. Brown Co., 1953.

CHAPTER 4

ANDERSON, CHARLES, and MILTON GORDON, "The Blue-Collar Worker at Leisure," in *Blue-Collar World: Studies of the American Worker*, ed. Arthur B. Shostak and A. William Gomberg. Englewood Cliffs, N. J.: Prentice-Hall, Inc., 1964, pp. 407–16.

BURDGE, RABEL J., "Levels of Occupational Prestige and Leisure Activity," *Journal of Leisure Research*, 2 (Summer 1969), 262–74.

CUNNINGHAM, DAVID A., HENRY J. MONTOYE; HELEN L. METZNER; and JACOB B. KELLER, "Active Leisure Activities as Related to Occupation," *Journal of Leisure Research*, 2 (Spring 1970), 104–11.

DUBIN, ROBERT, "Industrial Worker's World: A Study of 'Central Life Interests' of Industrial Workers," *Social Problems*, 3 (Jan. 1956), 131–42.

GERSTL, JOEL, "Leisure, Taste, and Occupational Milieu," *Social Problems*, 9 (Summer 1961), 56–58.

KLAUSNER, SAMUEL Z., "Recreation as Social Action," in *A Program for Outdoor Recreation Research.* Washington, D.C.: National Academy of Sciences, 1969, pp. 61–73.

KOMAROVSKY, MIRRA, "Social Life and Leisure," *Blue-Collar Marriage.* New York: Random House, Inc., 1964, pp. 311–29.

KRAUS, RICHARD, *Public Recreation and the Negro: A Study of Participation and Administrative Practices.* New York: Center for Urban Education, 1968.

NESBITT, JOHN A., PAUL D. BROWN, and JAMES F. MURPHY, *Recreation and Leisure Service for the Disadvantaged.* Philadelphia: Lea & Febiger, 1970.

REISSMAN, LEONARD, "Class, Leisure and Social Participation," *American Sociological Review,* 19 (February 1954), 75–84.

SHOSTAK, ARTHUR B., and WILLIAM GOMBERG, *Blue-Collar World: Studies of the American Worker.* Englewood Cliffs, N.J.: Prentice-Hall, Inc., 1964.

VEBLEN, THORSTEIN, *The Theory of the Leisure Class.* New York: The New American Library, Inc., 1953.

WHITE, REUEL, "Social Class Differences in the Uses of Leisure," *American Journal of Sociology,* 61 (September 1955), 145–50.

WILENSKY, HAROLD L., "The Uneven Distribution of Leisure: The Impact of Economic Growth on Free Time," *Social Problems,* 9 (Summer 1961), 32–56.

CHAPTER 5

BERGER, BENNETT M., "The Sociology of Leisure: Some Suggestions," *Industrial Relations,* 1 (February 1962), 31–45.

DUMAZEDIER, JOFFRE, *Toward a Society of Leisure.* New York: The Free Press, 1967.

FELDMAN, SAUL D., and GERALD W. THIELBAR, eds., *Life Styles: Diversity in American Society.* Boston: Little, Brown and Company, 1972.

HAVINGHURST, ROBERT J., and KENNETH FEIGENBAUM, "Leisure and Life Style," *American Journal of Sociology,* 64 (January 1959), 396–405.

NIEPOTH, E. WILLIAM, "Users and non-Users of Recreation and Park Services," in *Reflections on the Recreation and Park Movement,* ed. David E. Gray and Donald A. Pelegrino. Dubuque, Iowa: Wm. C. Brown Co., 1973, pp. 131–42.

————, "A Conceptualization of Leisure Service," *Leisure Service Delivery System: A Modern Perspective.* Philadelphia: Lea & Febiger, 1973.

CHAPTER 6

FARINA, JOHN, "Toward a Philosophy of Leisure," *Convergence,* 2 (1969), 14–17.

KERR, WALTER, *The Decline of Pleasure.* New York: Simon and Schuster, Inc., 1962.

KLAPP, ORRIN E. *A Collective Search for Identity.* New York: Holt, Rinehart and Winston, Inc., 1969.

MALCOLM, HENRY, *Generation of Narcissus.* Boston: Little, Brown and Company, 1971.

MELVILLE, KEITH, *Communes in the Counter Culture.* New York: William Morrow & Co., Inc., 1972.

MURPHY, JAMES F., "The Counter Culture of Leisure," *Parks and Recreation,* 7 (February 1972), 34, 41–42.

REICH, CHARLES, *The Greening of America.* New York: Random House, Inc., 1970.

ROSZAK, THEODORE, *The Making of a Counter Culture.* New York: Doubleday & Company, Inc., 1969.

YABLONSKY, LEWIS, *The Hippie Trip.* New York: Pegasus, 1968.

CHAPTER 7

ANDERSON, NELS, *Work and Leisure.* New York: David McKay Co., Inc., 1961.

HODGSON, J. D., "Leisure and the American Worker," *Leisure Today,* 1 (1972).

JOSIFOVSKI, JONCE, "Work and Leisure," *Society and Leisure,* 2 (1970), 9–17.

KANDO, THOMAS M., and WORTH C. SUMMERS, "The Impact of Work and Leisure," *Pacific Sociological Review,* 14 (July 1971), 310–27.

KELLY, JOHN R., "Work and Leisure: A Simplified Paradigm," *Journal of Leisure Research,* 4 (Winter 1972), 50–62.

MEAD, MARGARET, "The Pattern of Leisure in Contemporary American Society," *The Annals,* 313 (September 1957), 11–15.

PARKER, STANLEY, *The Future of Work and Leisure.* New York: Praeger Publishers, Inc., 1971.

POOR, RIVA, and JAMES L. STEELE, eds., *4 Days, 40 Hours: Reporting a Revolution in Work and Leisure.* Cambridge, Mass.: Bursk and Poor, 1970.

SMIGEL, ERWIN O., *Work and Leisure.* New Haven, Conn.: College and University Press, 1963.

CHAPTER 8

DUNSTAN, MARYJANE, and PATRICIA GARLAN, *Worlds in the Making: Probes for Students of the Future.* Englewood Cliffs, N.J.: Prentice-Hall, Inc., 1970.

FAUGHT, MILLARD C., *More Timewealth for You.* New York: Pyramid Publications, 1969.

FERKISS, VICTOR, *Technological Man: The Myth and the Reality.* New York: The New American Library, Inc., 1970.

HENDRICKS, JOE, and RABEL J. BURDGE, "The Nature of Leisure Research—A Reflection and Comment," *Journal of Leisure Research,* 4 (Summer 1972), 215–17.

KAPLAN, MAX, "Leisure and Design," Paper presented at the American Iron and Steel Institute, Chicago, Illinois, 23 March 1972.

————, "Implications for Gerontology from a General Theory of Leisure." Paper presented at the Third International Course, "Leisure and the Third Age," Dubrovnik, Yugoslavia, 15–19 May 1972.

McHALE, JOHN, *The Future of the Future.* New York: Ballantine Books, Inc., 1969.

McLUHAN, MARSHALL, *Understanding Media.* New York: McGraw-Hill Book Company, 1964.

MASLOW, ABRAHAM H., ed., *New Knowledge in Human Values.* Chicago, Ill.: Henry Regnery Co., 1959.

THEOBALD, ROBERT, *An Alternative Future for America, II.* Chicago: Swallow Press, 1970.